William Stevenson, London-born journalist and author, first became interested in Thailand while serving as a Royal Navy fighter pilot and later spent many years in Asia, the last five living in Bangkok. He was given unprecedented access to the king and his family. He has written many books from first-hand experience in international affairs, some as novels and others as best-selling non-fiction, notably *Kiss the Boys Goodbye* (Bloomsbury, 1990), *Ninety Minutes at Entebbe* (Bantam, 1977), *A Man Called Intrepid: The Secret War* (Macmillan, 1976), and *Bormann Brotherhood* (Bantam, 1975).

Praise for *The Revolutionary King*
'One of the most intimate portraits of the Thai royal family ever published . . . Mr. Stevenson's research included six years of unprecedented close and frequent access to the Thai royal court'

International Herald Tribune

THE REVOLUTIONARY KING

The True-Life Sequel of
The King and I

William Stevenson

ROBINSON
London

Constable & Robinson Ltd
3 The Lanchesters
162 Fulham Palace Road
London W6 9ER
www.constablerobinson.com

First published in the UK by Constable and Company Limited 1999

This paperback edition published by Robinson,
an imprint of Constable & Robinson Ltd 2001

A copy of the British Library Cataloguing in
Publication data is available from the British Library

ISBN 1–84119–451–4

Printed and bound in Great Britain by
The Guernsey Press Co. Ltd., Guernsey, Channel Islands

10 9 8 7 6 5 4 3 2

Contents

CONTENTS

Part Three

Part Four

List of illustrations

Photographs by courtesy of the Thai royal archive and from the author's personal collection.

To my wife Monika
and our daughter Alexandra
who helped discover
the modern and remarkable truths behind
the myths of *The King and I.*

Leading participants in the narrative

Ananda (1925–46): Elder Brother Nan, the Eighth Rama.

Bhumibol (b 1927): Little Brother Lek, the Ninth Rama.

Chakrabandhu Bensiri Chakrabdandhu: princely jazz-playing friend of Nan and Lek.

Chula Chakrabongse: a grandson of Chulalongkorn, favoured for the succession by Britain.

Chulalongkorn: the Fifth Rama, grandfather of Lek.

Galyani: oldest child of Prince Mahidol and Mama, sister to Ananda and Bhumibol.

Mahidol: princely doctor son of Chulalongkorn by First Queen Sawang, and father of Nan and Lek.

Mama see Sanguan Talapat.

Mongkut: the Fourth Rama, great-grandfather of Lek and subject of *The King and I*.

Prachathipok: the Seventh Rama, last Absolute Monarch, went to live in England after 1932 revolution; abdicated without issue.

Rangsit: last surviving son of Chulalongkorn when appointed Regent by King Ananda.

Sanguan Talapat: Mama, wife of Mahidol, HRH the Princess Mother, mother of Nan and Lek.

Sawang (1862–95): Old Gran, discarded First Queen and half-sister of Chulalongkorn, daughter of Mongkut, mother of Mahidol, Dowager Queen.

Seni Pramoj: great-grandson of Rama the Second, ambassador to USA, runs Free Thai Movement, first postwar prime minister.

Sirikit: King Bhumibol's wife, Queen of Siam, mother of their four children.

Vajiravudh: the Sixth Rama, son of Chulalongkorn, died without heir.

THAI LEADERS

Phao Sryanom: Police-General, former officer of Northern Command.

Pibul Songkram: active among the Promoters of Political Change and the 1932 revolution; at various times prime minister, War Minister, Field Marshal and self-declared National Hero Number One, Extensive Warrior, Supreme Patriot. Backed by the Japanese.

Pridi Banomyong: active among the Promoters of Political Change and the 1932 revolution; at various times prime minister and Regent; also SOE agent RUTH.

INTELLIGENCE UNITS

SOE: British Special Operations Executive.

OSS: US Office of Strategic Services, precursor to Central Intelligence Agency.

SOG: US Special Operations Group, emerged from secret US responses to threat from Asian communist movements.

Unit 82: Japanese secret service base on Taiwan (Formosa) after island's capture from China in 1896; gathered intelligence in support of World War Two military campaigns.

Phoenix Park: British inter-service liaison for Secret Intelligence Service covering Asia from Singapore.

Force 136: British 'Siam Country Section' of Special Operations Executive employing Free Thai agents against Japanese.

White Elephants: Codename for Force 136 agents.

King's Men: A misnomer because includes women of informal group of patriotic Siamese from all walks of life loyal to the monarchy.

WCC: World Commerce Corporation, formed after World War Two with prominent US and British intelligence personalities including former chief of SOE in Asia, Brigadier W.T. Keswick.

Prologue

HE was waiting for me on a journey that I now sometimes think must have started for both of us a great time ago.

I had been warned that he never smiled again after the killing of his brother. Nobody could say how he would behave toward me. Perhaps it was because nobody really knew him. Some said he was a god and others said he remained a western schoolboy. I had followed his instructions, flying halfway around the world to be driven along a coastal highway that ran between soldiers in camouflage, faces invisible, spaced like telegraph poles. The glimpse of a familiar sea, the tang of a jungle I once knew well, the apprehension and the fatigue fogged my mind, so that it seems even now as if what I first saw, lost in the sudden gloom of a room after the harsh tropical sunlight, was a Victorian youth standing amid Victorian furnishings on top of what had been a pirates' lookout. Gibbons shrieked in the palmtrees, and I had been told to be wary of pit-vipers under the rocks outside. I did not know I still had to penetrate a hidden world, detached from what seemed visible to me. By our calendar, the year was 1990. It had taken years to get this far to join him on a path whose end was, for me, still years away.

He said there was nothing I need hesitate to bring up, *when he was on his own*. Even on those occasions when I did find him on his own, though, there were others concealed from sight who counted the hours of our conversation, down to the last second.

He was a lonely man who was never alone.

He was sixty-two when we first met. He had only one good eye that examined me with steely fixity. He was lean and handsome in a boyish way. He had a straight back, a full head of black hair, and a face innocent of expression. Not a wrinkle on the high-domed forehead. Not a blemish on the flat planes of his high-boned cheeks. His nose was narrow and elegantly curved. The lips looked as if they had been cut in stone, like those on a temple statue. Later, I glimpsed anger behind the facade. Once, watching him stripped to the waist and hauling up a wooden dinghy he had designed and built, I saw the thick muscles bunched under the taut brown skin. Sometimes I would be led into his presence in a throne hall where he sat in golden robes, motionless for hours on end, silent as the wooden gods and demons under his gold-slippered feet.

He had become king when his older brother was shot dead in his bed. The dead king's ghost appeared during the subsequent rituals and said something to his successor that fixed an iron mask upon him. He lost an eye two years later, and the good eye seemed like a tiny window in the mask, revealing a turbulence of conflicting emotions. When I first spoke of this loss of an eye, he was upset. He had been totally blind for a while. Few knew about this. He deplored idle chatter about physical handicaps because superstitious people saw any handicap as punishment for past wickedness.

Before any encounter with him, I always suffered the itch of apprehension that pricks the nape of the neck when you deal with the unknown. I would leave his presence feeling wrung out. He talked in a kind of open code to baffle his minders when they made themselves visible. Sometimes, in the fields or temples, he would look straight through me as if we'd never met. In his aeroplane, though, he was certain of complete privacy and he'd talk excitedly about reshaping mountains, about digging out dams here or tapping a river there. After landing, the iron mask went back in place and he stood alone until men in red pantaloons, wearing leather helmets from wars of another age, closed ranks and marched him forward under a nine-tiered umbrella. I would catch up after the extravagance of ritual had ended, to find him moving nimbly on his knees among countryfolk who squatted as still as cabbages until he spoke to them, when they responded in dialects strange to my ear. Once he cupped an old woman's face between his large hands: leprosy had reduced her to a leathery tree stump. His father had died as a doctor among lepers.

He denied at our first dinner that he was a god-of-gods. 'People put a big burden on my head talking this way,' he said. Then he added something so startling I thought I must have misheard. He said he trusted nobody outside the room. Sitting with us were the queen, my wife, a crown princess, a doctor called Deny, and a privy councillor who long ago had been among the first of thousands sent to the west to find out all they could about modern technology.

Then he made another remark that I thought would put an end to our journey. He said, 'I hear you call me the Revolutionary King.'

*

He was Lek, snatched out of obscurity to become King Bhumibol, the Ninth Rama of Siam. Others call it Thailand, but royalty still clings to Siam. Born in the United States of America in 1927, he was Little Brother Lek to his Elder Brother Nan who was born in Germany in 1925, and asked to be king when he was a nine-year-old schoolboy in Lausanne. He was twenty when he was murdered in cold blood in Siam, a place the brothers scarcely knew.

Lek was eighteen years old when he replaced Nan. He knew nothing about monarchy and less about Siam. He had dreamed of becoming an engineer or a scientist in America. He told me, 'Instead, I became my brother.'

Their mother is always 'Mama' in my mind. She had no registered name when she was an orphan in a Bangkok slum. The poor went by nicknames and she never lost the habit. Her husband became 'Papa', although he was a grandson of Mongkut, the Fourth Rama who is inaccurately portrayed in *The King and I*. Papa was studying for an American medical degree when he first met Mama in Boston, Mass. How a Bangkok orphan girl came to be there takes a while to unravel. Papa married the unknown orphan and this sent tremors through a royal court obsessed with titles, for Papa was really a celestial prince, and he had been Heir Apparent until his mother lost favour. In his youth he had been commissioned in the Imperial German Navy. His father, King Chulalongkorn, had sired a virtual army of sons. Some were sent for training under the English monarch, or to Moscow to serve the Russian tsar. European monarchs were agreeably disposed to these princes. Old Siam seemed a rich prize to the circling vultures of imperialism. But the country is much more secretive than you might think when you visit and see all those open smiling faces. They conceal another universe, known only to the Siamese, full of angels that convert in a flash into demons if offended. This is enough to make anyone with an ounce of common sense put on a careful smile. Who knows what an angel may turn into?

The Ninth Rama was not offended when I called him the Revolutionary King. He was working towards a self-reliant republic but he had no power except the magic bestowed upon him as a monarch. You can see his problem: if he gave up majesty, he would lose the magic. He walked this tightrope throughout the cold war and learned to be careful about how he talked of revolution. Siam – Thailand – was the key domino. Americans said if it fell, all Asia would topple into the Soviet bloc. But when he spoke to me of unseen enemies, he did not mean the communists.

After he was crowned Ninth Rama, he studied Buddhist scriptures and was ordained a monk. I was surprised by how much he needed to confide his private fears until I glimpsed the intrigues and conspiracies and mischief-making around him. He could give away nothing that might be used against him by others. Privately, he said, 'Love endures,' quoting from the bible. If I had to put him into some spiritual category, I would have to say he never forgot his Catholic schooldays.

Lek's direct link with the royal house of Siam was through the discarded First Queen Sawang, whom he knew as Old Gran. She could remember, as a small girl, bouncing on the knee of King Mongkut, her father. It was he who hired Anna Leonowens whose spicey memoirs were made spicier in *Anna and the King of Siam* by Margaret Landon. This led to the even more inaccurate musical version. Mrs Landon's husband, Kenneth, became a cold war adviser to the US State Department and said he and his wife were going to write a history of Old Siam. Old Gran threw up her arms and cried, 'God save our ancient kings!' She knew that even the wise men of the west go to musicals. The original myth of a barbaric king had predisposed King George VI of England to believe Lek killed his older brother to seize the crown.

There was, however, a former director of British secret operations in World War Two, Sir William Stephenson, who was certain Lek did not kill his brother. After the war Stephenson (no relative of mine) started an enterprise to continue Anglo-American intelligence cooperation. It was eventually called World Commerce Corporation and became very active in Bangkok. Stephenson had been in touch with the king for a long time when he asked me to read his files on the regicide and later sent me to Tokyo to question the man he believed did kill the Eighth Rama. Stephenson wrote, 'King Bhumibol's enemies keep alive the lie that he killed his brother so they can control the throne.'

An invitation from the king reached me after interminable delays and diversions. The Ninth Rama did not want it thought that I was investigating the murder of his brother, but out of gratitude for Stephenson's help, showed me how he was carrying out his brother's vision of a Buddhist democracy. We became friends and I decided to write his story because it was so strange. He was like a western schoolboy flung back in time to a feudal court. I asked to put myself, as far as this was possible, in his shoes. He agreed to let me see everything, but I could not be seen too much in close company with him. Often it was four o'clock in the morning when we would exchange a few quick words after he had been playing jazz all night. The court was sleepy-headed by the end of these weekly jazz sessions. Jazz was one of the very few ways he could let out his emotions. Jazz also put him in touch with the past, like the monks who chanted themselves into a mental state to travel back through more than 2,500 years to Lord Buddha. Jazz linked Little Brother to Elder Brother. As students, they had played jazz together. Lek's youthful ideals had been intact then. Renewing contact with Nan's innocence scrubbed Lek clean for another week. He had been going to join Elder Brother in a jazz session at the hour Nan was killed.

For a king, Lek impressed me as being astonishingly frugal in his personal life. His habits were formed in the fatherless years when Mama had to pinch pennies and the brothers did odd jobs for the neighbours in Lausanne. His kingdom might compare with France in size but to this day it is far more difficult to navigate because of big differences in topography and climate. The population by the 1990s had reached 65 million. He seemed to be happiest among countryfolk, finding new money-making crops, and thinking up do-it-yourself inventions to make farm-work easier and initiating land-for-the-landless programmes. Siam is unique among small and physically weak nations in having successfully resisted colonisation. He did not want it to become the victim of a new kind of domination by foreign bankers.

He was vindicated in 1997 when the implosion of Thai currency, the *baht*, heralded a worldwide economic crisis. It confirmed all his warnings which he could only deliver until then in a kind of Buddhist riddle-speak: questions were answered with questions, obliging listeners to look for the answers inside themselves. He had shown me the resources that ought to make the country self-sufficient. He said the laws of the land condemned opium and heroin as illegal but drug warlords stripped the northern hills of other crops. It was illegal to cut down forests, but watersheds were destroyed by phantom loggers. Prostitution was illegal but village girls were sold to foreign dealers in the flesh trade and sex-tourism flourished. He took me to see what he had done to turn back these evils, in defiance of dictators who upheld just one law: the law forbidding him to do anything except sit on his throne. He took me into jungles where, to save money on imported devices, soldiers carved wooden limbs for the victims of landmines. In the western mountains flanking Burma, hydro-electric power was produced by dams he had built. Oil and gas were extracted from the Gulf of Siam. But water, he said, was what really mattered. His so-called charities got around constitutional limits upheld by army tyrants who declared that the monarch must never interfere in their governments. The one thing these generals could not do was change the minds of a people divided into different tribes and beliefs, ranging from animist to Brahmin and Buddhist, and only united by their awe of the king.

Many believed he was the prince in scriptures who becomes Buddha by following a path whose end is unknown. A revolution in 1932 had overthrown absolute monarchy. Then the new rulers found that people were paralysed without a king. So Elder Brother Nan had been called upon to become a monarch without power. A puppet was needed. Elder Brother was killed after he stood up to the most powerful figure then dominating East Asia, and made it clear that nobody was going to jerk his strings. Little Brother Lek survived by pulling threads of his own.

'My enemies will want to know what I tell you,' he warned me. 'This is dangerous for you and for me.' Foreigners who got too close to earlier kings came to a sticky end; and thirty-three kings of Siam had been murdered. He studied the methods of famous intelligence agencies and consulted the 2,500-year-old Chinese classic on 'The Use of Spies' by Sun Tzu which advises that, 'Divine manipulation of the threads is the sovereign's most precious faculty.' Lek fashioned threads of his own. His resources included former Siamese secret agents, collectively codenamed the White Elephants, of Force 136 run by British Special Operations Executive during the war against Japan.

You might think Lek was trapped in an endless medieval melodrama; but you have to measure his progress by the quixotic rules governing the inner Siamese universe. When his first civilian, truly democratic prime minister finally took office after years of exile, Lek murmured, 'Ah, Zorro rides again.' He was greeting a man who had been deported as a communist in another time when Bangkok's ruling generals were handsomely rewarded by one superpower for their devotion in fighting another superpower.

When he said he became his brother at the moment of Nan's murder, he meant this literally. 'I'm a boy who was called to be king,' he said. 'When I became my brother, we shared a schoolboy innocence. A great asset. I try to keep his youthful clarity of vision, but I am the brother everyone sees and I have to be pragmatic. Half of me is him, and half of him is me. So, if I'm anything, I'm really Rama Eight-And-A-Half.'

Western schoolboy humour, concealed from his enemies, kept him sane. Behind the iron mask, worn in the presence of those he could not trust, he was oftentimes sharing a joke with Nan. I only learned how this could possibly be when our paths began to part and I saw in what way Lek saved the small and helpless from the rest of the world's good and bad intentions.

Part One

1

Mama

Lᴇᴋ's mother had been the last person to see her son, Elder Brother Nan, alive. The shock of his murder sent her into a deep depression. She left the splendid Grand Palace in Bangkok and returned to the west where she was more at home in a small Lausanne suburb. And yet when she was in her nineties, I found her in the northern wilds of what she still called Siam, creating a community that could stand on its own feet. The day Little Brother Lek, as King Bhumibol, had become a Buddhist monk some thirty-five years previously, she said she had been reborn.

She had gone from rags to royalty. Then she was knocked down again. She had fought for ten years to keep her sanity, taking university courses in Lausanne and physically challenging herself on the Swiss mountain slopes. In Siam, I first saw her in sweat pants and a loose shirt, whiplike as young bamboo, cheerfully replanting four enormous old botrees, the kind under which Buddha is said to have ended his search to learn what life was all about. The trees had thick roots growing down from their branches, so it was like transplanting cathedrals. They had to be moved to make way for a road to open up another valley. She had army engineers at work on the trees. She could charm soldiers into doing anything. Yet army generals had bullied her at the time of her first son's murder. Terrified of losing her only other son as well, Mama had pleaded with Lek to reject demands that he take over from the dead king.

How did Mama make the first leap out of obscurity and into the Grand Palace? She had the unwitting help of Old Gran whose life began when kings went to war in wooden castles strapped on elephants and ended when nuclear bombs were secretly stored in the kingdom. Old Gran was Queen Sawang. If I quoted all her titles, it would make your head spin. A 700-year-old Palace Law dictates the proper way to address royalty within a stupefying system of rank and honours. The king always had the longest title. A consort who actually slept with the king got higher ranking than one who never climbed into the royal bed. The honorifics lengthened as a consort rose closer in rank to First Queen. Rank merited 'dignity', measured in *rai*, the units of land that each might own. One *rai* was 0.4 of an acre. Sawang lost her dignity when downgraded from First Queen, but she kept her head. She made shrewd property deals with the estates to which she was still entitled, and did good works, and in the end her kindness won her a sweet revenge.

Sawang was born in 1862, one of some eighty children sired by King Mongkut, the famous Fourth Rama, and she had married one of his sons by another wife. This son became the next king, Chulalongkorn, the Fifth Rama. Marriages between half-brothers and half-sisters and first cousins ignored the dangers of in-breeding. In fact Sawang was one of the legendary Three Sisters who became rivals when they all married their half-brother King Chulalongkorn, the bright boy portrayed in *The King and I*. A king picked queens from within the dynasty. He could have lesser consorts and also concubines of even lower degree, and if any one of them produced healthy young sons, she might move up the royal ladder. The most desirable post was to be First Queen, entitled to a seven-tiered umbrella.

This was Sawang's envied status when one of her sisters drowned in 1880 at the age of twenty after a royal boat overturned. It is said she was killed by snobbery, I was told. The girl was a queen, not entitled to a seven-tiered umbrella, but high enough in rank that she could not be saved because nobody at the scene was senior enough to touch her. A royal servant could touch a concubine's extremities in an emergency, but was forbidden to make contact with the person of a queen. This story was repeated until it became fact. Even today, courtiers shrink from writing down anything about royal matters which do not come directly from a king, and Chulalongkorn issued no report on the accident.

'The truth,' said one courtier, 'is that the young queen, who was pregnant, simply got stuck trying to get through a tiny window in the submerged boat. And King Chulalongkorn took solace in the youngest sister.'

Queen Sawang was demoted from First Queen in 1897 when it seemed the third sister was more likely to bear him a suitable heir. Sawang's children all seemed sickly. One of her sons had been selected by Chulalongkorn to be Crown Prince, but he died young, and so did three of his siblings. Then two other sons died. Her remaining boy, Prince Mahidol, survived and should have been Crown Prince but in 1897 he was only five years old and seemed doomed to an early death too. The Fifth Rama decided his successor must come from sons he had sired with Queen Sawang's rival who seemed to enjoy better health.

Sawang suffered awful indignities after losing her position as First Queen. She had lived in grand style, with her own magnificent mansion inside the square mile of the Grand Palace, with a retinue of 295 ladies-in-waiting; but when she was downgraded, portraits of her were torn from every wall by her deserting entourage. She moved eventually into a small house in what was then a wilderness, but she still loved Chulalongkorn enough to meet his request that she should raise a baby son of his by another consort who had died in childbirth. This baby would grow up to play a vital role in the lives of Mama and Little Brother Lek.

As for Mama, her parents belonged to the great mass of people who had no rank, no titles, no land, nor identity. She even received no given name when she was born in 1900 in a tiny wooden shop-house among the Chinese settlements on the wrong side of Bangkok's main waterway, the River of Lords of Life. Her Siamese mother died. Her father was Chinese. His shop-house had one all-purpose room with sides open to mango trees and a temple. Below, he dredged the canal for gold dust brushed accidentally through the neighbouring floorboards of more prosperous goldsmiths upstream. The specks he sold would end up threaded into lace for the Grand Palace. He died when the child was three. She was looked after by 'aunties', an all-purpose term for friends or distant relatives.

The orphan girl, at eight, got hold of a flat-bottomed wooden boat to paddle along the waterways, selling fruit and vegetables from the Chinese Village of the Wild Plum, known as Bangkok: *Bang* meant village, and *Kok* was Wild Plum. A much more grandiose name was invented for it, but Bangkok it remained in popular parlance. It had become the capital after the Burmese sacked the spectacular old capital of Ayudhya in 1767. A Siamese army general, Taksin, threw out the Burmese, moved the capital south to the safety of swamp and sea, and made himself King Taksin. Then he decided he was a saint and could fly. Another army general tied him in a red sack so that nobody should see royal blood spilled and had him beaten to death with sandalwood clubs to sweeten the smell. This army general founded the Chakri dynasty, translated the ancient Indian epic, the *Ramayana* which tells the original story of Lord Buddha's earlier incarnations. He called himself Rama the First, meaning he was Prince Rama who became Buddha.

The king who thought he was a saint had ben aiming to fly to Mount Meru, an imaginary place of gods inspired by the *Ramayana* story of a prince who broke out of his privileged life in the palace and was shocked by the facts of human suffering. It was in looking for answers that he became the Buddha. The little orphan girl peddling her fruit and vegetables along the waterways was on the outermost rim of a society structured around the concept of a god-king whose magical powers derived from Mount Meru. Each mortal served the person above, through a pyramid of royal pages, palace servants, chamberlains, nobles, and princes.

At the summit in Mama's early childhood sat King Chulalongkorn. He was one of the official thirty-nine sons and official forty-one daughters of King Mongkut who became so irritated by the interfering ways of the English governess Anna that she had to leave his employ. She wrote memoirs that she embroidered after she became known in America as the expert on Siamese court life and sold magazine stories about French women begging to go to bed with Mongkut. 'But His Majesty entertained a lively horror of French intrigue,' she wrote, 'and stood in vigilant fear of being beguiled, through such sirens, into fathering a Franco-Siamese heir.'

In truth, the Fourth Rama, Mongkut, had been celibate for twenty-seven years, while exploring the kingdom as a forest monk, before he became king. Then, as if to make up for lost time, he took on thirty-four wives. They were the kernel of Anna's fictions about the horrid harem at the back of the Grand Palace. When Mama entered this place, she was to find it occupied by ladies of the court who led blameless lives.

She made the unimaginable jump from the slums across the river after she heard the gossip about a small boy who paddled a boat just like hers and who caught King Chulalongkorn's eye. The king had sent the boy abroad to be educated, and then retained him as his personal secretary. Mama could see no reason why something magic like that shouldn't happen to her. Most children died early from diseases caused by the water supply: the river. It shrank during the dry season and gave birth to epidemics. To call the river Lords of Life seemed a contradiction to her. But each king was seen as a Lord whose hands cupped the water to save his subjects. She might have a chance to swim into the divine hands. A big new hospital had been built by the king. In it was a nursing college. Mama decided to become a nurse.

King Chulalongkorn had visited Europe and hired western experts to modernise Siam. He had already set up government ministries, railways, telegraphs and systems of education. 'He brought about a puzzling metamorphosis,' wrote a contemporary observer, Jules Hoche. 'He badly stitched the nautical town to a new land-based town where the electric trams make their way in between pagodas and sacred elephants, where bicycles run into the nobleman's palanquins and upset every law of movement.'

When the king built a bridge from the nautical town over the river to the town where trams might bump into elephants, Mama was able to walk to a new government school near the Grand Palace. He died in 1910 and never knew of the existence of Mama who, by winning a place in his school, would shatter old Siam.

When she won a place at the government school, she was nine. One day in needlework class she broke a needle in her finger. The girl at the next desk took her home to her father, a modern-minded royal surgeon, who invited the child to stay with his own daughter until he was sure there was no risk of blood poisoning.

For the girl from the slums, it was awesome to pass through one of the thirty-three gates in the thick white walls, into the dazzling other-world of the Grand Palace. Her first impression was of overwhelming colour and light; gem-like fragments of coloured glass were embedded in throne-hall and temple rooftops that undulated like ocean waves. There were strange creatures made of gold, half-human, half-animal. Fierce towering stone giants guarded a royal chapel where thousands of candles burned beneath the tiny but sacred Emerald Buddha. Alleyways ran crookedly between vast stone courtyards crammed with statues of warriors and gods, demons and scholars, elephants with wings, and eagles with human heads guarding a Siam that stood at the very centre of the world.

She glimpsed, without understanding, a replica of Angkor Wat, the mysterious long-lost core of the vanished Khmer empire. She saw giant stone Confucian scholars: and gold bird-women from Hindu mythology. Warehouses of bric-a-brac were stuffed with silk costumes worn by generations of peacock courtiers, and silver swords and little brass cannons and the uniforms of the Ministry of War Elephants.

Most of the marvels mirrored the hidden universe of the Siamese mind. The greatest marvel, though, was an immense stone mansion. The little girl had thought until now that all houses were wooden, built without nails, and perched on or over the water. This Boromphiman Mansion rose incongruously out of the Grand Palace jewel-box, the work of western masons brought in by King Chulalongkorn after he had seen Buckingham Palace and the imperial homes of Russia and Germany.

The palace surgeon arranged for the girl to live in the Back Palace, a walled town guarded by women that the English nanny Anna had called 'the harem'. Anna, in her day, saw it as: 'a place where women were disguised as men, men in the attire of women, hiding vice of every vileness. The most disgusting, the most appalling, and the most unnatural . . . a charnel-house of quick corruption.' But the Back Palace had been nothing more than a place where the consorts of earlier kings lived. Each minor queen then had a retinue of up to 300 ladies-in-waiting who had their own servants. Each senior servant had lesser servants. A minor wife also had a retinue. Anna, in one of her more sober moods, had written: 'They gamble on the daily lottery . . . fly kites . . . have their puppet shows . . . One might be selected by a king for the night.'

Few of the ladies actually slept in a king's bed. It was like climbing to the summit of Mount Meru and a girl who got there rose in eminence if she conceived. The descendant of such a consort still has a formidable authority among the cognoscenti, even today.

The Back Palace in Mama's time came under a Law of Monogamy introduced by King Chulalongkorn in his zeal to reform the lives of others. It was now the haven for young women who were taught useful skills; a maze of tiny stone houses, with its own police force, shops, laws and courts: a town of women, controlled by women. The young orphan's virginity was safe. The women guards locked and bolted the gates so that no adult male could enter. Some 3,000 women lived there, mostly ladies-in-waiting, their wits dulled by the proximity of Keepers of the Royal Goods and Chattels, the King's Personal Armourer, King's Astrologers, Prognosticators and Royal Magicians.

It had been possible to leave the Back Palace only with royal permission until King Mongkut in 1866 announced he 'no longer wished to possess, by means of threat or detention, any of the ladies'. He issued 'a royal proclamation pledging royal permission to Ladies of the Back Palace to resign'. Among them were 'Palace dancers and concubines, the Lady Consort Attached to the Royal Bed Chamber, Milady of the Lamp, the Third Lady Moved Up to the Royal Bed Chamber, Milady of the Royal Sword . . . and Palace dancers and concubines may resign on Monday, the 1st of the Waxing Moon of the First Month in the Year of the Horse.'

Many ladies stayed. They would have been lost on their own outside. Here, they got board and lodging. If they left, they could not marry. Siamese women devote time and inventiveness to sex. Those lingering in the Back Palace had to give up such joys. These relics kept an iron silence. To this day, there is a general distaste for pinning down details. A daughter of a former inmate of the Back Palace began to tell me, 'There was the happiest ambience, also naughtiness – ' 'No!' interrupted a courtier. 'Let the story die with you!'

The neglected consorts teased Mama with versions of the tonsorial ceremony marking the passage from childhood. The head was shaven to leave a topknot by which, said the faded lady pranksters, 'You can be royally lifted to heaven.' Pictures in palace archives show Mama as a strikingly beautiful girl in a court dress, defiantly letting her thick, silky raven hair cascade to well below her waist.

The royal surgeon asked Queen Sawang to give the girl a nursing scholarship. The queen had never met the girl. 'I preferred to help people I did not know,' she said later. 'The people I did know and who were once so eager to please me when I was First Queen had turned against me.' So she signed the surgeon's piece of paper, and in 1913 Mama was sent to the big new Siriraj Hospital. On her way each day, the thirteen-year-old fledgling nurse passed a palace storehouse full of the old medicines – tigers' bones, bears' paws, rhino horns, sea-shells, dried herbs and roots, various barks and leaves in indescribable filth and confusion. They were all that remained after 600 years when Royal Physicians were a corporate body. King Chulalongkorn had out-witted them and the popular preference for the old nostrums when he built the new hospital. He imported modern drugs and removed the English-language labels. Stubborn patients took their medicine, thinking it traditional because it carried the king's messages in Thai: 'For Colds', 'For Stomach Ache . . . ' But guardians of Palace Law still insisted that parts of the royal person were untouchable, even when a king was dying.

King Chulalongkorn's funeral was frugal in an age when the masses everywhere threatened monarchist spendthrifts. He had made monarchy self-sustaining by commercial ventures that became the Crown Properties Bureau, instructed to observe Buddhist ethics in conducting its many businesses. But in taking precautions to save the monarchy, he made one fatal mistake. By dismissing First Queen Sawang because of her evident inability to breed healthy children, he was committed to nominating as his successor the first son of the favoured Third Sister. This was King Vajiravudh, the Sixth Rama, who in his fifteen-year reign kept one wife and produced a hundred plays but no sons.

King Vajiravudh had gone to Eton and then to the Royal Military College at Sandhurst, was commissioned and attached to the Durham Light Infantry, and then graduated from Christ Church, Oxford. Still in the British army reserve as Rama the Sixth, he wanted to fight against Germany when the Great War broke out in 1914. His other half-brothers were serving in the armed services of all the big powers. Prince Mahidol, the surviving son of Queen Sawang, had been placed in the Imperial German navy. He wrote papers on U-boats and German torpedoes that were useful to the new king. But Mahidol was horrified by the First World War. He regarded it as the work of mad generals and thwarted monarchs.

The half-brothers might have found themselves fighting on opposite sides, had not the British discouraged King Vajiravudh from active service.

But he was allowed to supply the first combat fliers to come out of Asia, which got him what he really wanted, a place at the peace table. 'This is an excellent opportunity for us to correct the unfair treaties dictated by European powers,' he wrote, and made an impassioned plea to his allies: 'We have been fighting shoulder to shoulder for the rights of small nations, to protect the weak against the rapacious strong and to remove some of the old injustices that make for war. Is it not right and fair that Siam should be freed from outworn treaty restrictions?'

US President Woodrow Wilson agreed, and sent his son-in-law, Francis B. Sayre, to become Siam's foreign-affairs adviser. A skilled Harvard lawyer, Sayre thought the English encouraged Nanny Anna's malicious tales about the King of Siam to justify trying to run the kingdom and he finally undid the unfair treaties that European powers had imposed in fighting for control of the country. Many years later, he became a source of moral support for Mama's second son, Lek.

Mahidol was himself on his way to America. Disgusted by war, he wanted to use what was best in modern ideas to help Siam become an oasis of peace, free from the ancient superstitions that made it so difficult to reform its monarchical system. The son of Queen Sawang took to calling himself plain Mr Mahidol and studied public medicine in Boston, Mass. He had no idea that a scholarship founded in his name by his mother was paying for a particular young nurse also to study in the United States. Mama was stunningly pretty, to judge by surviving photographs. She went to a Baptist school in Berkeley, California, where missionaries who had once worked in Siam taught her English. Then she went east to nursing school. At Harvard College and Medical School was Mahidol. 'Sometimes he'd say he was "Citizen Mahidol",' recalled a fellow student. 'He'd read about the French Revolution.'

Mahidol made it his duty to look after newly-arriving Siamese students. He met Mama in the middle of the night at the railroad station. She had mislaid a Brownie box-camera costing her five dollars, her monthly allowance. She insisted on looking for the bag in which she had left it, ignoring his pleas to get some sleep first. By dawn, Mr Mahidol had found the bag and the Brownie, and had fallen under the spell of her ungirlish resolve.

He was eight years her senior, but he had big ears that stuck out like a small boy's, and a boyish enthusiasm he never lost. He got back to his rooming-house to tell a surprised fellow-lodger at breakfast: 'I'm in love.' He wrote to the address where she was staying, a boarding-house in Langdon Street, Cambridge. She had come to study public health, not find romance. She agreed, however, to meet what she thought was another impoverished student. They went out together, walking in the streets and parks around Boston. She would not let him squander money on coffee-shops. Eventually he had to tell her. The money she so carefully hoarded came from his own mother.

For two years, Mahidol and the girl thought carefully about a relation-ship that would shake the royal court in Bangkok. He was still a prince of high rank, even if he had little chance of becoming a king. The succession was firmly with the Sixth Rama's branch of the family. Mahidol was ready to give up all prospects of succeeding to the throne by marrying a com-moner, half-Chinese, and almost anonymous. She did have a name now, though, Sanguan Talapat. A name had been necessary for her travel doc-uments; and it was cobbled together out of what could be recalled about the families of her dead parents. 'It was only coincidence that "Sanguan" sounds like the name of Queen Sawang,' said a courtier later.

Her Brownie took pictures of her cramped room. Those in her albums are captioned in her neat English handwriting '*Where I study*' with a rickety table tottering under books beside a narrow bed. She was almost twenty when she said goodbye to Mahidol and sailed back to Bangkok aboard a Japanese liner, the *Tengo Meru*. She was now an American-qualified nurse who also nursed the explosive secret of the love of a celestial prince. In her diaries, she writes of jolly Captain Maki who called her and her girl com-panion, 'Siamese Twins'. She skylarks at Waikiki Beach. She lingers in Japan to join the firefly-watching parties, talks to the sacred deer of Neru, listens to the creak of outer boards that warn of intruders at the old impe-rial palace in Kyoto. It is hard to connect this sagacious young woman with the child who lived by her wits on the canals of Bangkok.

She met Queen Sawang for the first time to prepare for her wedding to Prince Mahidol in September, 1920. The ex-First Queen was impressed. The girl from the slums showed a proper deference without bowing and scraping, and the two of them talked for hours about America and the freedom of the individual made possible in the republic. Queen Sawang relished the consternation in royal circles. She was now fifty-eight and did exactly as she wished. Her tin-roofed villa at 967 Rama One Road was called the Palace of Lotus Ponds because aristocrats above a certain rank named their homes palaces and she was not going to be cheated out of this entitlement; but it was a shed compared with her old Grand Palace resi-dence where she had enjoyed twenty lavishly furnished rooms and a dozen balconies overlooking manicured gardens. She now lived beside an old temple where a rare image of Buddha presided, cast in the attitude of sub-duing the demon Mara. She saw her son's marriage as subduing demons of her own, including her loss of status and six children. This bright, healthy girl might bear sons more durable than the line started by her rival sister.

Queen Sawang presided at the marriage by simply pouring monk-blessed water over their hands as the young couple knelt in her house. The government register was signed by plain Dr and Mrs Mahidol. He was twenty-eight. His years abroad had accustomed him on formal occasions to black homberg, dark suit and black overcoat. His one wedding picture shows him in open-neck shirt and tan trousers. The twenty-year-old bride wears a simple flowered frock.

The couple wanted to go back to the west to broaden their education. Dr Mahidol's half-brother, the Sixth Rama, had written about 'this difficult time when antiquated traditions are struggling against change'. Mahidol wanted to learn more about the powerful new European movements that sought to tear down similar traditions. In the Sixth Rama's beloved England, the Transport Workers' Union called for the Red Flag to fly over Buckingham Palace. In Germany, the Kaiser was swept away by public dissatisfactions. In Holland, the House of Orange was threatened. In Greece, the throne was in danger. In Russia, the tsar and his family had been horribly put to death, but not before Nicholas II had smuggled a mysterious leather trunk to Bangkok with a message: 'Not to be Unsealed Except by a King of Siam.'

Mahidol intended his wife to become the best-educated of Siamese women and to lead a feminist uprising against male dominance and polygamy. She wanted him to see the most modern doctors about the kidney disease that seemed to run in his family. Mama's albums contain photographs chronicling their nomadic life.

Near cheap London lodgings in Lexington Gardens, her first baby, Galyani, born in 1923, is being pushed in a big-wheeled perambulator. The baby girl is cuddled by Mama in Bournemouth. She bounces on Papa's knee in Edinburgh. They move to continental Europe, living in boarding-houses near museums and centres of learning. For a young mother who from infancy managed in one small room a baby was no problem.

In Paris, Mahidol's curiosity led him to Siamese students who planned to get rid of absolute monarchy. One student, Pridi, was denounced as a communist, but Mahidol persuaded the Siamese ambassador not to send him home. Twenty-one years later, Pridi would be accused of helping murder Mahidol's elder son.

Elder Brother Nan was born in Heidelberg when the university halls rang with debates about *Das Kapital* and the ravings of someone called Hitler. Two months later, in November, 1925, Mahidol suddenly found himself enmeshed in the most rigid of the old hierarchies from which he thought he had escaped. The Sixth Rama had died just after his first child was born. It was a girl. The dying king patted her head, murmuring, 'It's just as well.' A boy would have had to take on a job for which the dying king saw little future. The role went to his younger brother, Prachathipok, who became the Seventh Rama but he had neither sons nor daughters. It was a great irony. Mahidol did not want the crown but was suddenly Heir Presumptive. He knew what happened to monarchies that failed to keep up with the times, and he knew the mood of the Siamese rebels in Paris.

He left Europe and went back at once to America, working as an intern at Boston Lying-In Hospital, rushing out on ambulance calls and scrubbing floors. His wife juggled between housework and studies in sanitation and preventive medicine. In the kitchen, she relied on the Kansas State Agricultural College textbook *Practical Cookery*. They lived with their little girl and small son in rooms at 63 Longwood Avenue, Brookline, Mass. on US$1,600 a year. ' It was not a lot,' Mrs Mahidol wrote in her photo album. In 1927 she became pregnant again and on the 5th December gave birth to her second son who was registered as 'Baby Songkhla'. This was Little Brother Lek. The name of Songkhla derived from a title given Papa Mahidol – Prince of Songkhla. It was a town near the Malay border. Papa, with his dislike of titles, gave it little attention. But the Japanese did. Every one of Songkhla's features – its harbour and roads, its post-and-telegraph offices, the peculiar location of its fort above Cat and Mouse islands, the dangerous presence of the Siamese crocodile called *gharial*, even the names of administrators, were scrupulously entered into intelligence files kept by the Japanese. What interested them most were Songkhla's long, gently sloping beaches which were perfect for infantry landing craft.

Two years after the birth of Baby Songkhla, his father was dead.

Papa had planned to go back to Siam and work in Bangkok at Siriraj Hospital. He settled his family at the Palace of Lotus Ponds with his mother, Queen Sawang – Old Gran to the children. Then he found that Palace Law forbade him to perform as a doctor. 'I would have to tell patients, "As a prince, I'm supposed to treat only your head,"' he wrote angrily to Dean A. G. Ellis, an American professor at the hospital. 'If I had the King as a patient, I could only treat his feet.'

So instead he escaped these stifling controls by joining a missionary hospital in the north to work among lepers. He was seen there, at the American Presbyterian Hospital in Chiang Mei, by the English author Alec Waugh who later wrote, 'I was moved and impressed. Royal circles were horrified to learn that he was bathing his peasant patients.'

On one of his brief trips south to Bangkok, carrying a specimen from one of his patients for lab tests, he asked an American specialist, Bill Perkins, to give him a medical examination. Perkins knew Dr Mahidol had been looking for a cure for the kidney disease that killed his siblings. The hard work among lepers had exposed him to infections that further under-mined his resistance. Perkins said gently, 'You'd better go home. There's nothing we can do.'

Papa died in late September, 1929, in the season known as the Buddhist Lent when the people wash away their sins by floating tiny candles in banana-leaf boats. Black swans drifted silently under weeping willows around the Palace of the Lotus Ponds. His cremation was as self-effacing as his life. His ashes were deposited in the temple next door.

2

Revolution

MAMA was lost at first without her husband. She was not welcome at the
Grand Palace and Papa, although Heir Apparent, had alienated many in
the royal court. So the fatherless children stayed on for a while at the Palace
of Lotus Ponds with their mother and Old Gran. They went to the Catholic
Mater Dei School where the headmistress was a nun of the Ursuline Order
known as Sister Xaveria, born Ana Pirc in Yugoslavia. Sister Xaveria
remained the rest of her life in Bangkok and in her declining years said
Mama had found in Prince Mahidol the one man who could develop and
strengthen her remarkable intellectual qualities so that, even in death, he
was the most powerful influence in her life. The nun remembered Galyani
as a pretty eight-year-old. Elder Brother Nan was a gifted boy of six. But
Lek, at four, she said was both naughty and precocious. She understood
why their mother wanted to get away from the artifice of the royal court
and give the children a western education.

Mama was thirty-one and looks younger in photographs: narrow-
waisted, with deft hands and the most slender wrists and ankles. She had a
thin and delicate nose, sensitive lips, and dimples. Old Gran, Queen
Sawang, asked Mama if she would marry again: 'The girl said she could
not look into the future,' said Old Gran later. 'A lesser person would have
replied "No" in order to share my money.'

The world depression had caught up with Siam. Revolution was being
plotted by the young Siamese once befriended by Papa in Paris, the western
centre of the Comintern and communist indoctrination. Bangkok was the
Comintern's base in the east. As the only country in the region never colonised, it was free from the anti-communist preoccupations of the security
police forces run by the colonial powers.

In 1932, Pridi, who had been saved from extradition from France as an
alleged communist by Papa, was back in Siam as the driving force behind
Promoters of Political Change, the name chosen by Pridi's fellow-students

when they were still in Paris. They issued a manifesto attacking royal land monopolies and locked up leading princes while King Prachathipok, the Seventh Rama, was at the Palace of Far-From-Worry on the east coast 150 kilometres from Bangkok. A Soviet-controlled Communist Party of Siam had been active for two years, providing sanctuary for revolutionaries from the west's colonies in Asia. A Vietnamese agitator arrived from Paris and distributed a call to arms: 'Overthrow tyrannical government in Siam . . . The Russians are the only people in the world today who have any real freedom and happiness . . . Let us follow in their footsteps . . . Unite in the struggle against the King!' The author would become famous under his alias of Ho Chi Minh.

The Promoters' revolution abolished the absolute monarchy in December, 1932. To keep it bloodless, the Seventh Rama stayed on for a time, tolerated as a puppet king whose presence would prevent a mass uprising. The revolutionaries knew most Siamese feared living without a king. Old Gran advised Mama to get out of the country. If the king were to abdicate, which seemed likely, the new regime would look for another puppet and might settle upon the eldest son of the late Heir Apparent. Old Gran had no wish to see her grandson suffer the fate of the last of China's Manchu dynasty, Henry Pu-Yi, forced at gunpoint to become puppet emperor for Japan's new colony of Manchukuo.

Old Gran had sound instincts. This was evident more than sixty years after the Promoter's revolution when a young crown princess would stumble upon old Japanese intelligence documents proving Bangkok was a centre of Japanese as well as Soviet spy networks. A Japanese military strategist, Masanobu Tsuji, was in 1932 laying down the foundations of his later position as Emperor Hirohito's personal spy. British investigators into Tsuji's World War Two crimes would dub him God of Evil. Much later, from Japanese archives long overlooked, it became clear that this God of Evil had been armed with every tiny detail of both Siam and Mama's sad little family.

Tsuji knew, for example, why Mama left with the three children in 1933, a year after the revolution. She had decided to raise the family in Lausanne. Papa had admired the common sense of the Swiss republic. He had liked Lausanne which had a school run on Jean-Jacques Rousseau's belief that understanding, not fear, is the way to teach children, and he liked Rousseau's idea of 'a republic protected by a king'. Buddha, after all, had spoken of such a seeming contradiction. Old Gran could help Mama financially, though she was ready to make her own living in Lausanne. She was an American-qualified nurse and had learned other skills while a child in the Back Palace.

Meanwhile the revolutionaries were united in confiscating the land of minor royalty, but they squabbled among themselves over the spoils, becoming divided between Pridi who talked about collectivising the land and a young army officer called Pibul who had fascist ambitions. Most of the docile population waited for guidance from Rama the Seventh who was still, in their eyes, the king; but he finally gave up and, in January 1934, set sail for Europe with his one wife, Queen Rambhai. He was only forty-one but he suffered from cataracts, and caught as he left only a blurred glimpse of the Royal Standard. This had been a white elephant on a red field but because the elephant was said to look like a pig to Europeans, it had been replaced by the fierce red *garuda* bird, resembling an eagle with a beaked but human head, and balancing the forces of good and evil by holding them apart with outspread, talon-tipped wings. He would never see his flag fly again.

He was invited by Hitler to visit Nazi Germany. The Führer told him stern measures were required to solve the economic woes caused by 'international Jewry', thinking this would appeal to a monarch whose predecessor had written: 'The Chinese are the Jews of the East, loyal only to their own.' Rama the Seventh, however, was repelled by Nazism. And he did not want to be the catspaw of Siamese staff officers joining Japanese militarists, drawn to Hitler's concepts of Total War and racial purification by blood and fire.

And so he went to England and eventually took a thatch-roofed cottage at Virginia Water in Surrey where he was to be seen in tweed breeches and Norfolk jacket, bicycling through quiet country lanes. At first he was warmly entertained by the British government. Then he wrote to the Bangkok regime: 'I am willing to surrender the powers I formerly exercised to the people as a whole [but] the government and its party employ methods incompatible with individual freedoms and the principles of justice.' And he abdicated.

'A pity we spent so much time and money on this poor little man,' minuted the irate British Foreign Secretary, Sir John Simon. 'Our aim is to prevent Siam becoming kingless [because] quasi-communist elements may gain the upper hand.' The British government had another candidate living in England, and much favoured by its own monarchy: Prince Chula Chakrabongse, whose father was Prince of Bisnulok, another son of King Chulalongkorn, and in line to succeed the Fifth Rama until he married a Russian, Ekaterina Desnitsky, who gave birth to Chula. Chula made matters worse by marrying an Englishwoman, Elisabeth Hunter. Siamese kings were forbidden foreign wives. On the other hand, reasoned Sir John Simon, the last Heir Apparent had married a common little orphan girl who was half-Chinese. Surely it could be argued that the sons of this woman from the slums had less claim on the throne than their first cousin, Chula, who was thoroughly British in outlook?

3

Lausanne

THE last absolute monarch abdicated on 2nd March, 1935. Mama received a telegram five days later from Bangkok asking nine-year-old Nan to become king. Old Gran had been right: the Promoters wanted to neutralise opposition with a boy king whose strings they could pull. Playing for time, she wired back: 'I have received your kind telegram and thank you sincerely.' The message was intercepted and copied for the files in Japan's military intelligence unit on the island of Formosa.

Mama was shunned by the Seventh Rama's side of the family. They liked the British government's idea that Chula should represent the throne and he began to stand in for the King of Siam at European royal occasions. He continued to do so until the coronation in 1953 of Queen Elizabeth II, eighteen years after Nan was named Rama the Eighth.

Nan and Lek were too small in 1935 to have any concerns about becoming kings. Mama had found a small two-bedroom apartment in Lausanne at 16 Avenue Tissot, named after the nineteenth-century discoverer of a cure for smallpox. Here in the capital of the Canton de Vaud, she had access to excellent libraries and the right schools. Living was cheap. She grew vegetables and fruit for the kitchen. On the lower slopes, among the vineyards, lived descendants of the old watchmakers who helped unite the artisans of France against the excesses of the old royalist regime. Lausanne University excelled in the arts and sciences, and while the children were in school, Mama read her way through the works of Europe's great thinkers. The community was small: about 100,000 residents scattered from the town at the summit of the hill down to Pully on Lac Leman where you could catch a ferry to Geneva. There were good roads and railways to Paris. The latest Paris journals crowded the many bookshops. Radio Lausanne had become one of the first three transmitters in Europe back in 1922. Its broadcasts would be regarded today as worthy but dull. Yet they were educational, and that was important to Mama. When the boys wanted a wireless receiver for themselves, she had them make their own crystal set.

She wrote to Old Gran of a Siam that would profit from self-sufficiency, and the example of Lausanne's mix of rural stability and innovative thinking.

'I never realised how much I love you,' she told Queen Sawang. Old Gran's sage on-the-spot advice would have been so welcome in this interval of uncertainty. Mama did not want to be dragged back to the stupid intrigues, the petty-minded squabbles, the trivial gossip of an inbred royal court. 'Some day,' she wrote, 'Siam will find its strength again within its own resources instead of losing its soul to other nations.' Just in the way that her small family would develop its own talents and resources.

Jazz migrated to Lausanne from Paris where black American jazz musicians were heroes. Elder Brother Nan and Little Brother Lek were infected by the local passion for jazz records, even among townsfolk who took pride in recalling that Mozart gave concerts in the hilltop town hall, between the cathedral and the castle. The boys shared one bedroom and their sister slept in Mama's room. When any child got into mischief, Mama would negotiate their punishment: 'How many smacks do you think you should have for breaking this window?' They earned pocket-money doing small jobs for neighbours and were made to give half of it to local charities. Toys were home-made. Mama talked of how she and Papa had husbanded their resources. Papa had shared what little he had to help more needy students build up a solid base of public health in the kingdom. The upbringing of the Mahidol children may sound priggish today, but Mama made the children see a dead father's dreams.

So the official request for Nan to become King Ananda, Eighth Rama, came as a shock. On 8th March, 1935 the London *Daily Mail*, then a broadsheet, carried a full page on SIAM'S NINE-YEAR-OLD KING, and a spread of candid camera shots. The gossip diverted readers from a Europe swept by mass movements spawned by grinding poverty. 'My brothers knew they had some sort of rank,' recalled their big sister, Galyani. 'But it wasn't very high – one above the lowest.'

In the power struggle among the Promoters of Political Change the fascist-leaning army officer Pibul Songkram had come out on top. Old Gran warned Mama: 'He thinks of himself as "The Führer", and of using the title Father of the Nation, which is rightfully that of kings.'

Mama tried to do what her husband would have thought right. Prince Mahidol had rebelled against a court that relied on superstitious credulity, but he had also written, 'to honour and respect the king is to honour and respect the country. Every citizen possesses a share of this corporate power delegated and vested in the king. Honour that power, and you honour yourself. Only through the tradition of kingship can we change things.' But Papa also said the individual must take responsibility for every action. Nan was awfully young to have to make a decision like this on his own. On the other hand, Mama at the same age had run her own life, and the boy was not a fool. She left him to write out the pros and cons. At least Nan would know he had made for himself a choice so momentous, and for which she could think of no historical precedent.

He was a gawky little boy with a fine-featured face, solemn brown eyes, large ears that stuck out, and thick black hair cut short back and sides in the approved Miremont School manner. There is a picture of him at the desk he shares with Lek in their small bedroom. He looks like any scrawny European schoolboy in short pants and open shirt, legs dangling, while he sucks his pencil.

He wrote out the reasons why he could not be a king: 'I'm a child and don't know anything . . . The throne is too high and I can't sit still, so I'd fall off . . . The royal umbrella would cut me off from the sun's rays and its vitamins whenever I went outside . . . There would be people in front and behind me so I could not run free . . . '

His mother smiled and thought this ended the matter. She reported conscientiously that Elder Brother Nan deeply appreciated the kindness of the government and people, and hoped they would understand that he felt greatly honoured but unsuited for such a heavy task. Besides, he had to finish his education.

Upon receipt of this news, astonished Bangkok delegates waiting in Berne scurried over to beg an audience with the boy who should be king. He was either in school, or immersed in studies, or busy with his household duties, said Mama. She would receive the officials.

They crowded into the small apartment and their spokesman said with studied courtesy: 'The people will feel lost and unprotected without a godhead.'

Mama tried to see behind the masks worn by officials. Old Gran had warned that a symbolic king was needed to keep the people docile. War Minister Pibul had already said publicly, 'Governments come and go. The national assembly can be abolished. Only the military abide.'

'And what about monarchy?' he had been asked.

'A monarch can die!' he replied.

Describing the encounter between his mother and the delegation, Little Brother Lek later asked me: 'Can you imagine? Mother was on her own, faced by all these gentlemen who wanted only one answer.'

Although she had no official position, she did have the right in this Swiss democracy to speak for her son as the mother of a minor. She sent the delegation away. She needed time to meditate in the alcove she had turned into a Buddhist shrine. In her view, Buddhism offered no answers, only guidelines for finding the answers inside yourself. She searched her soul. Nan as king might have a chance to bring about a more equitable society if most Siamese still believed kings were living Buddhas. But Mama had studied the western philosophers. Half her life had been spent in the west. What people believed and how governments behaved were two different things. Nothing magical was going to help Nan as king in the conditions that now existed. In Bangkok, the nobility still fought to keep its privileges. Someone on the throne whose origins were controversial might sharpen jealous rivalries among huge numbers of other children descended from past kings. Royal offspring had multiplied from alliances between cousins, half-brothers, step-daughters, uncles; between long-departed kings and consorts; and between adopted children and those descended from one night in the monarch's bed. This multitude shared a wide variety of special claims.

War Minister Pibul was now accusing the departed Seventh Rama and his relatives of selling land and stealing possessions that rightfully belonged to the state. Pibul was said to believe a conspiracy against him was being hatched in England among Siamese exiles. In Siam he had rounded up 'royal conspirators', and some were sent to an island prison while others were threatened with execution. If Nan proved unmanageable as a boy king, he could be assassinated. Other kings had been killed in their minority. Eleven years must pass before Nan would be old enough for the formal coronation that, in the minds of most Siamese, protected him from treachery and murder. During the period of waiting, he could be killed without too much fuss. Past history had proved that.

Little Brother Lek, standing on the sidelines, only saw what a suffocating weight of ancient ritual must fall on Elder Brother's shoulders if he signed on as 'King of the White Elephant . . . A King who has all Emperors in the whole world under subjection.' The grandiose titles filled a dozen pages, and Nan would have to live in Bangkok which had another fulsome name favoured by royalty. This boiled down to: Great City of Angels, Abode of the Emerald Buddha, The Invincible Realm, Grand Capital of the World Endowed with the Nine Precious Gems, Abounding in Royal Palaces Which Resemble the Divine Living Places of the Reincarnated Gods, City of the God Indra.

The first languages of the brothers were French and English, and these titles, when rendered in Thai became mind-boggling tongue-twisters, beyond their grasp. Lek was seven, small enough to enjoy nursery tales of fantasy, but there was something monstrous about this fairy tale. So Lek regarded Nan with awe when Elder Brother announced he was reconsidering his decision in the light of the delegation's pleas. The children had been reminded of another of Papa's teachings: that Siamese lucky enough to study abroad had an absolute duty to go back and make the best of what they had learned. Finally, Nan tore up his objections.

His mother's critics were to accuse her of cold-hearted calculation, because she had been told that the British royal family was pushing its own candidate, Prince Chula Chakrabongse, so that Britain could run Siam through a king of its own choosing without the bother of administering a colony. Mama wrote to Old Gran: 'I hope you will not worry too much. I just think it will help the country. With someone else, there might be trouble . . .'

But Lek denied she influenced her elder son. 'She always made us think for ourselves,' he said later.

4

Boy King

ELDER Brother Nan became King Ananda but Mama was still plain Mrs Mahidol. Nothing drastic happened to disturb the harmony of life within her closeknit family. Still they were watched. The Bangkok regime moved them into Villa Vadhana, a two-storey steep-roofed house in Pully, down the hill from Lausanne. A secretary and an aide-de-camp came from Siam to stay nearby and warned her that correspondence was not entirely private if it passed through the legation whose small staff included Pibul's men.

She had moments of sudden, irrational terror. Then she would write frankly, using the public postal system, to ask Old Gran about the possibility of Nan giving up the throne. Mama wasn't sure about the technicalities of abdication; he was an uncrowned king; but surely she had the right as sole parent to speak for him? Three years passed. Official letters continued to be intercepted. Some were copied for Japanese intelligence files. There were military officers in Bangkok who conspired with Japanese militarists deeply interested in the boy king's future.

Mama had prepared for the possibility that she would have to manage on her own if her son the king should become a commoner again. Then the regime in Bangkok would surely find a way to cut off the modest support she'd received through Old Gran. She taught herself pottery, and guessed her work was good enough to find local buyers. She had been smart enough to hawk peaches as a child. She could certainly sell her wares now. She felt safer as a nonentity among local burghers who read their French newspapers among their potted plants and heavy furniture, and then came out to greet one another politely as in any small village. Doors were never locked. The police station above the Plage mostly answered the questions of tourists and hadn't seen a burglar in years. The French Alps stretched along the horizon, and Mont Blanc dominated the skyline. In winter the boys played ice hockey or went out on the ski slopes. The Pully Plaza had bicycle paths and a velodrome cycle stadium, and in summer there were swimming and sailing on the lake where pirates once preyed on Geneva-bound steamers. British mountain climbers regularly fell off craggy heights, and British soccer players trained local teams. There was no hooliganism, every English visitor was a gentleman, and the local hotel training school, reputedly the best in the world, was called L'Angleterre. Telephones had been fully automated since 1923. The postman knocked twice a day, even on Saturday.

The King of Siam swept the neighbours' autumn leaves or shovelled snow with Little Brother Lek. They transferred to l'Ecole Nouvelle de la Suisse-Romande, Chailly sur Lausanne. Their sister, Galyani, went to the International School in Geneva. Nan stopped worrying about what he would do to amuse himself in a palace. Lek was interested in hydraulics, forestry and engineering. 'The boys wanted to build bridges, and were not so keen on pure scholarship,' Mama recalled. 'I made sure they mastered Latin, French, English, German and Spanish. Once, they kept putting off the translation of English poems into German and French until I had to do the translations myself to shame them.' At home they still spoke French and English.

Queen Sawang wrote that Pibul had added National Hero Number One to his titles and talked of recovering the lost lands of Greater Siam. The Japanese were only too ready to help him. They had a disproportionately large legation in Saigon to which well-to-do Siamese motored from Bangkok because it was like Paris, except that you could reach your destination along a good 550-mile road; it was a leisurely day's drive through Indochina whose French colonists noted that Japanese swarmed everywhere with cameras and maps. Japanese financial loans to Siam had soared after the Anti-Comintern Pact of November 1936 with Germany. The Siamese *Chronicle* warned: 'Soon the Japanese will say "You borrowed all that money from us, now we are obliged to send some of our people to protect our interests, *Banzai!*"' National Hero Number One campaigned to have Siamese men wear top hats and swallowtails like the Japanese emperor. The British manager of Bangkok airport, Robert Jackson, secretly examined Japanese bombers disguised as civilian airliners on 'goodwill flights'. They concealed mapping cameras.

Old Gran knew such things partly because the Bank of England ran its own intelligence service. 'The Bank and the British Treasury constitute an inner network of British imperial power,' Queen Sawang was told by her friend, a financial adviser to Siam, Edmund Hall-Patch. By 1938, Old Gran had come round to thinking Nan should make a brief visit to Bangkok. Hall-Patch had reported to the Bank of England, 'Without a king, Siam is becoming a vast humbug.'

In coming to her own decision, Old Gran took the advice of the orphaned son King Chulalongkorn had handed to her as a baby fifty-three years ago. The deposed First Queen had faithfully discharged her trust, and brought up the boy, Rangsit, to be what she considered the very model of a modern royal prince. Rangsit could see the ridiculous in idle ceremony. He had once caught his reflection, dressed in robes of office: 'Have you ever seen the Sumatran orang-outang?' he asked. 'It walks upright with slow-swinging arms and its orange fur hangs from the top of its head to its feet so that it seems majestic and all-knowing. I look to myself to be such a fraud.' It was he who had drafted a plan to begin parliamentary government and he had served as director-general of the public-health department. He regarded American-style public health to be right for Siam, and shared Dr Mahidol's frustration when Palace Law prevented him from giving full medical care in Bangkok. After the 1932 revolution, he had worked quietly to rally younger members of the royal family who valued the Tenfold Buddhist Rules of Righteous Kingship. Now it was the Mahidol children's Uncle Rangsit who advised that King Ananda should appear in Siam long enough to show that he really existed. The people felt lost and could be led astray. Japan was cultivating Siamese militarists led by the Promoters who needed the boy king for their own ends. But the country had never been without a god-of-gods. Nan could come during the 1938 Christmas break to reassure the people that his divine spirit still protected them.

Galyani and Lek hadn't thought much about Nan as King Ananda. Would Elder Brother wear a coat of gold, pointy gold shoes, and a tall spiral hat, like in the magazine pictures? Or would he sit like Queen Victoria whose monument stood near the Catholic school in Bangkok they had briefly attended? The British Queen-Empress's statue was revered as a Goddess of Fertility and garlanded by Siamese girls who prayed to be as fertile but not as fat. It all sounded madly exotic to children who recited Christian prayers at school.

Mama translated into English an essay on Palace Law as a guide for all the family. It set out 'the dignity and honour of the king, princes, government officials and regulations concerning the deportment of bureaucrats to ensure they do not commit offences towards the king'. The Law divided the king's children into four ranks, according to the status of the mother. This was where Mama might run into trouble. There were rival princes who did not wish to recognise King Ananda because his mother had no status at all. She knew she had better pay careful attention to court etiquette. Nobles could only be addressed in *ratchasap*, or royal language, which caused the children to gulp, since they knew nothing about any

Siamese languages. The boys discovered that if they chewed betel-nuts (about which they knew nothing), they could only use spittoons made of gold with blue enamel, because they were *Chao Fahs*, Lords of Heaven. To stop them from getting big heads, Mama quoted from their great-grand-father, Mongkut, the famous Fourth Rama, who had assured his American missionary friends that the title was no more than a label. However, Palace Law forbade courtiers, on pain of death, to make phys-ical contact with a royal personage; a person of lower rank must stay behind someone of higher standing and keep the head below the level of the higher being.

Galyani was a sensitive, scholarly girl who, at fifteen, had absorbed modern western thought, and she was not at all sure she wanted to travel so far back in time, except as a curious onlooker. King Ananda was now thirteen, and felt like Kim in Rudyard Kipling's 1901 novel about the Great Game. A British army officer, Arthur Connolly, had originated that phrase in 1840: 'If we play the great game the results will be incalculably beneficial to us and to the tribes whose destinies may change from turmoil, violence, ignorance and poverty to peace and enlightenment.' The Great Game was still being played between imperial powers over who should dominate Asia, and Kipling's works were read by English-speaking schoolboys almost everywhere. The Great Game would only stop, said Kipling's Indian agent, Hurree Babu, 'when everyone is dead'.

That should have stopped the heart for a moment of any schoolboy sent off from Europe to play king in the Great Game.

Mama shepherded the children aboard a Danish steamship at Marseilles. King Ananda wore an ordinary school jacket, shorts and striped tie; his sister and Lek also looked as if they were ready for school. Nan and eleven-year-old Lek were uncannily alike, and so close that they finished each other's sentences. Their long black hair fell in the same way in cow-licks over broad foreheads. They did everything together. The journey seemed less of an adventure and more of a test of the schoolboy king's nerve as Siam approached. Why should anyone take King Ananda seri-ously? 'Wear a blank expression, so people will read into your face what-ever they want,' Lek recommended. They practised on Galyani. When she spoke, two round faces stared blankly back, mouths closed tight. She was not amused by the pranks of little boys.

A foretaste of duplicity came on the British-run island of Penang, once part of Siam. Penang was named after the mildly narcotic betel nut chewed by members of the royal court whose teeth were stained red by it. The ship anchored in the straits between the Dutch colonial East Indies and Malaya which had also been Siamese and now was British. Mama now knew for sure, from Queen Sawang, that Siam's War Minister Pibul was being armed by the Japanese who were said to be planning to 'liberate' the region. The local white colonials seemed uncaring and soporific in the hot perfume of cloves.

The ship was boarded in Penang by Pibul's jack-booted representatives. Toward Mrs Mahidol, dressed in a sensible cotton frock instead of the expected ankle-length court dress with sashes and decorations, they showed no respect. All through the voyage, she had detected signs of coming upheaval. In India, the Japanese were recruiting for a 'Pan-Asian liberation campaign' but the British were too smug to take this seriously. In the British island-colony of Singapore, the King of Siam could not take tea at Raffles Hotel because of his dark skin. Mama saw no indication that the colonial masters anticipated trouble. Yet Japanese troops were already close to the British Crown Colony of Hong Kong. They had captured Nanking, the showcase for China's new republic. Nobody in Singapore seemed to feel the news had any relevance when the *Japan Advertiser* reported 'a friendly contest' in Nanking between two Japanese sub-lieutenants 'to see which of them will first behead 100 Chinese with their swords . . . In the final phase of their race, running almost neck and neck, the score is S.L. Mukai, 89, and S.L. Noda, 78.'

Britain was not preparing a realistic defence of its protectorates. Japan's treatment of the Chinese in Shanghai, where Mama had stayed on her first voyage home from America, was already a scandal. She had read in Switzerland the definition by Carl Jung of the 'psychic epidemic' that grips a nation when its grievances reach fever pitch. Japan was in that grip now. She remembered her first voyage to Japan when Papa thought the world was on the brink of a wonderful new age. Now she was making another journey because Papa would have said the times were evil and the Siamese people needed to know they still had a king.

Mama looked artless and pretty and not at all like a thirty-eight-year-old widow in photographs of the time. But she already knew how royal courtiers could convey disdain in subtle ways. No governor's wife could be icier than a lady-in-waiting who, without any apparent loss of good manners, knew how to make you feel an intruder.

Worse than the jealousy Mama could arouse was the fear that King Ananda would draw the spotlight away from National Hero Pibul. Pibul announced just before the family arrived in Bangkok that an attempt had been made to kill him by his valet who shot at the great man while he was pulling on his trousers; only skill and confidence had saved Pibul from suffering more than a wound in a delicate part of the anatomy. Then he alleged that his cook had put strychnine in his dinner. He could feed any

cock-and-bull story to the media, such was his power to charm or intimidate editors. He had been persuaded to let King Ananda visit because his
advisers said this would enhance his own stature. They had not warned him
about the great wave of excitement sweeping the entire country as Nan
sailed closer. It was uncanny, the way the public seemed to know where and
when their king would arrive.

Miffed by the magic, Pibul made it known he had to deal with an
attempted coup. He staged it himself. Then, with comic-opera showmanship, he suppressed it. This, he said, justified a military takeover and he
made himself prime minister.

The ocean-going ship was too big to navigate the Lords of Life River
and weighed anchor in the Gulf of Siam. The royal yacht *Sri Ayudhya*
took the family upriver. The children, having read Joseph Conrad in
school, remembered *Heart of Darkness* and the river that led 'into the
mystery of an unknown earth!' Conrad had also recorded his delight at
first glimpsing 'the oriental capital which had as yet suffered no white
conqueror; an expanse of brown houses of bamboo, of mats, of leaves,
of a vegetable-matter style of architecture, sprung out of the brown soil
on the banks of the muddy river. It was amazing to think that in those
miles of human habitations there was not probably half a dozen pounds
of nails.' The homes had been built without nails for centuries. They
were designed to be taken apart for easy transport in a waterborne
society. A powerful brown tide carried out to the Gulf of Siam a cargo
of rotting vegetables and carcasses. Between patches of tall palmtrees
glistened the *klongs*, the canals cutting the flat countryside into precise
squares, bright green ricefields interrupted by orchards where Mama had
once paddled. Along the snaking river slid double-decked teakwood rice
barges, slab-sided like Noah's ark. Mama said: 'Exports in Thai are
known as *rice-goes-out* – the source of prosperity.' This left a lasting impression on Little Brother Lek.

Pibul avoided greeting King Ananda, the Eighth Rama, when he
stepped ashore at the Grand Palace dock on the 15th November, 1938.
Queen Sawang was the first to embrace the family. She was seventy-seven.
The children had been only toddlers when they last saw their grandmother.
In the long interval, she had grown in their imagination. They were taken
aback by the tiny bald and wizened figure, so very oriental. She pierced
them with her black eyes, and made them promise to see her in the privacy
of the Palace of Lotus Ponds. They would soon understand why.

The family were put in the mansion Mama had glimpsed when she was
first taken to the Grand Palace as a small orphan. Using the essay on Palace
Law, she continued to coach King Ananda in the phrases to be used when

addressing nobles whose titles seemed to change with each occasion. Princes and princesses had more than one title, with subtitles indicating the exact relationship to kings past and present. Fine distinctions divided royalty into sub-groups. Each member was known by several different names according to context, and Nan could not afford to get the honorifics wrong. He remembered Lek's advice to wear a blank expression. People read profundities in his silences.

Pibul ran a Nazi-like youth movement led by a Berlin-born chief, Prayoon Pamornmontri, who set off air-raid alarms, blew whistles and regularly blacked-out Bangkok, heightening the sense of external danger. Pibul, as minister in charge of security as well as premier, and as supreme commander of the army, too, announced a security clamp-down and proclaimed that the immediate threat came from Jews and Chinese: 'The Jews profit from international tension, and Chinese here control eighty per cent of the economy.' Most local Chinese businessmen originated from the Canton region, now ravaged by Japanese troops. Naturally, these Chinese started a campaign to stop trade with Japan. It was the last thing Pibul wanted. He spread stories about Mama's father as a Chinese disloyal to Siam.

The brothers found out about such things from Old Gran by slipping out of the unguarded Grand Palace prison at night, and walking in old clothes to the Palace of Lotus Ponds where they were met by the small robed figure of the Dowager Queen. She knew a lot that was hidden from others, about how the Japanese had inflated Pibul's dreams of glory by promising to help restore Greater Siam, and to recover the Shan States in Upper Burma, Laos, Cambodia and parts of southern China all the way to Tibet's lowlands. This Greater Siam had evolved through a flexible and practical process that was not understood by western imperialists with their notions of sovereignty. Siam had received tribute from smaller kingdoms on the basis of personal relations and mutual needs. The Japanese would restore Greater Siam, but secretly they meant to turn the territories into Tokyo's tributaries, not Bangkok's.

That was where Nan could play a role, said the figure that appeared beside Old Gran. This was Uncle Rangsit, acting as a family guardian to the boys. So long as Nan existed as king, he said, the Japanese would be cautious: they were making much of being fellow-Buddhists, and emphasised Emperor Hirohito's divinity. Hirohito would respect Nan's kingship. It would be a good idea, said Uncle Rangsit, if Nan, while he was still here, proclaimed that Mama was to be known henceforth as Her Royal Highness the Princess Mother. It would give the Japanese an impression of an active, properly structured royal family, and might help to protect the Siamese people from suffering in the way of Japan's other victims if war should come. And Prince Rangsit, whose wife Elisabeth Scharnberger was a German aristocrat opposed to the Nazis, expected Hitler would start a world war soon.

The news of Mama's elevation threw the Pibul camp into confusion. Perhaps King Ananda was not quite the simpleton he made himself out to be. Pibul grew even more frustrated when the civil service insisted it had priority in arranging the king's activities. It had been dismissed by the Bank of England's intelligence as 'archaic and quite inelastic'. Its inflexibility, however, meant there was continuity in routine government business. Civil servants were loyal to the crown and they were shortly to demonstrate, under Japanese occupation, that they knew a thousand ways to sabotage military dictators. As it was now, they were running rings around the military government. This was not difficult. A British diplomat reported that Pibul's government was 'like twenty-two Eskimos suddenly given stumps and a ball, but no rules and no umpires, and told to play cricket'.

Nan continued to build up the impression of an active kingship. Old Gran was promoted to the rank of official Queen Grandmother. Those who had gloried in Sawang's downfall were now required by Palace Law to crawl in her presence. Those courtiers who had removed every one of her photographs from the Grand Palace scampered to put them back. Nan's action had also made it safer for Old Gran to stay in Bangkok, from where she and Uncle Rangsit would keep Mama properly informed. It was vital now that her family go back to Lausanne within the allotted time. Efforts were being made to delay Nan's departure and Prince Rangsit feared for the young king's life while he remained.

'Bangkok is seething with rumours of impending assassinations,' wrote Prince Chula Chakrabongse in Siam that winter. There were royalists who still considered he had more right to be king, despite his English wife, and the British throne had even shown him the respect due to a monarch at the coronation of King George VI in 1937.

'I hear talk of murdering King Ananda,' Chula said to a British diplomat. It was an oddly prescient remark. The brooding mansion where the family stayed already gave Mama premonitions of some terrible event within its lofty rooms. She looked down at the narrow streets of the Back Palace where she had once lived among embittered old consorts. Now her chambers were reached between paintings of pre-Buddhist gods, dominated by the God of Death. One night, walking near the Chapel Royal, she was startled by a figure in rags. It croaked: 'King Ananda will reign but never live to rule.' Then the apparition vanished.

Mama was soaked in western rationality. She had long ago rejected superstition. For a moment, though, she was back in the company of the ladies of the Back Palace with their amulets to ward off evil spirits. The encounter was not enough to unnerve her, but she never forgot it.

5

Rangsit's Arrest

AFTER King Ananda left with his family in mid-January, 1939, Uncle Rangsit was arrested and sentenced to death. Twenty more 'royalists' were accused of treason and awaited execution. The self-proclaimed National Hero, Pibul, had ordered the purge. He was nowhere to be seen for Nan's ceremonial departure. Instead, he issued a proclamation abolishing the traditional 'King's Birthday' which, as in England, was a fixed date regardless of when successive monarchs were actually born. In its place, there would be a new National Day on each anniversary of the revolution ending absolute monarchy.

Prince Chula was lucky. He had already gone back to England. He had not, like Prince Rangsit, offered the young king guidance on how to deal with the regime, did nothing to hurt Pibul's self-image, and escaped any charges of conspiracy against those in power.

Mama received the news of Rangsit's death sentence when she arrived back in Lausanne. 'How,' wrote Queen Sawang, 'can I meet King Chulalongkorn in the next world? He put Rangsit as a baby in my care. Now I shall have to report that I failed to save his son.' She almost preferred to see Rangsit die. 'Dead, he can join my king and husband. But alive in jail? It's too dreadful!'

Rangsit had been arrested, handcuffed in public view at Bangkok central railway station, and subjected to public humiliation. It was only fair, Pibul was reported as saying: hadn't Pibul suffered public humiliation because King Ananda followed Rangsit's advice?

Mama appealed for clemency. Or else King Ananda would resign. Nothing would suit Pibul better; but the National Hero and his Japanese backers dare not risk a nationwide protest right now. Even the placid Siamese with their ability to flow around unpleasantness might rise up in anger if Rangsit's martyrdom caused the king to abdicate.

Uncle Rangsit's fate was kept from the children for a time. The following Valentine's Day of 1939, the boys wrote a teasing card to their sister with French poetry and English words trickling alongside the right flank of the reproduction of a classic female nude: 'A thing of beauty is a joy for ever (Shakespeare),' they wrote; and on the statue's other flank: '*Belle Galyani – Votre beauté eclipse celle des fleurs, votre teint fait honte aux roses . . .*' The card was unsigned but Lek drew pictures of himself and Nan with hearts and flowers and Cupid's arrows shooting across the page to a sketch of Galyani.

It was an innocent fragment of a childhood soon to be overshadowed by war.

Pibul flew to Berlin to talk with Hitler about Siam's part in the German–Japanese pact against communism. In September, 1939, Hitler invaded Poland. Back in Siam again, Pibul broadcast allegations of communist and other 'anti-government activities' since the 1932 revolution and managed to blame both royalists and Marxists. By December, the public heard through bazaar gossip that eighteen of the 'royal conspirators' had been put to death. There was no official announcement. Pibul had learned from the Nazis that the best way to ensure public docility was to spread fear by unexplained disappearances.

Uncle Rangsit was spared from the first batch of executions. If King Ananda gave up the throne now, the public might turn against Pibul and the Promoters, so Rangsit was allowed out of jail on sufferance. His German wife's anti-Nazi family, the Scharnbergers, were under the scrutiny of Hitler's Gestapo, and while Rangsit was allowed to visit the northern hospital where Dr Mahidol had worked among lepers, the secret police ransacked his house, and took away correspondence 'on suspicion of conspiracy'.

When this news reached Mama, she guessed letters between herself and Bangkok had been opened, and she was more sure than ever that King Ananda had narrowly escaped death in Siam. Her duty to her husband's memory required her to see that her family served in whatever way it could, and for now that meant keeping the children safe abroad. The war in Europe made it difficult to do otherwise. None of the children relished stepping backwards in time to Siam again. Nan felt as if he had just finished performing in a very strange play. Lek got back to what engrossed him most, which was everything technical. Galyani returned to boarding school as if the Bangkok trip had been a fantasy. At the back of all their minds, though, crouched the word that now had more ominous implications: duty. It was Papa's legacy.

The price of performing one's royal duty was driven home by news that Prince Rangsit was back in jail. Old Gran had told the Bangkok regime that if only her adopted son could be allowed the lesser indignity of house-arrest, she would pledge her own life as a guarantee that he would not leave. Pibul's answer was to strip Rangsit of all his titles and lock him up again. Queen Sawang was ordered to let her hair grow out. A shaved head had been a symbol of royalty since princess-warriors had to guard against being dragged by their hair from the battlefield to be raped.

Old Gran's brief humility swiftly vanished. 'I told him to chop off my head,' she wrote. 'Then he could watch my hair grow out on my head sitting on his desk.'

Pibul did not respond immediately. He had a son serving in the British navy, which was now at war, and a daughter studying in Paris, where the war restricted her movements. Queen Sawang had many Anglo-French diplomatic friends. He might need their goodwill to bring his children home. But then he antagonised the same diplomats by putting on a display of military power that revealed an airforce more powerful than any in the nearby western colonies. Siam's navy was the most powerful in Asia next to Japan's (although Siamese officers on the first submarine supplied by Tokyo refused to submerge at a naval review because nobody was sure it would ever come up again).

In 1940 Paris fell to the Nazis and Pibul seized the opportunity to invade French-run Laos and French Cambodia. A brisk little 'Siamese War' against the French confirmed him as National Hero Number One among the warrior-class. Nobody mentioned that the warplanes ensuring victory were obligingly flown by Japanese pilots. He added 'Extensive Warrior' to his titles.

Japan attacked Pearl Harbor on 7th December, 1941, and, with the United States now drawn into the war which had engulfed Europe for more than two years, Mama was urged to move to America by a visitor. Mama thought later that it might have been Allen Dulles, who was certainly in Berne within months as local chief of the new wartime US intelligence organisation, the Office of Strategic Services, the OSS. Her visitor pointed out the danger of Germany invading Switzerland and taking King Ananda hostage. Washington was ready to treat her and the children as US citizens. She replied politely that the King of Siam did not wish to be seen as running away.

Siam was struck by Japanese amphibious forces at the same time as the attack on Pearl Harbor. They landed on Songkhla's sandy beaches. Mama thought it ironic when eventually she heard the news: Papa's title had been Prince of Songkhla. A swift drive down through British Malaya followed. Success was credited to brilliant planning by Emperor Hirohito's secret intelligence aide, Masanobu Tsuji, 'a person of great and mysterious influence', according to a contemporary.

Tsuji had gone ashore in advance of the landings at Songkhla to talk with key Siamese officials already groomed by his agents, and he rejoined the amphibious forces, knowing they would meet with little opposition. Tsuji reasoned that the capture of Songkhla would ensure King Ananda never raised the flag of resistance to Japanese occupation. Prince of Songkhla was, in fact, a title as meaningful as that of Prince of Wales: it was traditionally given to future kings. Nan was legitimate heir to the throne as son of the Prince of Songkhla. Tsuji now had Songkhla under Japanese control, and considered that this meant the King of Siam was also under control.

When Tsuji arrived with the invasion forces, he had already established a record of horrific war crimes in China. He had incinerated prostitutes inside their Shanghai brothels because, he said, they sapped the vigour of Japanese soldiers. But Japanese policy was to avoid provoking an uprising in Siam. It was needed as a staging post and springboard for attacking India. Japanese troops were then to advance into Persia and the Middle East, helped by the local armies secretly recruited among nationalists seduced by talk of driving out the white colonials. Tsuji had to keep the goodwill of Pibul and Siamese military officers won over by Japanese help in recovering Old Siam's lost territories. Siamese armed forces would reinforce the Japanese in Burma. Nan was, for the moment, a king safely out of sight and out of mind.

6

Trapped

For more than two years, King Ananda was cut off from Siam by the war in Europe. The Seventh Rama who had abdicated in 1934 died at the age of forty-eight, some said of a broken heart. His body was cremated at Golders Green in May, 1941, when London was being blitzed by German bombers. He had an adopted son, Prince Chirasakdi, who was killed flying a Hurricane fighter in the RAF.

Any Siamese serving in the British armed forces were liable to be charged with treason by Pibul's government after it declared war on the United States and Britain in January 1942. The US Secretary of State, Cordell Hull, chose to ignore the declaration, saying that Pibul's regime was illegitimate so long as it acted without its king's approval. And King Ananda remained silent.

The British were less forgiving of Siam's self-proclaimed leader and National Hero Number One, Pibul, who had insulted Winston Churchill in radio broadcasts. In London, Siamese students were declared to be enemy aliens. But Special Operations Executive (SOE) shuffled Siamese volunteers through the army's Pioneer Corps, the secret route into unconventional warfare. The students reported to the address credited to Sherlock Holmes in Baker Street. One piece of fiction deserved another. These Siamese agents were collectively codenamed the White Elephants.

Meanwhile Japan's self-proclaimed God of Strategy, Tsuji, expanded the opium trade to finance his own secret operations in collusion with some Siamese unit commanders. The art of covert politico-military war would be further polished long after Japan's defeat, perfecting treachery and political booby-traps on a scale so big that Siam would pay for it for decades to come. The Japanese were building up their strength in Siam to prepare for the most ambitious stage in their military adventures: the advance to meet Nazi Germany's forces in the Middle East. This required building the infamous Death Railway from Bangkok into Burma so that troops could be transported overland, rather than be exposed to Allied submarines in the Andaman Sea and the Bay of Bengal. Against them the overstretched British armies, having retreated through Burma, stood fast on India's borders, and were reinforced by Gurkhas and other tough colonial troops.

American and British forces used unconventional methods – long-range penetration behind enemy lines, glider-borne commandoes, hit-and-run marauders – to inch back toward Siam where by 1944 Japanese commanders sensed that the tide of war was turning against them. They had been instructed to treat Siam as an ally, and to make it an example of what the future held for those who joined Japan's Asian Co-Prosperity Sphere, but Japanese field commanders were ruthlessly using local forced labour and western prisoners. Smooth-talking senior Japanese officials in Bangkok treated Siamese princes as equals, playing upon a supposed sharing of monarchical and Buddhist tradition, and most of the royal palaces were left untouched. But, secretly, some of these same palaces became meeting places for American OSS agents, and British-run Siamese White Elephants who were dropped by parachute from long-range aircraft operating from India. Other agents were landed or exfiltrated by British submarines.

National Hero Pibul was in command of Siam's armed forces but he could do little about the units that protected Allied agents. Airstrips were carved out of the jungle for small Allied aircraft and disguised as ricefields. Stone gods, made in England and crammed inside with explosives, were distributed to friendly Siamese who were taught to make other booby-traps of their own. Guns and ammunition were dropped behind Japanese lines to help an armed uprising. Some supplies were hoarded for future use by local nationalists who believed communism was the only path to real freedom.

The British had one important agent, none other than Pridi Banomyong, who had been accused in Paris of being a communist and saved by Mahidol, and was one of the original Promoters for Political Change until he fell foul of his former colleague, Pibul. Now Pridi, known in London under the codename RUTH, had been manoeuvred by SOE into position as prime minister of Siam! Pridi was not only prime minister by 1944 but was positioned as Regent, acting for King Ananda in his absence from Bangkok. This had been accomplished by British agents who concluded that Pridi was a nationalist who had toyed with communism when it seemed the only way to freedom from the old feudal ways. SOE was convinced Pridi now represented a silent majority of Thais who were disillusioned with Pibul, and this was demonstrated by the ease with which SOE's agents persuaded the Bangkok government to accept his premiership. By then, it was clear Japan was losing the war, and Marshal Pibul meekly drew back from centre-stage. This clarified things for Siamese civil servants who had been torn between loyalty to the existing government and personal sympathy for the Allies. Now they had someone who spoke for the king that everyone wanted desperately to protect and guide them. Pridi now wanted to order a Siam-wide uprising against the Japanese but he was told to bide his time by Lord Mountbatten, chief of South East Asia Command, SEAC, based in Ceylon.

From America, Bangkok's ambassador, Seni Pramoj, a great-grandson of King Rama the Second, ran a Free Thai Movement. The name Thailand, which meant Land of the Free, had been first used before European adventurers began to write about 'Syam', and it had been more recently put into use again by Pibul's regime. Ambassador Pramoj broadcast to the Thai resistance over FBI shortwave transmitters, but he was suspicious of British SOE control over agents like RUTH, the premier. The ambassador claimed to have overheard Lord Mountbatten speaking of Britain's occupation of 'Siam' after the war, during an Allied conference in Quebec.

The Japanese continued to play upon their own Buddhist affinity in dealing with Siam; and they had set up Buddhist centres throughout South East Asia: these were bases from which local intelligence networks were run and there were extensive transfers of 'monks' to Bangkok. Japan's radio traffic was monitored by Bletchley Park in England, and Tsuji's name was cropping up in ways that made him seem to wield a lot of secret power. He was always turning up in different places as far apart as Burma and Switzerland.

Mama had been visited by a stiff little Japanese during these years. He presented her with gifts of rice. She thanked the visitor and sent him on his way. The rice she gave to a Lausanne charity. One day it was reported that this was Tsuji himself who lingered in the hope of seeing King Ananda and recording what he looked like.

Nan was now nineteen and forming his own ideas about the future with Little Brother Lek. They built a club out of packing cases in their backyard and played the parts of ministers and opposition in a mock parliament. Nan was a fan of George Bernard Shaw. In the Packing Case Club he spouted Shavian socialist ideas and grew accustomed to speaking his mind. He was studying political science and law when atomic bombs hit Japan in August, 1945.

The long ordeal of a world war was over for young men his age who had survived the fighting. For Nan, the ordeal was just beginning. He had no taste for the intrigues of the medieval court he had glimpsed almost seven years ago and he had his own ideas about modernising Siam. He needed more time to earn his university degrees and acquire enough maturity of style to face down any opponents who would stack their wartime military experience against his lack of any. The summons from the Regent, Pridi Banomyong, was unambiguous, though. Nan was needed right away.

When Mama received Pridi's abrupt summons, she braced herself. She had spent the last few years studying the works of European writers: 'A woman's dedication in shaping her family is the same as that of a great statesman in organising his country,' she quoted André Maurois in her diaries; and she recorded the words of Descartes, La Rochefoucauld, Pascal, Montesquieu, Voltaire and Rousseau. She had tutored her children in visionary hopes for a new society. Now she wondered if she had added to Nan's burden by making him more sharply aware of the feudal nature of the royal court.

Old Gran confirmed the need for King Ananda's return, however. Dowager Queen Sawang thought he should visit during the winter academic break again. He was not yet old enough to be crowned: twenty-one was the proper age for coronation. This raised the old spectre of kings killed in their minority. But she reported some good news. Prince Rangsit had been let out of jail by Marshal Pibul in 1944, acting to protect himself with Allied victory in sight. Mama agreed to let Nan fly to Bangkok in December, 1945. She made an absolute condition, though, that she and Lek must go with him, and both brothers must leave again early in January.

Galyani would stay behind. Nan's sister was a princess but she had relinquished all royal titles when, in 1944 at the age of twenty-one, she married a Thai army colonel working with the small household staff assigned to King Ananda and she had just given birth to a baby daughter.

Lek flew with King Ananda and their mother to Bangkok in RAF planes, not sure what to expect. From Karachi the young king mailed a cryptic card to a girl he knew at university, Marylene Ferrari, the daughter of a Swiss Calvinist pastor. Nan addressed her as 'Ooliram', reversing her nickname, and called himself 'Bicot', a character in Swiss children's stories. Their friendship dated back several years. Perhaps they were in love. The subject is never discussed within palace circles. 'It's too sensitive,' confided a lady-in-waiting later. 'Some people have said the king was depressed because he could not marry a foreigner. There is no evidence of this. But he was leaving friends whose ways he understood and going into a world of ancient restrictions on its kings. He was beginning to see how difficult it would be to use his kingship to change things.'

The journey went by way of British bases where the first trickle of prisoners released from Japanese camps waited in haggard patience, hoping to get home for Christmas. In Lausanne, the boys had been unable to visualise Asian events. Now they crammed into a few days the gritty realities. The Far East had been almost a forgotten war in Europe. Since Hitler's suicide eight months ago, attention had been focused on surviving new hardships, and on Soviet Russia's moves into East Europe. The cold war was on the horizon and Nan would suffer for it.

Former British-run agents joined his flight. They said the knowledge that a monarch still existed had played an important part in Siam's resistance to the Japanese occupiers, in encouraging civil servants to sabotage the Japanese war effort, or villagers to help camouflage the Allied landing strips. Telephone operators had protected secret communications. Local police had locked up agents of Force 136 of the Siamese Country Section of Britain's SOE, and then let them out at night with their suitcase wireless transmitters to communicate with Allied intelligence. Even before the end of the war, it seemed as if loyal Siamese, not Japan, controlled the countryside.

But there were also roving bands of unpaid Siamese soldiers who had fought alongside the Japanese. Their Northern Command leaders were ambitious, aggressive and ready to switch loyalties: 'They're on our side if the price is right,' commented an ex-Marine, Keyes Beech, who had become an American correspondent. 'The Japanese let them take over the Shan States and proclaim the liberation of "The Original Thai United State." This incensed Admiral Lord Louis Mountbatten as British Supremo of what was supposed to be a joint Anglo-American South East Asia Command, SEAC.' The Americans said the initials really meant Save England's Asian Colonies.

King Ananda was tossed into a world even stranger than the one he vaguely remembered from when he was there for four weeks, seven years earlier. It all seemed such a long time ago: these past seven years for the brothers represented their adolescence. What came before was all but forgotten. A photograph shows his arrival on 5th December, 1945, to a reception dramatically different to the previous one. He and Lek are on the tarmac beside a war-worn Dakota shimmering in the heat. They wear the rumpled wartime austerity suits of college students and look numbed by days and nights in aircraft bucket seats, with no sound-proofing against the rattle of piston engines, and only jets of unpressurised air to cool them. A royal page seems to have hurriedly retrieved his costume from a dusty palace attic and tilts a large umbrella rather tipsily over the king. The umbrella does not even have the customary seven or nine tiers and looks more like a stage-prop. The woman who should be honoured as Princess Mother merges into the shadow of the plane's interior. Lek stands a few paces behind his brother, as protocol requires. Nobody has marked this as his eighteenth birthday. True, Pibul was not present to greet them on this arrival either, but this time he had a sounder excuse. The former National Hero had been imprisoned as a war criminal when the Allies entered Bangkok.

At the Grand Palace, they moved to Boromphiman Mansion, the huge stone pile which had oppressed Mama with a sense of foreboding when she was last there. The war had reduced it to a gothic horror. The floorboards were rotting and a sense of evil lurked in the decay. The brothers were separated and slept in cavernous bedchambers where palace attendants came and went at all hours, crouching with bodies bent but eyes alert. The boys felt they were being cossetted like babies in a segregated world. They had no sister to share their jokes. They could only turn to each other for laughs. Even that wasn't easy. They had to contrive ways to be left alone together. The rules dictated that Little Brother must defer to Nan in public, and every occasion seemed to be public. They had to invent ways to escape from ceremonial duties foisted on King Ananda.

His calendar lengthened ominously. Mama seemed helpless to get confirmation that the boys would be back at their classrooms in time to begin the new term. Departure dates were changed. It was said to be difficult to negotiate how they would fly back: the US airforce wanted to provide the aircraft and take the king by way of Washington to see the president. Nan worried that the delays would prevent his graduation. Lek felt curiously detached, as if he was sleep-walking through the endless rituals in stifling heat.

Mama wondered who was behind the delays. And why? She tried talking to Pridi Banomyong, who as the most prominent wartime personage in Siam still to hold the stage, ought to give advice. But Pridi was strangely evasive, and Marshal Pibul was still in jail when Mountbatten swept into Bangkok on 18th January, 1946. Rumour had it that Mountbatten wanted to become Earl of Burma, which he later did, and Viceroy of Siam, which was impossible. At the Grand Palace, he was received with such a display of Siamese smiles that he got carried away. The forty-five-year-old grandson of Queen Victoria lectured Nan on how to behave as a king. His diary, however, reveals contempt for the Princess Mother and 'The Boy King'. He wrote that he expected they would repeat their behaviour of 1938 when 'they paid a brief visit to Siam but were so horrified by Siamese Court life that they hastily returned to live secluded in Lausanne.'

What is true was that the brothers felt disconnected from everything they had learned in those past and impressionable years. They longed for things that were tangible, fixed and scientific laws that you worked out on paper, as far as you could get from the oriental rules being drilled into Elder Brother. Uncle Rangsit sternly reminded Nan: 'The people want to see you as their king. The less you betray in emotion, the happier they are. Imagery says everything.'

Uncle Rangsit understood the innate needs of the Siamese people when they turned to their king. Acting Vice-Admiral Lord Louis Mountbatten, coming from the fringe of a quite different royal culture, did not. Which was unfortunate because he claimed in his diaries that he was going to Siam 'to build up British prestige'. He was not without grand designs of his own, however.

'When he flew into Bangkok in January, 1946, he acted as if Siam was a British colony,' reported Harry A. Hindmarsh, a Spitfire pilot who became a newspaper editor. He had escorted Mountbatten's RAF York transport, MW-102. 'On board were Mountbatten's cabinets of medals, his ashtrays inscribed with the family crest, and his family tree that he took everywhere so he could keep looking for a connection with Emperor Charlemagne. He had established that he was related by blood or marriage to Kaiser Wilhelm II, Alfonso XIII of Spain, Ferdinand I of Norway and Alexander I of Yugoslavia, and of course to Queen Victoria.'

Mountbatten called Elder Brother Nan 'a frightened short-sighted boy, his sloping shoulders and thin chest behung with gorgeous diamond-studded decorations; altogether a pathetic and lonely figure . . . his nervousness increased to such an alarming extent, that I came very close to support him in case he passed out . . . It was clearly impossible to observe the royal protocol of not speaking unless His Majesty spoke to me, and I therefore carried on a monologue as best I could, obtaining replies from the King only if I put him a direct question, such as: "Is your Majesty going to remain in Siam?" Reply: "Yes." Question: "Does your Majesty plan to go back to Switzerland?" Reply: "Yes." Question: "I believe we have the honour of dining with your Majesty tonight?" Reply: "Yes," etc. etc . . . Hollywood could not possibly have improved on the King's First State Audience . . . He had never seen any Royal procedure . . . and had not even seen Hollywood's version of how to behave as a King. In fact, he hadn't even got a clue! . . . The King had no idea what to do, but willingly carried out all the instructions I whispered in his ear.'

Tackling the Princess Mother 'on the question of the King leaving his country again so soon after having come to it for almost the first time in his life, I pointed out how lucky it was he had been recalled by the Regent [Pridi] and the underground movement, since in Yugoslavia, Belgium and

Greece they had so far refused to have their King back. I pointed out the obvious danger of His Majesty leaving his country so soon to return to his studies, but was unable to shake her.'

Driving in a procession, 'I leant across to [the King] and said to him: "May I suggest you should acknowledge the cheers of your subjects? Why don't you salute and bow?" He replied gratefully: "I'm afraid I am not very accustomed to this sort of thing."' Mountbatten told him to stay in the kingdom and forget about learning Swiss law: 'I told the boy: "In learning to be a good lawyer, you will hardly learn to be a good King; but you have this consolation, that if your present decision loses you the throne . . . you will be able to earn your living as a lawyer in Switzerland." [He said] it was good to have somebody to talk to who wasn't always saying: "Yes, Your Majesty." . . . I really am sorry for him. He is so hedged about by medieval customs and etiquette. His hair has grown long and untidy but he can't get it cut until the high priest has cast an auspicious day.'

At a State Ball, 'I said to the King: "All over Europe it has always been the custom for the King to open each State Ball. Do you not think you ought to be dancing?" Reply: "No, I have not yet taken sufficient dancing lessons." I spent the next ten minutes trying to persuade the young King to dance. Finally I said: "Your Majesty reminds me of a small boy sitting on the edge of a bathing pool on a very cold day and trying to make up his mind to jump in. If only you will take the plunge you'll find you will quite enjoy it." He then took refuge in the answer he so often used: "Please ask my mother." The Princess Mother supported the king, and said: "He is not experienced enough to take the floor." . . . as she had already refused to dance with me herself, I got fed up and said: "I absolutely insist that one of you two dances . . . " The Princess Mother finally said: "Well if it has got to be one of us it had better be me," and to everyone's intense astonishment she took the floor with me.'

Nan found these irrelevant lessons in western court etiquette less than helpful when the burden of office weighed so heavily. But he knew how to behave like a king when it mattered. When Mountbatten finally got his Great Victory Parade on 21st January, 1946, the boy king silently displaced the Lord High Admiral and took over the reviewing stand, climbing onto a box so he could look down on the tall British supremo. Nan also put survivors of the Free Thai Resistance Movement at the head of the parade.

Seni Pramoj, who conceived the idea that Britain wanted some form of trusteeship over Siam while he was still ambassador to the United States, had now come home to act briefly as the first postwar premier. He saw nothing being done to repair bombed bridges and freight yards. He later recalled: 'Electricity was uncertain, water mains were broken, the telephone systems a patchwork. The troops under British command behaved abominably. It seemed as if we were being blackmailed into begging for British help.'

Sharp divisions were becoming evident between American and British policy-makers, largely because of mutual suspicion that each plotted to win economic domination. The divisions extended into the ranks of Siamese princes and threatened the kingdom's unity. In the *Bangkok Chronicle*, Nan read that the people needed the comforting halo of royal sanctity: 'We are like sleepers awakening from a nightmare . . . a benighted city of oil lamps . . . after four years of war that nobody won and everybody has lost, we are back to where our grandfathers were. Our only hope of survival as a nation lies in keeping the halo of sanctity round the tradition of kingship and the supernatural stamp placed upon it.'

In that same January, Pridi again became prime minister. As a British agent, he had seen how a clique of Northern Command officers collaborated with his enemies, the Japanese. Now he had to win them over for the sake of national unity. But they switched allegiance to the United States which promised to pour millions of dollars into campaigns to stop communism. This led to the release of Marshal Pibul. The War Criminals' Act was pronounced to be illegal in Siam because it was retroactive.

This news was received with cautious satisfaction by a monk whose identity papers named him as Noribu Aoki, one of the Buddhist wartime exchange students from Japan. In reality, he was Masanobu Tsuji. The man who had spearheaded the Japanese invasion of Siam had proceeded to stage his own suicide in the River of Lords of Life to deceive the British when the Japanese cause was lost. Tsuji in his new guise was now pretending to meditate in a temple beside the Grand Palace.

The first overt warning that King Ananda's life was in danger came when a rockfall killed his chief aide, just after the aide's car switched places with the king's in a convoy of vehicles.

'The aide had a sudden premonition and deliberately put himself in danger,' recalled the brother of a witness, Chitr Jotikasthira. 'Right then and there, I knew the king was a target of assassins. He was supposed to be in the lead Jeep that was crushed.'

Nan was on his way to a mock battle staged by US General 'Wild Bill' Donovan of the OSS. During the war, General MacArthur, jealously guarding his own intelligence service, had shut him out of the Pacific. Donovan therefore turned Siam into a base from which to run secret operations against the new Soviet threat in Asia. He had asked President Harry Truman to extend the OSS into a peacetime foreign-intelligence agency. Truman said no. Donovan argued that the British would enlarge their Asian empire under cover of secret operations. An irate British director of secret operations retorted that Donovan was 'launching a self-glorifying public-relations campaign', and the SOE chief, General Sir Colin Gubbins, warned that the OSS was now 'an instrument of American postwar power'. It was an open secret that OSS and SOE pursued separate and rival policies.

The OSS put into Nan's hands what was later said to be the instrument of his own death. The king arrived at Donovan's mock battle. An OSS agent, Alexander MacDonald, showed the king his personal Colt .45. Nan asked to try it out. MacDonald saw that the king could not control the gun's violent kick, and he gave Nan the .45 to practise with. 'He took it with enormous schoolboy pleasure,' MacDonald wrote later.

The king had a new problem with Pridi as premier. He was reputed to be still secretly loyal to the Soviet Union. Some said the story was spread by Pibul. Yet Marshal Pibul had been freed from jail by Pridi. For young Nan, utterly lost in this oriental intrigue mixed with Allied tensions that were beyond any newcomer's comprehension, it was impossible to make sense of these contradictions. What should he believe? The old wartime cronies of the pro-Japanese Northern Command were now greedy to win American financial aid in the new war against communism. Pibul had their support and could end premier Pridi's political career and his relationship to the king.

Pridi wanted his own candidate to become Regent after King Ananda returned to his Lausanne studies. Mama felt strongly that Uncle Rangsit should take over as Regent; that he alone could protect a son whose inexperience could have fatal consequences. King Ananda told Pridi that he wanted Rangsit to have the post. The prime minister dug in his heels. Why? Mama heard all the rumours: that Pridi was a communist; that pro-Soviet members of the British Labour Party wanted him to stay in power; that his choice of the Seventh Rama's widow, Queen Rambhai, for Regent would reinforce his popularity with the British who preferred to see Siam run by royalty they could influence.

So much was going on behind the polite smiles that Mama could not divine. The British had Japanese troops fighting alongside them now in Vietnam to help the French keep colonial power against communist guerrillas. The British were also using the expertise of 110 Japanese senior officers still in Siam; and they were using Japanese soldiers to locate 144 secret Japanese burial sites which might conceal SOE's air-dropped arms.

Some American OSS officers said the British were preparing to stay. The victorious allies were competing with each other for control through local pawns, it seemed to Mama who feared the king was at the centre of a situation that could explode. It was now six months since he had been scheduled to leave. She pleaded with Prince Rangsit to find a way to speed things up. He had the Royal Astrologers announce that the 13th June would be an auspicious time for the brothers to leave.

President Harry Truman had already invited the king to visit Washington, having cancelled Lend-Lease aid to Britain because, he said, it had moved in 'a pro-communist direction' when Winston Churchill was replaced by a Labour government. The British responded with an invitation for King Ananda to stop over in London and meet King George VI. If Nan went to see Truman only he would offend King George. If he saw King George, he would upset Americans distrustful of the Labour government. Uncle Rangsit reminded Nan that Siam's independence had been accomplished by the statecraft of ancestors who balanced between rivals in the Great Game. He should certainly stop over in London, but must keep in mind that the British needed the kingdom's prewar gold and foreign currency reserves left with the Bank of England. They owed the United States crippling war debts and the Bank of England had reported that Siam, nominally an ex-enemy, was actually wealthier than the United Kingdom.

Not surprisingly, Nan wrote to his Swiss girl friend, Marylene Ferrari, 'I can hardly wait to get back to Lausanne.'

Suddenly, two elderly palace retainers, brought out of storage to attend upon the king, died. It was whispered that they had been poisoned. The royal court was full of secrets and rumours. Mama uneasily recalled the stories of another court where there had been the same ceremonial control of spectacle; where the monarch had been captured by mystique; where access to his person was also minutely prescribed by palace protocol; and where proximity or distance from the king defined a person's stature. It was Versailles on the eve of the French Revolution.

Nan fell sick. He had five days left before he was due to leave when, on Saturday, 8th June, 1946, he could not hold down his food. Mama brought him hot milk and brandy. She reminded palace courtiers who thought this was not the work of a king's mother that she was, and always had been, a nurse.

That Saturday evening, two worldly-wise brothers, the former ambassador to Washington, Seni Pramoj, and the younger Kukrit, descendants of King Rama the Second sat silently weeping because they saw what they took to be an ill-omen: a sky bisected by a broad slash of yellow resembling the ceremonial sash of the Chakri dynasty. When Seni had been broadcasting to the Thai Resistance from America, the pixyish Kukrit had been a White Elephant agent for the British. They forgot their differences now. Kukrit later told me that the strange sky reminded them of celestial warnings that preceded the murders of earlier kings. The First Rama had predicted the Chakri dynasty would end in 1932. That year, the phantom of a sacred royal White Elephant had hovered beside a new bridge, just before the Promoters launched their revolution. 'No king had actually ruled after that,' said Seni later. 'The slash in the sky was like the final burnished sword of the dynasty's executioner.'

That night Nan quarrelled again with Premier Pridi about the choice of Regent. The king said he was giving Uncle Rangsit the position. Tightlipped, Pridi left. Nan took to his bed again, clutching his stomach.

7

The Killing of the King

ON Sunday, 9th June Little Brother Lek was up early to watch the barefoot monks who moved so freely through the Grand Palace. Ordinary people filled the monks' bowls because it was more blessed to give than to receive, and the monks did you a kindness by giving you the chance of a better life to come. It was called *metta*, or compassion. Some of the monks were Japanese Buddhist students, still sheltered by royal temples in this same spirit of giving. The student-monks had been brought in by the Japanese Hikari Mission. What Lek had no means of knowing was that the mission had been part of the Asia-wide wartime network run by Emperor Hirohito's relative, Count Ohtani Kozui, for the purposes of espionage, sabotage and assassination.

Monks were everywhere. They flowed through the Gate of Glorious Precious Victory, one of the many gaps in the palace's crenellated white walls, four metres thick and four times as high, with tiny built-in forts. The monks were so much a part of the daily scene, they went unnoticed by palace retainers scurrying through courtyards and alleyways to the royal kitchens from which drifted the delicious smells of rice bubbling in chicken-broth, coriander and fresh lemon grass, deep-fried beancurd with garlic, sliced pineapple and eggs in Thai breakfast soup, crispy pancakes and the special Bangkok soft springroll.

To Lek, the sixty acres of palace grounds were like a cosmic sea viewed at different depths. Above were waves of undulating rooftops whose tiny twinkling tiles had miraculously survived revolution and war. *Nagas* swam as sea-serpents with many heads, and turned into hooded cobras beside the white spired *chedis* rising skyward like frozen thunderbolts. Somewhere in all this, Lek supposed, could be found the secret passages of the Siamese mind which he found sinuous and slippery. Placid on the surface, it concealed layer upon layer of complication. 'A strange people,' he had read in a book on the Grand Palace by the Marquis of Beauvoir. 'The tropical sun alternately casts rays of gold, crimson, pale pink and misty blue which play like thousands of electric lights on the marble minarets, the porcelain domes, the crystal spires, the glistening gables.'

Japanese overlords during the war knew that if they defiled this place of Siamese gods and demons, they would be forced to put down an uprising with regiments of frontline troops they could not spare. So they kept their hands off the voluptuous bird-women made of solid gold, their thighs spread, their breasts tip-tilted. They left untouched the enormous old warehouse crammed with royal paraphernalia and such sacred regalia as the Whisk of the White Elephant's Tail and weapons of sovereignty like the Devil's Discus. Above flickered a tiny flame which had never been extinguished, at least to anyone's knowledge. It burned within the shrine of the Spirit of Goodness, sole guardian of the warehouse of treasures whose value was beyond computation..

Close by, King Ananda was in bed with a fever. His wooden-shuttered bedroom was on the upper floor of the east wing in that rambling mansion of Boromphiman. The outer stone shell stretched 200 feet east to west, and it was eighty feet in depth. Opposite the main entrance stood the Temple of the Emerald Buddha and behind it, to the west and south, the little town of the Back Palace. The mansion kept traces of its former grandeur. Heavy Italian marble columns marched through cavernous but now sparsely furnished rooms. There was a vast assembly hall on the ground floor. Side doors were used mostly by royal pages and servants nipping back and forth from the kitchens in a separate bay. The upper floor was reached from the central entrance hall by a sweeping staircase with marble steps and iron rails interrupted by fluted marble columns. There were two service stairways tucked into the west wing where the Princess Mother and Little Brother Lek stayed. Their spartan bed-chambers were separated from the king's equally austere bedroom by corridors back and front of the main balustrade. A dome over the central area was bordered with frescoes of lesser gods serving the supreme Hindu trinity of Brahma, Vishnu and Shiva the Destroyer.

Here the family had been living for half a year, waiting week by week to leave. The woodwork was riddled by termites. The roof leaked. The whole place smelled like a graveyard. The best chance of being left alone was when the brothers played jazz together. It had been their passion in Lausanne; it was their salvation here. They were both competent with several instruments, although usually the king played the piano and Lek played sax. Their other escape was target-practice in the Turtle Garden behind the mansion. Gunshots or jazz covered their brief snatches of frank conversation. There was no other privacy.

When the boys were on the firing range, their instructor, an impoverished navy lieutenant, observed that neither the king nor his brother seemed capable of shooting straight with the weighty Colt .45 provided by the former OSS agent. The instructor watched from under the mansion dome where the God of the Dead, Yama, was depicted on a throne while at his feet stretched Kala, the chief custodian, whose long legs ended in huge clawed feet and whose pointed nose was almost as long as the hangman's rope dangling from one hand over the edge of a broken column.

On this Sunday morning there were few official functions and the king was expected to sleep late and take breakfast with Mama and Lek at 8.30. Elder Brother Nan disliked walking past the mouldy walls around the central dome where he read stern warnings, barely decipherable after the years of neglect, of what could happen to inadequate kings, taken from Vedic scriptures. He was as unclear about the intrigues swirling around him as he was about the connection between animism and Hinduism, between the prayers of the Brahmin priests and the chanting of Buddhist monks. He had confided to Uncle Rangsit that he had forgotten how to hold a normal conversation and didn't know what to say to President Truman, much less King George.

At six, his mother aroused him. She had worked here as an orphan and some female courtiers grumbled that she had no right to play the grandee, but most palace servants appreciated her readiness to help in menial tasks. Her stunning beauty had endured beyond the age that most Siamese men said marked the end of sexual desirability. The Princess Mother seemed to cast a spell over such men. It was the ladies of the entourage who were critical. Perhaps they were jealous.

Mama asked the king what kind of night he had had. He replied 'Better,' and threw aside a flowered coverlet. His faded blue pyjamas were damp from perspiration. He had turned off a small fan driven by a little kerosene-fuelled motor. He drank some brandy and milk, dropped back, and at once fell into deep sleep.

Lek emerged from what was unappropriately called the playroom. He hated being treated like a child. He dreaded being lectured by those courtiers who took it upon themselves to prevent him from upsetting unseen deities. The monsoon season had started, the robes of the Emerald Buddha had been changed accordingly, the image had been ritually bathed, but still no rain fell. So there was talk of reviving the Ploughing Ceremony when the king coaxes the heavens to open. That could mean more delay. Brahmin priests would make astrological calculations as to which day was lucky. Lek hoped no busybody official would bring this up before the 13th, *his* lucky day for getting away.

For this morning, he had arranged to go with the king to play some jazz with another princely courtier. They were to meet at nine for an hour. Nan was running late. Their mother was back in her bedroom, talking with a lady-in-waiting.

At 9.20 a.m. a bang was heard in the eastern wing upstairs.

A royal page was heard shouting, 'The king has shot himself!'

Mama flew along the back corridor, pursued by all her old fears. History seemed to come to a full stop.

Lek heard a thud that might be a slamming door. He left his room and saw the commotion. He followed the Royal Nanny along the corridor and into Nan's bedroom. The Nanny had been a nursing student with his mother. Mama bent over King Ananda's thin body, and kept crying, 'My dear Nan! My dear Nan!' The Royal Nanny took hold of Nan's wrist, knowing that the Princess Mother could not care less about forbiddances against touching a royal person. 'There's still a pulse,' she said. Mama picked up her son's wrist. He seemed to have been sleeping when shot. He was flat on his back and completely limp. Even as his mother felt the faint pulse, it fluttered and vanished like a departing soul. She was too good a nurse to fool herself. Nan was dead. There was a wound in the middle of his forehead and she began distractedly wiping away the blood. Lek hurried out to call for the Royal Physician.

When Lek returned, the fact sank in that Nan was gone. Little Brother was struck by a terrible thought. The Siamese were convinced that one's spirit wandered during sleep. The most awful thing that could happen was to die before the spirit had a chance to re-enter the body. *The Buddhist Book of the Dead* taught that nothing mattered so much as a tranquil passage to the next life. Mama had not yet had time to consider that her son's soul might be condemned to wander.

Lek was frightened for his mother's peace of mind. He vowed to give Elder Brother 'a decent funeral', he told me later. 'It seems a strange fancy, but there had to be a proper transition.' It was Lek's first big concession to Siamese beliefs: he could not let his brother's spirit become lost and wandering through all eternity. This explained his subsequent actions.

The Royal Physician was outside the Grand Palace fixing his antiquated car. It took a long time to find him. Distraught palace servants ran through the mansion like headless chickens. The Princess Mother took refuge in actions that later gave birth to ugly rumours. She began mechanically to strip and bathe Nan's body. Uncle Rangsit had been on his way to see King Ananda and, after standing horrified, took comfort from instructing Mama on the iron routine to be followed. He knew by heart all the rituals to be employed when a king died: the General Expulsion of Evil: the Bathing and Adornment of the Royal Corpse – Mama cleaned the body, not thinking she might be disturbing police evidence. Sudden death made it impossible to carry out the most sacred ritual which was the Ceremony to be Performed *Before* a Dying King Expires. That was when scriptural texts were inscribed on nine sheets of gold leaf and placed on the nine principal parts of the body while the monarch is still alive.

The royal page had shouted that the king shot himself. His mother had first taken this to mean an accident. But – accident? Nan's wrists were as thin as her own, and lacked the strength to steady a large pistol. How could he fire it *accidentally* into the centre of his forehead? Nan must have been killed in his sleep. Logic led her to the question of where Nan's spirit had gone, but this was too dreadful to dwell on yet. She turned to the duties required *after* the death of a monarch. Mercury should be poured down the throat to speed the drying of the corpse; a mask of gold should be prepared to place over the face, symbolic of the radiant vision of a god. This was all so antithetical to her own Buddhist simplicities, it was so much at odds with the austere cremation of her husband, that she began to feel she was losing her reason. To keep her poise under the searching gaze of those entering the room, she fell back upon stern duty.

A family doctor had come on the scene at about ten. Major Nitya Vejjavivisth could see no sign of cadaveric spasm. This was murder, he decided without saying anything to the mother. 'Blood was soaking from the back of the head into the bed,' he said later. 'There was a cross-shaped wound of about four centimetres on His Majesty's forehead and a hole of about one centimetre in the frontal bone.'

The Royal Physician, Dr Snood Sanvichien, finally arrived. He knew enough about gunshot wounds to find this one strange. A Colt .45 held to the head was more likely to blast it apart, or at least leave a gaping hole where the bullet emerged from the back of the skull. What appeared to be the murder weapon was on top of a wooden cabinet, as if carefully laid aside. He saw no bullet, nor a spent cartridge case. 'I decided this was the work of a communist agent,' he wrote later, refuting stories that the palace closed ranks to hide some terrible secret.

The police issued a bulletin that King Ananda had shot himself accidentally while playing with a Colt .45. The OSS agent, Alexander MacDonald, who had given the king his own Colt, was devastated. Then he became uneasy after talking with old wartime colleagues. 'The service .45 must have the grip safety depressed when firing. There were rumours that the official statement about an "accident" was a cover up for suicide, but both were virtually impossible for a fairly fragile boy. It would be terribly difficult, and it's abnormal, to shoot yourself in the forehead.'

When word got around that King Ananda was dead, all kinds of people crowded into the Grand Palace to join government ministers and senior officials. Among them was a senior grandson of King Chulalongkorn, Celestial Prince Bhanabhandu Yugala, who had protected Allied agents while he acted as liaison with Japanese commanders.

'It was murder. And there was a risk of civil war without a living king. Every honest person wanted the younger brother to step in – quickly!' the Celestial Prince told me fifty years later, refreshing his memory from notes made when he was the first person commissioned to investigate the death. 'The regicide was planned to destroy the country by removing the only symbol of unity. The police claimed the boy was playing with the gun when it went off. It didn't make sense. He wasn't wearing his glasses and he couldn't see a thing without them, and you don't play with a gun when you're sick and lying down. I never doubted the brothers were not intended to leave Siam alive. The government put a blanket over it all . . . Lion and tiger were fighting inside the cave for possession.'

The lion was Marshal Pibul, no longer facing charges as a war criminal, and allied with the Northern Command clique secretly preparing to run postwar Siam. The tiger was Pridi. The premier had quarrelled only the previous evening with the dead king. Now he was not in the royal audience chamber. His critics would say later that this was significant. The two men were dubbed by foreign journalists 'Tweedledhi & Tweedlebun' (Pibul is pronounced *Pee-bun*).

Marshal Pibul was quick to spread the word that Pridi had used his position as Britain's most highly placed agent to get arms for a communist uprising; and his involvement in the king's death was why he was not seen that morning. Thus began a whisper campaign that frightened people into a silence that lasted half a century. A woman senator finally confessed to me: 'I got close to the truth as a very young reporter. My parents were warned by the police that I would be killed. I stopped asking questions. If there was such a thing as a God of Evil, the god spread a pall of suspicion and fear that has clouded the kingdom ever since.'

Lek saw his mother nursing Nan's still-warm corpse. She had once resisted demands that this child lying dead in her arms become king. Then she had given way to duty. Papa had died because of duty. Uncle Rangsit had spent years in prison for duty. Now Nan was dead in duty's name. All the men she loved had been doomed by duty.

Lek was in the grip of something more powerful. Mama looked up and saw it in his face. They both could hear the frightened cries for a new king coming from below.

He walked out of the death chamber as if moved by another's will, deaf to his mother's cry: 'No! Don't do it!'

8

Succession

Lek moved towards the broad stairway. Uncle Rangsit stood in the corridor, transfixed by the sight of the boy, cold-faced and yet drenched in sweat. For a moment Little Brother looked like King Ananda. Through Rangsit's mind, he said later, ran the German expression, '*Zeitgeist*' – a ghost speaking for the spirit of the times. His German wife's family had died for going against the spirit of Hitler's time.

It was only fourteen hours since Rangsit had been appointed Regent by the king who was now dead. In the absence of a king, the new Regent represented kingship. His responsibility was for the country. His personal loyalty was to the approaching figure. He had watched Lek drift through palace pomp, and he knew how desperately the boy had wanted to escape.

Lek paused, suddenly aware of Prince Rangsit's frozen presence. Boy and man regarded each other. The Regent saw an enigma. The boy saw a sixty-one-year-old friend who had been threatened with execution and spent years in prison for his loyalty to Siam's welfare. Rangsit threw his cloak over the boy's thin shoulders and said in a hoarse whisper, 'You can never turn back.'

Lek began a slow descent. He stopped halfway. A hush fell among monks, senior princes, cabinet ministers, courtiers and commoners who had squeezed unchecked into the audience chamber. Garlands of sweet-smelling frangipani swung gently in open windows. Such one-day garlands had been made by Mama when she lived in the Back Palace. Hot winds swirled through the courtyard. The sunshine blazing outside turned the chamber into a pit of darkness. Above Lek's head was a circle of light from the high glass dome. He stood framed against it, a perfect target.

He said tonelessly that he accepted their demand. The silence was broken by shouts of '*Chaiyo!*' Long live the king!

Prince Rangsit at the head of the stairs clenched his fists. Lek was acclaimed King Bhumibol, Ninth Rama, but he was still unprotected until crowned. Other kings in this position had been killed. And the boy surely knew it.

The new king started to climb back up the stairs, then paused and turned. He would need the full support of everyone, he said in English, and added a Thai expression: '*Duai chai sucharit*' – and with sincerity.

Prince Bhanabhandu, at the foot of the bannisters, stood immobilised by astonishment at those last three words. He was the product of an English public school and the military academy at Sandhurst, and survivor of a dangerous double-life under the Japanese. He was not easily fooled. He recalled: 'In seconds, the boy had become a king. He spoke like a king . . . Everyone knew what he meant in a world of lip-service and deceit. People pleaded for him to accept the throne and he acted fast to save their skins but he didn't want them to betray him later. I could not believe he had thought of those words himself and later I asked if anyone had written them out for him. But nobody had.'

The new king continued to surprise those who had seen his lack of inter-est while Nan was alive. He asked if anyone noticed anybody enter the palace who should not have been there? This was impossible to answer. It was always full of visitors from the streets outside who came to worship or just look around, and anyone could have strayed into the royal family's quarters, too. Royal guards wanted to close off the palace. But Lek said this was the very time when it should be open to those who wanted to mourn with him. He would keep vigil before the dead king's body. The Princess Mother found herself caught between her western-style rationality and the old superstitions. In her distress, she accepted the advice that funeral rites were a Spiritual Coronation to celebrate the ascension of a good king's spirit to join the gods. Privately, she finally confronted the idea that the spirit could be wandering and lost when someone died suddenly in sleep. Where was Nan's spirit now? She could never attend his funeral until she knew the answer. For four more years, the desiccated corpse would wait for the crematory flames.

King Bhumibol wanted his brother's death to serve some useful purpose. He had heard the report that the lion and tiger would now fight for posses-sion. Uncle Rangsit said Siam must stay united, or the great powers would bring in more troops to keep order. What held the Siamese people together were the laws of their hidden universe. Therefore things must unfold according to sacred rules. The royal urn, the Great Golden One, would have to be re-assembled. The First Rama had designed it. The remains of later kings and senior members of the royal family had been kept in it until their cremation. Miraculously, the urn's sections still stood behind the huge old wooden bed where the dynasty conceived its armies of offspring. The bed was stuck in a corner of the Throne Hall. The heavy gold frames of the urn were bolted together with the inner silver shells, under the guidance of a loyal old palace servant who remembered all the procedures. Nobody else remained alive who could recall all the elaborate rites. Since King Chulalongkorn's frugal funeral, there had been no ceremonial send-offs.

Pibul's army cronies were taken aback when Lek launched an independent inquiry into Nan's death. He brought in British army doctors and an American physician who had worked with Papa at the missionary hospital, after he had ordered the cutting open of King Ananda's body. The archaic rules about examining royal bodies were ignored: his father, as a young doctor, had lacked the power to change them. Lek, as King Bhumibol, could. He formed a commission of doctors to study the results of the swift forensic examination. After tests on other corpses, and the firing of bullets into pigs and much argument about what the military knew of gunshot wounds, sixteen of the doctors said murder was the most likely cause of death: four said suicide, and two concluded it was an accident.

The new king had quickly empowered a British-Indian Army pathologist to remove Nan's viscera for further tests, remembering the stories that two royal pages were killed by poisoning. Could plotters have had access to the potion his mother took to Elder Brother that fatal morning? 'In the viscera of His Late Majesty,' certified Captain V. N. Chaturvedi, 'none of the common metallic or alkaloidal poisons were detected.'

Immediately after death, it had been customary to wrap a *phanung* of red cloth around a king's loins and thighs, with a cream-coloured scarf binding his chest. The new king then traditionally led the family in pouring holy water over the feet of the corpse. Normally, there would be a First Queen to comb the hair and then break the wooden comb into pieces to make sure it was never used again. The body had to be re-clothed in two *phanungs*, under a vest of silk and a coat embroidered with gold, two baldricks glittering with diamonds across the breast. This had not been done before the hasty post-mortem on King Ananda.

Since there was no First Queen, Mama had to perform the duty. Her face betrayed no emotion while she wrapped her first son's body, hurriedly stitched and patched after the immediate forensic examinations. She combed his hair. Bones had to be broken to bend the body into the sitting position, thighs pressed tightly against stomach, knees drawn up to chin, feet tied to a stick, arms encircling the legs and all bound in linen and fastened with special cords. She put gloves and gold shoes on the dead king's hands and feet, a silk cap over his skull, a gold ring in his mouth. She gazed upon his face for the last time and covered it in a gold mask. A crown was lowered upon the masked head. Thus he was 'fully crowned and annointed Sovereign' and in palace terminology recognised as Grand Master of the Most Illustrious Order of the Royal House of Chakri. Kneeling, shedding no tears, Mama allowed the trussed and bound body to be placed within the Great Golden One's inner silver casing. The space was small, even for a boy so slight: about a hundred centimetres high by fifty-five centimetres at the widest diameter. The eight outer sections of gem-encrusted gold enfolded Nan. Through the perforated floor, bodily fluids would be drawn off daily through a stop-cock until the corpse became dry.

When all was done, she withdrew, features drawn, her spine straight as a rod, back to the dark seclusion of her bedroom.

A Siamese king's astral body was thought to hover until its ascent to join the gods at the time of cremation. King Ananda's spirit seemed destined to wander until the mystery of his death was solved. Only the earthly envelope was in the urn on a nine-tiered platform beneath the white Umbrella of State. Because Nan had not been crowned, he was entitled only to an umbrella of seven levels. The new king, in the language of the court, 'raised King Ananda to the level of nine royal umbrellas.' Eleven years earlier, the prospect of being lost under the white umbrella had made Nan first reject the crown. 'He might be alive today,' Lek remembered thinking, 'if he had followed his instincts.' The body was to remain in the urn far beyond the Hundred Days of mourning observed in past centuries. A thousand days would pass before cremation became thinkable, long after the juices from Nan's body had ceased to drip into the pan under the urn.

Lek had made a rational decision that, to save Siam from chaos, he must restore what once would have seemed to him a pagan ritual. Now he wondered if there was such a vast gulf between the beliefs of east and west? He remembered Shakespeare's words: 'I am thy father's spirit, doomed for a certain term to walk the night.' Was his dead brother like that king of Denmark, and was Lek like the son named Hamlet? He stood before the urn, night and day from June to August, praying that Siam would not be divided by the murder. During some of the worst thunderstorms in living memory, he walked unprotected through the crowds on his way to keep the vigil, refusing to take physical precautions against attack.

Lek had set his own inquiry in motion, but this did not stop the rumour mill. Because nervous court officials never admitted the possibility of foul play, talk of a palace cover-up was soon circulating. 'A source of the highest royal rank says the king was definitely assassinated and a politician now in power is going to turn the country into a republic,' the British embassy reported to London. Admiral Lord Mountbatten, who never began to understand the world of Nan and Lek, was said to have written to King

George VI that 'King Bhumibol shot his brother to obtain the crown.' Alexander MacDonald recalled, 'It was easy to spread disinformation over a telephone system in Bangkok reduced by war to the greatest communications feat ever accomplished with bailing wire.' More soberly he goes on to report, 'A nasty war of innuendo was being fought. It was said there was a plot to get rid of the monarchy altogether, perhaps by blaming the younger king for Ananda's murder.' MacDonald still felt awful about giving Nan his gun, but he was having doubts that it was the murder weapon.

Pridi quit as prime minister in August, distressed and helpless to defend himself against a whisper campaign naming him the regicide's mastermind. The man he had freed from jail, Pibul, remained in the shadows, content to manipulate a weak government whose new figurehead once led a goodwill mission to Tokyo after the Japanese invasion: Admiral Thamrong Nawasawat. He launched an inquiry that became known as the King's Death Case. It buried the conclusions reached by Lek's panel of doctors.

The dead king's servants were interrogated. They were known as royal pages, though they were mature men, but they were vague on details of that fatal morning. Lek was not surprised: 'By nine on any morning when my brother was alive, retainers were apt to be mentally absent while physically at their posts. I could walk around the grounds in full view of the pages. If Nan came to find me, nobody remembered seeing me.'

The Chief of the Palace Guards feared for King Bhumibol's life as he moved alone between the streams of mourners. British army security officers were concerned that they would be blamed if a second king were killed, but Lek refused to be cut off from countryfolk. Some had walked for days to pay homage. He would not rob them of monarchy's magic. Royalty itself had to believe in the myth. Otherwise, royalty was not convincing.

Lek's real vulnerability was known to Prince Chakrabandhu Bensiri Chakrabdandhu. He was a kindly and sensitive man, a soldier and poet. When he told me what he could remember, he still seemed to be the courtly officer of old, with a long sad face and large romantic eyes. He had an ear for music. Before Nan's death, the brothers asked him to join in their jazz sessions.

'Show us what you can do,' King Ananda had told him.

The Prince improvised, and Lek said, 'You're good, but a little wild here and there.'

'I had no formal training,' murmured the gentle prince. 'I compose by ear. And I know nothing about classical music.'

'Jazz is classical,' said Elder Brother Nan.

'I need practice.'

'We'll give you practice,' said Little Brother Lek.

'But I'm in love,' stuttered the soldier-poet.

'That's nothing to look glum about.'

'I mean, I'm in love with the Blues but don't know how to play them.'

The brothers laughed. 'We'll teach you,' the late king had said and, from then on, there were regular jam sessions. If there was no formal engagement early in the morning, the trio would get together for what the prince later recalled as 'an escape into privacy for King Ananda. Otherwise, he had constantly to wonder who was serving the god of influence, *ittipon*, by trying to be seen at his side . . . On that last Sunday, the boys were late for a nine o'clock appointment. I was thinking they were playing another of their tricks on me . . . But when they should be making music, His Majesty was already dead. I heard the shouts and hurried to the mansion. Among all those dignitaries, I felt out of place. Much later, I tried to tip-toe away.'

The new king caught him at a side door. 'Don't go! I need you. The only close friend I had was my brother. Please be my friend.'

'But you have many friends,' said the prince.

'Acquaintances. At school. On the ski slopes. Not friends. And nobody here.'

'Then,' said the old prince, 'my king for the first time cried.'

When Lek stood expressionless and dry-eyed in front of King Ananda's urn, he heard the seamless chant of monks running back through nearly 2,500 years to Lord Buddha talking to his disciples, a continuity symbolised by the thread passing through the hands of the cross-legged monks. 'Monks say that chanting opens the mind to a path between souls,' said Lek. 'It happened to me. Nan once talked about a mind of the universe creating all things: a godhead that shattered into a billion billion fragments. Each of us is a bit of a bit. We move through manifestations of ourselves toward unity with all other sentient beings until the godhead becomes whole again.'

On the night before he was to return to school, King Bhumibol stood again before his brother's body. 'His face was an iron mask,' said the soldier-poet, Chakrabandhu. 'He had to hide from his enemies any sign of weakness and he had to conceal his feelings.' The prince saw Lek walk away from the Great Golden One for the last time, and stumble as if in surprise, then turn. What had happened?

Lek explained to me later, 'I heard following footsteps as I left the urn.

In royal ceremonies, I had always to walk behind my brother. In this moment I forgot he was dead, and I told him, "It is for me to walk behind you. That is the proper way." My brother replied, "From now on, I walk behind you."'

Part Two

9

Who Killed the King?

THE murder of a king in Europe would cause a media frenzy. In Bangkok, reporters were silenced by a new military gestapo whose existence was concealed from the new king. An editor disappeared for implying that Marshal Pibul had been rescued from war-criminal charges by enemies of the king. In cinemas, the accusation was hissed against the man who freed him: 'Pridi killed the king!'

The sense of the dead king's presence sharpened Lek's memory of Nan's thin body on its back, legs stretched out, limp arms extended, hands curled, eyes closed. He scoured manuals on the Colt .45, learning that pistols issued to OSS agents were usually loaded with special bullets, hollow-pointed, that blew a target's head apart. The calibre was close to that of an elephant gun. The kick could shift a seven-pound weight a distance of two feet. Whenever Nan had fired it on the range, his arm jerked violently upward so that he was just like other novice shooters who pull the trigger instead of squeezing it, causing the muzzle to jump so much that an amateur could fire an entire clip of five to seven rounds at fifteen metres and miss a man completely. The Colt had been tidily positioned in Nan's bedroom by someone else.

As well as the British Indian-Army pathologist Lek had asked Colonel J. D. Driberg of the British Royal Army Medical Corps 'to provide an expert armourer of English or American nationality to inspect the late king's body'. After Driberg was called to the British embassy for a confidential chat, he deemed it best not to go on public record with any opinion about accident, suicide or murder.

The Ninth Rama was not asked to the talks in Washington originally scheduled for King Ananda. He discussed this with Uncle Rangsit and Old Gran at the Palace of Lotus Ponds. To make their way there secretly when Nan was alive, the brothers escaped attention by wearing the clothes of the street: worn singlets, pants, and sandals. Now Lek followed the old routine.

He picked up public opinion right outside the Grand Palace walls in the seventy-five-acre Pramane Ground where crowds gathered to gawk at King's Death Case witnesses brought to an adjacent court-house.

The Pramane Ground was a magnet for countryfolk. The king passed for a farmboy in the dark. He watched the tastiest dishes sizzle and smoke in shallow pans over charcoal braziers while the poorest people sucked opium pellets to kill the pangs of hunger. Opium was easier to come by than food, thanks to the wartime expansion of opium supplies by Tsuji Masanobu, working with Siamese army quislings in the opium-growing region of northern Siam and Burma. Tsuji's name appeared as a war criminal in Allied intelligence reports but nothing about his past was disclosed to the new king who could only patch together information through an informal group of King's Men. Many had been in Force 136, the Siamese section of SOE, or were US-run agents. One former agent reported that Major-General Geoffrey Evans, the British Commander of Allied Land Forces, had asked: 'If one king was murdered, why not the other?'

The only possible motive for killing Elder Brother Nan must have been to destroy the monarchy, and Evans' army intelligence officers were looking for Tsuji as 'one of the most dangerous men on the planet'. He had been helped to go underground by the last Japanese ambassador in Bangkok, Kumaichi Yamamoto. The British knew Tsuji had disguised himself as a monk but now dismissed the first theory that he had slipped out of Bangkok. When reports first came in that the war was over, Tsuji had quickly built secret bunkers in Bangkok, paying Chinese black-marketeers with gold from the Greater East Asia Ministry in Tokyo which supported 'stay-behind' groups in Asian jungles. The gold had been already cached in strategic places. Even back then, Tsuji was planning a new kind of struggle.

A British Army colonel, Cyril Wild, doggedly followed the trail of Tsuji. Wild was a former prisoner of the Japanese who spoke their language fluently, and flew to Tokyo as representative of the United Kingdom War Crimes Liaison Mission. In this same summer of 1946 when Nan was killed, US General Douglas MacArthur was earning a name as the American Caesar who surveyed all Asia from his Occupation headquarters in Japan. Wild had explosive and well-documented files on Tsuji but he was told by an aide to MacArthur's intelligence chief, Major-General Charles Willoughby, that 'the General asks that the United Kingdom drops her efforts to trace this officer [Tsuji] and, in addition, all plans to prosecute him.' Wild had unearthed twenty-four Japanese War Ministry reports, prepared after Japan's defeat, instructing Tsuji on how to evade capture. Wild wanted to lay out the facts before the International Military Tribunal for the Far East (IMTFE). The Japanese had destroyed, hidden or falsified high-level military records. Wild out-smarted Japan's 25th Army intelligence chief, Ichiji Sugita, by recovering the documents of a secret postwar Japanese group known as Unit 4.

Told to drop Tsuji's case altogether, and unable to make his information public, Wild flew to Hong Kong. Colleagues reported that Tsuji was communicating with one of his oldest and closest comrades, Shigeru Aseada, now part of Unit 4 whose members were protected as 'experts on communism' by the Americans in Tokyo. Wild left Hong Kong on 25th September, 1946 for his headquarters in Singapore. His aircraft crashed shortly after take-off. Wild was killed, and all his personal notes on Tsuji were lost. Lek and his King's Men, who were perhaps the most in need of this information, never received it.

The Ninth Rama had found a way to learn of Bangkok's intrigues better than any Allied intelligence officers or diplomats. When Nan was still alive, Lek had visited cinemas incognito in order to listen to the piano-players who warmed up the audiences, and one of these, a young Portuguese struggling to feed his brothers and sisters, agreed to join King Ananda and Lek in their jazz sessions. Lek later gave him a Thai name, Manrat, meaning Truthful Vision. He proved to be more trustworthy a source than western observers pouring into Bangkok with their own governmental prejudices colouring their judgement.

The head of the US diplomatic mission in Bangkok, Edwin F. Stanton, had arrived after a previous posting to China. He believed communism had taken root in the local Chinese community. He asked for a royal audience. Lek was not going to be drawn into any political discussion. And so Stanton's impression of the king was that of 'a boy, mouth drawn down at the corners'. Stanton wrote later that it was difficult to coax the Princess Mother to appear: and when she did, she was 'a frightened woman of woeful countenance [in] an oppressive and deadly stillness'.

Stanton sat in awkward and lengthening silence. Finally, he blurted out something about a new Kodak camera, having heard that both the king and his mother were keen photographers. The king was happy to talk about something uncontroversial. Stanton wrote: 'Their interest in affairs of state had become timorous . . . They had a dread of these ornate palace rooms.'

What mother and son dreaded most was to talk about King Ananda's death. The Princess Mother had once seemed to Lord Mountbatten 'to be a vivacious woman who looked half her age and who danced and joked with me like a young debutante'. That was in January. Now she seemed crushed and old. Lek hid behind the mask of an innocent boy. Both knew that nothing they said was secret. They were surrounded by courtiers who concealed their feelings behind *chowris*, exquisite leaf-like fans, big or small according to status. The fans were supposed to wave away evil but each royal word could be absorbed through them and relayed outside with a less than devout twist. The royal audience confirmed Washington's view that the new king was too young to be taken seriously: 'He deferred to his mother,' said Stanton, 'and she was paralysed by guilt.' Stanton thought she blamed herself for not stopping her boys from becoming kings in such treacherous circumstances.

British civilians in Bangkok were robustly on the new king's side. 'No two brothers loved each other more,' wrote Judge Gerald Sparrow, the Englishman appointed to the International Court in Siam, and a prolific author. 'King Ananda was murdered in his own bed by the filthy hand of International Communism, the Comintern. It might have reduced the kingdom to chaos. It did not [because] the King's younger brother, with real personal courage, took over.'

Kenneth Landon, the State Department adviser married to the author of *Anna and The King of Siam*, had a different slant. He reported: 'The military is a fence around the king.'

But Lek had ways through the fence. He asked Dr Edwin Cort, the American doctor who had worked among lepers with his father in Chiang Mei, to meet him in Old Gran's garden. Cort had served on his medical panel of inquiry. Cort was unflappable, shrewd, and grateful to Siamese colleagues who risked their lives to hide Americans from the Japanese occupation. He was infuriated by tales that Lek killed Nan, and had said as much to the State Department to which he was an interim adviser. He sat with the boy under a sacred bo tree, and one night suggested that a possible motive for killing King Ananda had been Nan's support for the Chinese residents who were now said to be helping communists: 'It's an old lie,' he said. 'Marshal Pibul deported their families in wartime for the same thing.'

Dr Cort turned to forensic matters. If Nan was killed by a bullet in the head, the American asked, why was the body limp? It should have been in cadaveric spasm. Why did the police say the bullet lodged in Nan's head, when it was supposedly found later in the bedding? Why was a bloodstained pillowcase unearthed later in the Turtle Garden? There was no explanation for the cross-shaped wound in Nan's forehead. Any projectile fired into the skull would cause a concave dent centred on the entry wound: a circular entry and an irregular, large and messy exit. And as for a .45 bullet, it would send a man flying backward like rag doll. The standard Colt .45 automatically ejected a casing within a couple of feet to the right of the pistol. No casing had been found. Ballistic experts said the Colt .45 placed near the body had never been fired in weeks. Chemical tests on the rifling of the barrel supported this. The registration number, 2 C 81459, corresponded with that of the gun given to Nan by Alexander MacDonald. But was it the murder weapon?

Cort said it was a physical impossibility for anyone, least of all a boy who was frail and ill, to hold the gun any distance from his head and pull the trigger while overriding the safety devices. Suicides pressed the barrel against the side of the temple, or put it in the mouth. Cort thought the original report of an accident or suicide had been circulated to give the regicide and accomplices time to escape.

The king in singlet and shorts took many secret ways to Old Gran's home. One night he slipped out of the Grand Palace from the river landing, and then along the canal running beside the Palace of Lotus Ponds, using a flat-bottomed wooden boat like the one his mother had once paddled. There he met the Regent, Prince Rangsit, in the cultivated jungle where male peacocks strutted and spread their multi-coloured tail feathers in great rustling fans of erotic display, their triple-pronged crowns erect on their proud little heads.

Uncle Rangsit felt that King Bhumibol should return to Lausanne with his mother before she died from grief. In Siam, first loyalty was to a parent in need. And Lek needed to master political science and law.

'I'm not an academic,' the king protested. 'The country needs technicians.' Lek had hoped to go to university, to study engineering.

'My father, your grandfather, King Chulalongkorn, always said we would remain stupid boys if we did not go to European schools,' said Rangsit. 'Siam was never colonised because your forefathers were statesmen.'

'Kings count for nothing today,' Lek countered.

'They do here,' said Rangsit. 'A King of Siam must keep his small principality independent by balancing the rivalries of surrounding forces.'

There were also the gods and demons to consider because, as Rangsit put it, 'They're part of our inner world.' He came back to their next meeting with a passage from *Siamese State Ceremonials* that made a deep impression on Lek. It quoted the American anthropologist, Kaspar Malinowski: 'A society which makes its traditions sacred will gain an inestimable advantage of power and permanence. Beliefs and practices which put a halo of sanctity round tradition and a supernatural stamp upon it, will have a survival value for the type of civilisation into which they have evolved. Bought at an extravagant price, they are to be maintained at any cost.'

The Regent traced the growth of Siamese beliefs out of magical symbols. The White Elephant, the White Monkey and the White Raven protected majesty because they were visual expressions of what people believed. 'Marshal Pibul tried to uproot the old beliefs after the 1932 revolution and removed the royal White Elephants from the Grand Palace,' said Rangsit. 'People remember. For fourteen more years, they suffered.'

The Regent also reminded the king of Buddha's words: 'For as long as there are bullies and liars, kings are needed. For as long as the poor look for hope and the rich seek excess, for as long as the wicked fight for dominion and other nations manoeuvre for control, for as long as evil men oppose the impulses of the good, we need to believe in a king whose power comes from above.' Buddha's dream of building a republic through kingship had been tempered by a pragmatic knowledge of human failings.

But Lek wondered if Rangsit was right in insisting that he study political science. What use were western ideas of parliamentary democracy in a land deeply influenced by ancient traditions, alien to western experience? His prime minister, Pridi, was a case in point. Pridi had found it impossible to carry on; his authority and the effort to create western-style democratic institutions were sabotaged by whisper campaigns. As if to bolster Pridi's position, the British Labour government had ignored the normal thirty-year secrecy rule and identified Pridi as their wartime secret agent RUTH. Lord Mountbatten made even more astonishing disclosures at a public function in London. 'Pridi organised sabotage and guerrilla forces comprising some 60,000 fighting men, which was more than Siam's total number of regular troops . . . The strain imposed on Pridi and the risks he ran for over three years were very formidable . . . He never failed us . . . and British prisoners of war in Thailand have good reason to be grateful.'

It was all very puzzling. Pridi had been so frequently condemned as a communist. The activities of wartime spies and saboteurs were still closely held secrets in Britain. Were these disclosures intended to restore Pridi to the premiership he had abandoned in August?

In January, Mountbatten had been pressuring King Ananda to stay in Siam. 'I spent four days hammering away to make King Ananda realise that it is crazy to leave the country for Switzerland.' Now, Mountbatten wanted King Bhumibol to leave.

The change of heart came with a new policy outlined to Mountbatten by Malcolm MacDonald, the son of Ramsay MacDonald who had become the British first Labour prime minister in 1924. Malcolm MacDonald was British Governor General for South East Asia, based in Singapore. The

British could not afford an unstable neighbour: they were preparing for a long-drawn war in Malaya with Chinese-led communist guerrillas who were directed from jungle headquarters on the border with Siam, by now generally called Thailand. Britain wanted to withdraw troops from Siam, but not risk being blamed if another king was killed. And so Mountbatten had the Ninth Rama delivered safely back to Lausanne.

Before Lek left, Uncle Rangsit recommended an ancient Chinese classic, *Romance of the Three Kingdoms*, constant companion of their ancestor King Mongkut, Rama the Fourth. It contained the essence of statecraft. Rangsit quoted its start and finish: 'Empires wax and wane: states cleave asunder and coalesce . . . All down the ages rings the note of change.' The book helped Lek enter the mind of his great-grandfather, the Fourth Rama, who had found the way to balance between rival powers.

10

Sirikit

THE king's flight was once more in British hands. As a safety precaution, the crews were confined to barracks at Bangkok's Don Muang airport. At night, searchlights played on their converted Lancaster bomber, a piston-engined transport called a Lancastrian. Armed guards were posted round the clock. One muggy morning, King Bhumibol and his mother were hurried over bumpy roads in a vintage Packard whose palace polish slowly vanished under layers of red dust. The journey was in poignant contrast to the earlier drive described in Mountbatten's diaries: 'A Rolls-Royce . . . chauffeur and footmen dressed in a uniform indistinguishable from the Russian Guards . . . a long silver trumpet . . . I was gratified to see colossal crowds.'

No colossal crowds had been summoned by silver trumpets this time. The departure date of 14th August, 1946, had been kept secret as another security measure. Yet the crowds rose out of the flanking ricefields in the fiery orange glow of the sun as it burned off the low-lying mist. 'Some mysterious empathy between the king and the people brought them out,' reported Alexander MacDonald of Associated Press. 'A forest of arms rose up. Hands clutched lotus buds, a symbol of the rebirth as Buddha of Indra, god-of-gods.'

Indra in mythology falls to the level of an ant, rises again to seek liberation from self, but is drawn back down again. Lek had been taught the story. But he did not want to be forever rising and falling. He had discarded the ceremonial robes and was back in school uniform. He wanted to shake off the confusion and the oppressive heat; and forget the conspiracies. He was tired of being organised by others. Lek did not expect to be reborn as Buddha. He was a schoolboy again. Mama sat beside him, stiff and pale, once more dressed in her simple European frock. He rolled down his window and heard what stuck in his mind later as a single chant, 'Do not forsake us!'

The words jolted him. He knew these people now. They were perceived in the west as indolent. Harsh extremes of flood and drought forced them into spasms of idleness. But he had watched with admiration their inventive and patient hands. What could they not do with modern technology to empower them! New ideas had emerged from the war. Innovation had always changed the fate of millions. He knew enough now about the legends that Siamese armies won supremacy when someone first thought of lashing fighting platforms to the backs of war elephants. He was more certain than ever that he should forget the study of political science in favour of a technical education so that he could lead the kind of revolution the country needed.

At the airfield, a former British SOE agent with Force 136, Eric H. Morris, waited. Mother and son boarded the converted RAF bomber plane and Morris followed them in. The flight zigzagged through a British Empire now dying. Bodyguards were dressed in white mess jackets on the plane, and it refuelled only at secured British airfields. Outward bound, there had been no sense of danger, and the crews had remarked on Mama's youthful looks and energy. Now, she was listless and haggard beside the empty seat.

As the months passed, Lek drifted back into his old identity, but life was more difficult without Elder Brother. To make things easier, Lek pushed aside the dark memories of Bangkok. He did write some lyrics, though, that memorialised his journey back. *Time*, the US news magazine, got hold of them and quoted: "'*The little bird in lonely flight/ Thinks of itself and feels sad.*'" *Time* added: 'In Bangkok's dance halls, where Siamese hepcats curve their fingers backward and dance the ramwong, the hit of the week was a song composed by the royal jitterbug king himself.'

The press saw him as yet another dispossessed playboy royal and soon lost interest. Thrones were toppling, empires dissolving. Back in the snug privacy of the only real home he'd had, Lek could go out and do as he pleased, see anyone, speak freely. He relaxed back into the reassuring certainties of familiar western classrooms. In Bangkok, he'd had to cope with an elite whose long names were hard to remember and kept changing, so that he would think he was dealing with several different personages until they turned out to be one and the same. It had been equally hard to get a grip on places, institutions and beliefs: the names were slippery and the gods switched faces and purposes. Here at university, everything was concrete: information stayed the same from one lesson to another.

Jazz was the only activity which had saved his sanity in Siam. Here in

Lausanne, jazz was still regarded as a hand-me-down, word-of-mouth music, like sculpting air. This chimed with the ancient Siamese custom of conveying music from master to pupil without notation. Now, jazz connected him with the Elder Brother of the old carefree days. How baffling those brief months in Bangkok all seemed. He had to go back. But what did he have to offer?

The Princess Mother suffered mental depression of a kind that would destroy a lesser person. Added to the trauma of seeing her son die was a palace environment from which cruel gossip was relayed to the ordinary people for whom she had real respect. It was being said that she thought her first son was weak; that she wanted to be founder of a strong new line of kings; that she had attended to the preparation of Nan's body inhumanely with cool detachment. The truth was that her simple Buddhist faith taught her death was only a door we all had to pass through. She tried not to search for some mistake she might have made leading to the tragedy, and concentrated on practicalities.

Old Gran and Uncle Rangsit wrote to her with advice about the need for Lek to marry within the stern limitations of tradition. There was a shortage of girls who would be accepted as the future queen of the Ninth Rama. Papa had married Mama for love. It had prevented him from making use of his royal status to serve a wider public. However, Mama was told of a Siamese diplomat in Paris with two suitable daughters: the mission chief was Prince Suranath Kitiyakara who could trace his family back to the thirteenth-century dynasty of Sukhothai, said to be the first organised state in Thai history. One of his daughters was even studying music, which should suit Lek. In Old Siam, it would have been considered a perfect match: the girl shared with Lek a common ancestor: King Chulalongkorn was their paternal grandfather.

Lek had a threadbare jalopy and agreed to visit the Paris mission but he was a bit of an innocent when it came to girls. Part of him was still a schoolboy, more fascinated by machinery although willing enough to learn about diplomacy. He spent all his time with the Paris ambassador and told Mama, 'He never tries to ingratiate himself but sets me straight. Once, I was going to buy a better second-hand car, get it registered, get a licence to drive, all at the same time. He refused to use his influence to help me. He believed in doing things according to rules.' Lek had been without a father most of his life, and the ambassador filled a gap.

In the autumn of 1948, the ambassador was taking his family to Fontainebleau. He invited the king, who drove first to a French car factory. Its owner had invited him to inspect their production line. The king sketched his idea for a cheap little people's car. He said later, looking chagrined: 'I should have patented the design because the company later made such a car, the Citroën *deux-chevaux*.'

He had then driven on to meet the ambassador and his family. He had a puncture and arrived late. One daughter, Sirikit, caught his eye. She was sixteen and outstandingly beautiful. He had never noticed her before. Feeling an inexplicable excitement, the young king drove off home from Fontainebleau. At the villa, his mother asked, 'How did things go?'

He said it had been a good meeting with the ambassador.

'Yes, but – the daughter?'

'Sirikit must really hate me,' he said. 'She was very annoyed because I arrived late. She got angrier when I suggested her father send *les enfants* to dine separately . . . The other daughter was nice.'

It was the other daughter that Mama had in mind.

Lek drove more frequently to Paris and contrived to see Sirikit again without appearing bumptious. She found him to be not the condescending youth she first thought, and not at all the roistering relic of a crumbling dynasty, as portrayed in the popular press. She was studying classical music, not the kind Lek called jazz. Mama had miscalculated there, too. Still, Sirikit was a linguist. She talked with Lek in French, which lent itself to flirtation.

Lek's courtship continued unnoticed until he crashed his Fiat 500 Topolino. *Time* had criticised him for doing little else but 'organise a swing band, tinker with cameras, drive fast cars'. Now the press became more interested. Lek had been driving with the husband of his sister Galyani beside him when a truck shot out of a side road. The pile-up in October, 1948, brought Sirikit rushing to his bedside in a Lausanne hospital. In another bed lay Galyani's husband, badly injured, and for a while not expected to live. British reporters speculated about 'the smashingly pretty princess from Siam'.

The Princess Mother's secret concern was that the crash might not have been an accident. The circumstances were as odd as the time boulders killed the man sitting where Nan should have been in a Jeep, two months before he was murdered in bed.

Sirikit begged her father to let her spend more time with the boy while he remained in hospital. Her father was a stickler for the proprieties, but finally a cautious statement was issued: 'Under the Princess Mother's care and supervision, Princess Sirikit will continue her education at the Riante Rive Boarding School in Lausanne.' The press played up the romance of the gorgeous young princess who was giving up the splendours of Paris to be with her sweetheart, a fairytale king.

In fact, he had been secretly moved to a special department for the blind in the Clinic Bois-Cerf because it was feared he would lose his sight. He spent weeks with bandages over both eyes while Sirikit helped him with his classroom work by reading to him. The real extent of the king's injuries was investigated by Marshal Pibul's hacks, using the King's Death Case as an excuse to see him. The Princess Mother received them, and made sure their questions were confined to events in the Grand Palace surrounding Nan's death. But she would not allow them to cross-examine Lek. He had given his testimony already and she did not want any possible enemies to spread reports that the king was blind. They would say he was punished for sins previously committed, and revive the lie that he killed Nan.

Pridi also came secretly and separately to Lausanne.

A year before Lek's motor accident, while he was still discovering the attractions of driving to Paris, Marshal Pibul had staged a coup, declaring its purpose was to resolve the King's Death Case and naming Pridi as the chief conspirator. The British naval attaché in Bangkok was aroused in the early morning of the 19th November, 1947 with the message: 'RUTH is here.' The attaché was Captain Stratford Hercules Dennis, a veteran of both world wars, a commando in special operations against the Nazis, and Mountbatten's deputy chief in SEAC's Combined Operations. He opened his door to six men carrying sub-machine guns, grenades and pistols. One of them claimed to be Pridi, but Dennis failed to recognise the sunken face with a moustache and pebble-glasses until Pridi removed the false whiskers and put his false teeth back into his mouth. All the men were being hunted, he said, and he asked for protection. A message was sent to the ambassador, Sir Geoffrey Thompson, a hawk-nosed Ulsterman who was about to eat breakfast: 'RUTH needs help.'

The British ambassador, his naval attaché and the American naval attaché, 'Skeats' Gardas, consulted a survivor of the Japanese Death Railway, William Adam, now local representative of the Shell Oil Company. Adam had an ex-prisoner's view of Marshal Pibul's wartime record and he was sure Pridi faced execution. There was a Shell tanker waiting to leave for Singapore, but to reach it, Pridi would have to be taken to where the ship lay at the mouth of the Lords of Life River. Skeats Gardas had a launch, an old wartime submarine-chaser, moored at Bangkok's Klong Toi docks. While Captain Dennis hid Pridi and misdirected his pursuers, Skeats dismissed the launch's Siamese crew, replaced them with his wife and young sister, and then hoisted the Stars and Stripes. Pridi and his companions were smuggled on board and the unusual American crew of a naval attaché, his wife and sister, tore for twenty miles along the winding river to where the tanker lay at anchor. Some four hours later, Adam in his Shell Oil office received the pre-arranged radio message meaning all was well: 'After a short stop due to engine trouble [the tanker] is now running smoothly.'

Pridi was put in quarantine in Singapore while in London the British Foreign Office sweated over the possible repercussions to this reversion to the simple days of Anglo-American cooperation, when danger justified deceit and wartime comradeship was more important than peacetime rivalries. Pridi was a diplomatic embarrassment at high levels, and so he 'disappeared'. He moved around the China coast and Europe, terrified for his life, and often in disguise.

After Lek's car crash, Pridi sought to clear himself with a written statement which he gave the British and the mother of King Ananda in whose death 'I hereby deny absolutely that I was in any way implicated'. He never came face-to-face with Mama, though. Later he stole back into Siam and tried, but failed, to get rid of Marshal Pibul. Again he escaped, but this time the western powers were afraid to touch him: regicide was much too serious a crime, and the King's Death Case was doing a good job of placing Pridi in the frame. Many years later, Lek said he did not believe that Pridi was a communist nor had anything to do with Nan's death, but in those early years, he was trying to pick his way through tangles of lies. In 1949, Pridi was given sanctuary in China: that sleeping giant was passing into communist hands.

Lek regained the use of one eye after a series of operations. This was kept secret. European newspapers noted acidly that sunglasses were the new fashion accessory of escapist royals. Reporters did not know he wore them to shield his remaining eye. He was indifferent to the speculation. His sister's husband was also on the way to a full recovery. And Lek, the student, was in love. If a king could have a personal life, his began to taste sweet.

Sirikit's youth and energy were good for Lek and for his mother's morale. The girl was sure she had been a warrior queen in an earlier life. Her ancestors went back to kings who reigned before the Chakri dynasty, and she dreamt about princesses of her own age who rode war elephants into battle and who cut their own throats rather than fall into the hands of the enemy. She had the light-heartedness of those who have no fear of death. In rescuing Lek from the perils of being too earnest, she in turn fell in love with him. They announced their engagement in a quiet ceremony on 19th July, 1949. A photograph shows him standing beside Sirikit. He wears dark glasses and a rumpled student's jacket, pullover and dark baggy pants, his tie askew. His arms hang by his side, his expression is serious. The girl smiles radiantly and cuddles a black and white cat. She is spectacularly photogenic and soon she will be on magazine covers the world over.

She was born on 12th August, 1932, the year absolute monarchy was overthrown. Her father resigned from the foreign ministry in protest, only rejoining it when he felt he could represent the true Siam, not the pro-Japanese policies evolving under Pibul. He was with the embassy in Washington when it rallied the Free Thai resistance movement. Sirikit attended the Catholic convent school of St Xavier in Bangkok during the war. So she was the first of Lek's generation to explain to him how the war had looked from inside Siam. By 1944, the convent girls had known the tide was turning when seventy-seven of the first one hundred American B-29s hit, among other things, the Great Bangkok Boulevard. This was a Japanese-built row of what appeared to be huge department stores. They were shown in Tokyo's propaganda films as among the benefits of the East Asia Co-Prosperity Sphere. The sham was exposed when bombs tore apart a bamboo-and-matting facade. The Japanese had scoffed at warnings that giant US transcontinental bombers could strike this far. The first raid was costly: 308 Americans in twenty-three B-29s were lost. Another five aircraft went down going back to Indian bases. Americans became Sirikit's heroes.

Sirikit loved France but did not admire its colonial policies. In her father's Paris office there hung a copy of *Le Petit Journal* of August, 1893, showing Siamese territories annexed by the French all the way to *l'Empire D'Annam*, Vietnam. A shrunken Siam was drawn in profile as an Auspicious White Elephant facing west. The ear was the central rice plain; the trunk dangled down to Malaya where the British had snipped parts of it off; the rump was lost in French Cambodia; the backbone curved against the Gulf of Tonkin and enclosed Vietnam which France had seized. The crown was Laos, dominated by France. *L'Ecole Française d'Extrême-Orient* described 'this strange Siamese race, supple and fluid like water, insinuating itself with the same force, taking the colour of all the skies and the form of all the river banks, and keeping their essential identity while they spread like an immense sheet of water from South China to Assam'.

Lek wondered if Buddhist passivity had allowed that sheet of water to be broken up. Sirikit said the lost territories had to do with European notions of sovereignty. When European empires tried to seize Siam, its monarchy yielded the territories that were more trouble than they were worth. It made little difference because the lines on western colonial maps marked frontiers that did not exist in the minds of folk accustomed to wander freely across open landscapes.

As well as lessons in colonial history, she brought him books about the kings of jazz that introduced him to the realities of life for some Americans: Benny Goodman who came out of the Chicago South Side ghetto and could remember his father returning from the meat stockyard with the stench from shovelling unrefined lard still clinging to his clothes; Lionel Hampton whose family knew the hoodlum Al Capone and whose showmanship required grunting, groaning, gesticulating, frothing and exhorting tenor saxophonists to squeal and honk. These, and others like Coleman Hawkins and Louis Armstrong, formed an aristocracy of the disadvantaged. Creativity got them out of the slums. Lek hoped that some day they would admit him to their ranks. His mother had shared their origins.

He was jerked back to another kind of reality when he saw the caption under a newspaper photograph of Chairman Mao Zedong in a grey tunic at Beijing's Gate of Heavenly Peace on 1st October, 1949. The Paris papers reported that portraits on flattened fuel cans of the Nationalist Chinese KMT's Chiang Kai-shek had vanished from the main entrance to the Forbidden City, and that 'Losing China' had panicked Americans. US President Truman said: 'Thailand is the only sovereign and independent country in South East Asia . . . That is where we must make our stand against international communism and that is why it is international communism's chief target.'

When he heard this, Lek knew he had to go back. He would cremate Ananda's body, get crowned and marry Sirikit quickly, so that she could take over as queen if he were killed.

His mother received the news just as a former friend betrayed her trust by testifying in the King's Death Case which still dragged on: 'The Princess Mother should read the histories of younger brothers who killed older brothers to win the crown.' It was a stab in the back from Dr Nitya (Nit) Vejjavivisth who had gone to Harvard on a scholarship bestowed by Papa, and who had known Mama in Boston. Nit had been the first court physician to see the dead king's body. He courted jail by his reference to the Princess Mother. It was *lèse majesté*. Yet no charges were laid. Nit had been put up to this by the chief of paramilitary police, Phao Sriyanon.

Police-General Phao had been a young officer with the old Northern Command clique that in wartime expanded the drug trade, and had been forced to retire from the army for collaborating with the Japanese. His political fortunes were restored by presenting himself as one of the experts on communism needed by the US intelligence services. Stories of his postwar control of drug trafficking and other criminal activities were filed by foreign correspondents who escaped criminal charges by publishing abroad what Bangkok editors dared not print. That most distinguished of American journalists, C. L. Sulzberger of the *New York Times*, described him as 'a superlative crook'.

The king could not fire Phao. Then Phao put it about that 'nobody can become king who is not the son of a queen. And this pretender's mother is a Nothing.' The insult infuriated the king. Mama, whose nerves were constantly tested and who periodically was close to breaking down, now wanted him to abdicate. He could do nothing, she felt, to help a country governed by the army coups, which she saw now were the reality behind a pretence of parliamentary democracy. Lek asked if she would stop thinking of him as irresponsible if he came back to Lausanne within six months of marrying Sirikit in Bangkok, going through with his own coronation, and seeing the body of Elder Brother properly cremated?

This was a challenge to her customary courage she could not reject. She slept scarcely at all in this troubled period. At night, she read English detective novels to take her mind off terrifying realities. It became an addiction that lasted the rest of her life.

Dowager Queen Sawang, 'Old Gran', in formal court attire, *c.* 1900.

Mama, future mother of two kings, as a young girl living at the Grand Palace after leaving the Bangkok slums.

(*Top*) King Chulalongkorn with a few of his sons at Eton. (*Above*) Dowager Queen Sawang, 'Old Gran' (centre), with her only surviving son, Prince Mahidol who became a doctor and was father to the brother-kings. With them (left) is Princess Valaya, the last surviving of her daughters – the rest died in childhood. (*Left*) Mama with Papa – Dr Mahidol, Celestial Prince – after their marriage, when he began her 'educational tours' to Europe.

(*Above*) Mama pushing pram with baby Galyani – her first child – in London. (*Below*) Mama with (from left to right) Elder Brother Nan, Little Brother Lek and daughter Galyani after Papa died in 1929.

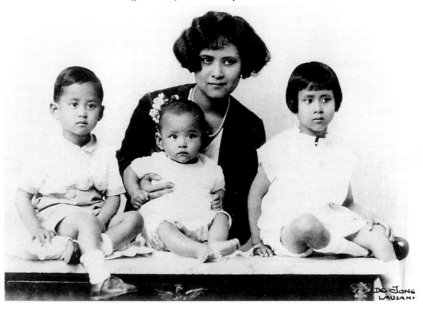

Elder Brother Nan and Little Brother Lek in snowy Lausanne, the winter after Nan became King Ananda.

(*Below*) Relics of the brothers' childhood games: (*below left*) the 1939 Valentine from the brothers to their sister Galyani; (*below right*) the officers of the Packing Case Club.

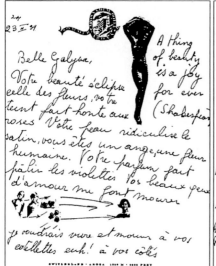

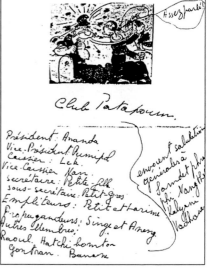

The family (from left to right) Galyani, Mama, Elder Brother Nan
and Little Brother Lek in Lausanne winter. Nan is already King Ananda.

(*Above*) King Ananda on his first visit
to Bangkok as king in 1938, with
Little Brother Lek. (*Left*) Little
Brother Lek, aged 21, with Sirikit,
aged 17, in October 1948 in
Lausanne, when they had agreed to
become engaged. Lek, still
recovering from a car crash, was
obliged to wear dark glasses while
his eyesight was still in doubt.

Little Brother Lek proclaimed ritually in Bangkok streets as King Bhumibol, Ninth Rama.

Bhumibol moved from Europe to an exotic new world, where (*below*) gold-painted humanoids and dragons are among gods and demons guarding the royal chapel where The Emerald Buddha resides.

Classical Thai dancing teacher as she and her forebears would appear at royal audiences.

(*Below*) A royal barge with a crew of fifty oarsmen, built during the reign of the Fourth Rama (of *King and I* fame). Siam's royal barges, seen as the last traces of the days of the sea-kings, were used to transport monarchs from the very earliest times, as depicted in old temple paintings.

Re-enactment of how Kings of Siam once went to war. In the last recorded eighteenth-century battle against the Burmese, some 100,000 war elephants were deployed.

(*Left*) King Bhumibol at a formal ceremony in the Grand Palace.

11

Cremation and Coronation

'CARPENTERS worked hard to complete the wooden tower that would serve as a funeral pyre for the late King Ananda Mahidol, who died of a mysterious pistol shot,' *Time* noted slyly on 20th March, 1950. 'The Siamese had waited long and impatiently for King Bhumibol to return to his throne and light the pyre. Three times in the last three years, the young (22) king had been rumored on the way home from the villa in Lausanne . . . Three times something (a Siamese coup, an automobile accident or a mere change of plans) had interfered. Meanwhile, as the king spent his days going to school, organising a swing band, tinkering with his cameras and driving his cars from Switzerland to Paris, royal duties piled up in Bangkok . . . Last week, gangling, spectacled Bhumibol was on the Red Sea in the steamship *Selandia*, with his pretty fiancée, 17-year-old Siamese Sirikit Kityakara at his side.'

It was thirteen years since Lek cheered up Nan on his first voyage to Siam as King Ananda. Aboard *Selandia*, it was Princess Sirikit who buoyed Lek's spirits. She was chaperoned by her father who reminded Lek that Siam's monarchy served a different purpose to anything in Europe: 'When the legends die, all collapses. Angkor Wat was the centre of a great empire and now it's overrun by monkeys.' The scholarly ambassador to France was quoting Charles de Gaulle. All Lek was likely to see of Greater Siam's lost treasure was the largescale model in the Grand Palace.

Lek glimpsed a dilemma he must resolve. Angkor Wat had been overwhelmed by foolish superstitions based on old Vedic scriptures which had become corrupted. Elder Brother Nan had shuddered whenever he passed under the Vedic figures and legends on the walls of the palace mansion in which he was shot. Habits of subservience made it easier for dictators today. Buddhist values vanished into thickets of backward-looking Vedic laws. The new king, though, might need to play on popular superstition to build authority against the dictators.

'The king is coming back.' Foreign newspapers reported that the message travelled from sampan to sampan along the twisting Bangkok canals and upriver to the rice-rich central plains; it was on the lips of barefoot mendicants in the cool teakwood forests of the uplands. An American zoologist was quoted: 'I stood paralysed by the sudden appearance of the mottled diamond-like pattern of a Russell's viper, head up, body rigid, ready to deliver the bite that causes cerebral hemorrhage and makes the eyes bleed. I turned at some movement behind, and saw the calm countenance of an old man in an orange cloth: "My king is back," said the monk, pointing at the snake as it uncoiled.'

The ship had to anchor outside the long and narrow bar that leads into the great river to Bangkok. Lek transferred to a launch while Sirikit stayed on board. Sirens hooted and the banks were packed with cheering figures, as the launch came alongside the Grand Palace river landing where guards in spiked helmets stood like toy soldiers in the sweltering heat, water boys ready to drench any guard who showed signs of fainting. And there was Uncle Rangsit. His baldness was hidden by an ornately tiered broad-brimmed warrior's hat. 'The Regent removed the hat and with a flourish turned over the powers of state,' reported Gordon Walker of the *Christian Science Monitor*. 'Prince Rangsit is popular because he is now the only one left alive out of all King Chulalongkorn's multitude of sons. Field Marshal Pibul deployed troops to stop the influx of people. His own soldiers defied his orders.'

Pibul's dangerous jealousy had been reawakened. Uncle Rangsit reminded Lek that the Emperor Claudius played the stammering fool to conceal his growing wisdom. It was still the best ruse.

In Lausanne, the Princess Mother read the *Neue Züricher Zeitung* report of Lek's arrival: The brother-kings' real home had been where 'they spent unclouded days on the shores of Lake Geneva and played with neighbourhood children . . . They knew Siam by name only.' Mama marked the passage and the truth of it.

Lek had to have explained to him the reason for the elaborate rituals Uncle Rangsit had prepared. The Regent quoted from *Siamese State Ceremonies*: 'The more public and stately parts of the Royal Cremation have most value in maintaining the respect of the masses [who] have an innate love and respect for all forms of royal pageantry, and it is the magnificence of the state procession, the splendour of the Urn enthroned upon the catafalque that impresses them.'

There would be two coronations. The first would be the Spiritual Coronation of Elder Brother Nan as King Ananda. The people believed the rising flames lifted a dead king to an invisible throne among the gods.

The long delay before this Spiritual Coronation had made people apprehensive. It was essential to make it the celebratory occasion it was meant to be. It summoned up beliefs grounded in the early magic of an agrarian society. The living king wondered grimly if Nan's spirit would go anywhere until the King's Death Case was properly closed.

King Ananda's cremation and his Spiritual Coronation were all done within twelve days of King Bhumibol's return. Nobody alive had seen a cremation like this one. 'It was such an extravagance of tinsel and gold, it punched you in the eye,' said one foreign observer. 'Long plaintive trumpet blasts gave the signal for the procession,' reported the *Neue Züricher Zeitung*. 'Golden Urn on richly gilded carriage . . . bands playing the Siamese funeral march, 542 carriers of the royal regalia, trumpeters, pipers, drummers and conch-shell blowers clad in woven silver and blue silk with white stockings and black-buckled shoes . . . The Supreme Patriarch with peacock feathers . . . 200 uniformed men drawing the last mortal remains to be lifted to a throne high above.'

Mama read the report and hoped such splendour would not go to Lek's head. But Little Brother Lek saw what Uncle Rangsit meant about using this magic to keep an upper hand. The ebulliance of the crowds was intoxicating. The new king walked in intense heat behind his brother's body in the procession on foot to the pyre. Western diplomats complained of the ordeal, but Lek's first impulse when Elder Brother died had been to give him 'a decent funeral', and he had to go through with it. At the auspicious hour calculated by the Royal Astrologers, Lek lit the first candle. Flames leapt high. The Gongs of Victory beat a tattoo to signify the dead king's ascension. The gold mask of a god, covering Nan's face, vanished forever.

That night, hundreds of thousands of Siamese stayed with the ashes. Lek, unrecognised in open shirt and loose trousers, came back secretly to look at the glowing embers. Food vendors gave spicy sweetmeats to poor children, and he thought of his own mother when she had been a child with no money. He had made a vow before and he made it again: he would make kingship serve these people. But how was he to do this without losing his mother, and without becoming a slave to superstition?

He borrowed a flat-bottomed boat that night to paddle to the Palace of Lotus Pond and found Old Gran reading her English motoring magazines, of which she was inordinately fond. 'It was a good funeral!' the Dowager Queen said cheerfully.

Lek may have appeared to be the tool of others to foreign observers who only saw his expressionless face and a doll-like figure encased in stiff garments. Walter Bosshard cabled the Zurich paper: 'It was tiring for the king, not at all strong healthwise.' Only those who helped the king in and out of a multitude of robes saw how muscular he had become and how he mastered so many mentally demanding moves in these old ritual dances in order to hold a multitude who might be otherwise won by a new species of politician.

Marshal Pibul had to dance to the tune of Lek's popularity even though the National Hero had consolidated himself by rigging an election that made him premier again. Even Phao, who had all the powers of a secret-police chief, dared not interfere with crowds watching King Ananda consumed by flames to be re-born in that higher place where he would be served by six-armed and fiery-tongued gods, elephants with wings, and a central trinity of Brahma the Creator, Shiva the Destroyer and Vishnu the Preserver, forever seeking a perfect equilibrium.

Lek was uneasy about this hint of a caste system governed by *Varda* – colour. It reinforced the Vedic notion of humankind stacked up in shelves of importance, black at the bottom and pure-white at the top. Veda came from ancient Hindu psalms and was corrupted in India into creating the Untouchables, a caste inescapably condemned to be underdogs. Vedic ideas had become muddled with the later teachings of Buddha. He was eager to talk this over with Princess Sirikit but propriety required her to remain at her family's home until the next act unfolded.

Marshal Pibul had used the persistent Vedic class system after rebelling in 1932 against a hierarchy where six out of ten high-ranking officials came from the top four per cent of the population. Pibul had despised this upper-class but then built his own. If Lek wanted to bring about a real revolution, it might take him a long time to end the old habits of subservience. Kings in the past had prohibited prostration but it still continued.

Thus Marshal Pibul himself came on hands and knees to talk to the king who had been told that Pibul had once planned to push Elder Brother aside and declare himself the monarch in 1943. Only Hirohito had stopped him. Lek listened to Pibul's platitudes and then asked if the new prime minister had any questions? No, said Pibul after a puzzled pause. Then, said the king, he had nothing to say in reply.

He had settled upon silence rather than the role of the stammering fool, still with the purpose of concealing his growing wisdom. People read into his silences more than was there. Field Marshal Pibul never repeated his claim that succession was regulated by the law of AD 1360 which required a king to be son of a queen. He had been in the presence of a wordless god. The pose had a curiously intimidating effect on even the most cunning intriguers, at least for as long as they were in the king's presence.

Lek never wished to be called god-of-gods. He had been reading in Lausanne university about the new hydrogen bomb and Albert Einstein's warning against 'radioactive poisoning of the atmosphere and annihilation of any life on earth'. He could not reconcile this with ancient magic. He did not want to surrender entirely to Uncle Rangsit's weary conclusion that nothing would get done without the authority bestowed upon monarchs.

But away from the icon's aura, Marshal Pibul reverted to type: 1950 was the year US Senator Joseph R. McCarthy silenced prominent Americans with anti-communist witch-hunts. Pibul and his cronies claimed to be the only bulwark against communism in South and East Asia. Few in Washington had the courage to say that US dollars corrupted such men. In Bangkok, it took Prince Rangsit to speak out against the misuse of US military aid in a time when 'the syphilis rate is a national disgrace and only one hospital in the entire kingdom takes in serious cases like tuberculosis. The root of the problem is that it is every man for himself. Everyone breaks the law. The best jobs are seized by the military, retired or not. Generals take directorships in new businesses, while roads and bridges remain in disrepair. Critical editors are still disappearing or are jailed. One was beaten to death.'

Marshal Pibul decided he must destroy Prince Rangsit for good, once the king was safely back in his silly schoolroom. It had been a mistake not to execute Rangsit when Pibul had the opportunity years before. Now, Pibul was reduced to leaking anti-monarchist tales to the growing number of Americans at an embassy dramatically expanded from what had been a legation 'costing just pennies'. And since Pibul could not stop the masses from gazing in awe at monarchy, he declared: 'Censorship is necessary against communist insurgency.' He raised another demon that haunted Americans: British colonialism. He said publicly, 'The British have plans to move troops up from Singapore to occupy southern Thailand if our government should be overthrown.'

With his duty to Elder Brother paid, Lek wanted to move fast to marry Sirikit. The coronation must follow quickly, so the crowned king could make her his queen. They both knew an uncrowned king was in danger. It was a quiet wedding, Lek wore an open-neck white shirt and white trousers, like his father, the upcountry doctor. Queen Sawang, Old Gran, poured annointed water over the hands of the young couple, just as she had done for Lek's parents, and then the couple slipped away briefly to Far-From-Worry, the seaside palace near Hua Hin, which was only two hours by powerboat across the Gulf of Siam to the safety of French-run Cambodia if anything went wrong.

King Bhumibol's coronation festivities began on 5th May, 1950. Again he was trapped in an exhibition of the supernatural. The king was divine. Only his own hands could place on his head the towering gold Crown of

Victory representing a contest between the king and the demons of hell. An octagonal throne of figwood stood for the tree that protected Buddha. Lek had to memorise a catalogue of responses in Pali, the language Buddha had used to reach followers in every land. An eightfold throne ceremony came from the ancient Vedic *Rajasuya*. He had to recite, 'Ascend thee the East!' and repeat the incantation as he faced eight points of the compass: 'We invoke the Guardians of the Quarters by which We assert our rule.' Lek's sense of connecting with the distant past fought against Papa's detestation of superstitious bombast.

His face impassive, he listened to a Brahmin pandit intone: 'May the Sovereign give me leave to pronounce his victory. May the Sovereign turning now towards the East, where he is the equivalent of the Sun, extend his protection and exercise his royal authority over all those realms.' A conch-shell filled with water from each territory was emptied over his hands while the pandit proclaimed: 'Through the power of the Triple Gems [the Buddha, the Law, and the Brotherhood] and through the water poured down upon him may the king be awarded success.'

The Ceremonial Bath tickled his schoolboy sense of humour. The water came from Siam's five principal rivers, consecrated by monks and thickened with honey and clarified butter. It signified that all parts of the old empire must pay homage to the monarch. He kept a straight face, and hoped neighbouring countries would not mistake the symbolism for a threat.

Foreigners were excluded from the most secret rituals. The highest ranking officials gathered in the large hall. Lek had to make himself invisible behind a curtain of gold-embroidered brocade. Upon a signal, the curtain was slowly drawn apart and, amid the beat of drums and blowing of conch-shells, Lek appeared as the godhead in full array, surrounded by the royal regalia, seated on a throne representing all the levels of heaven and hell, clad in gold-embroidered *pha-nun*, the Siamese lower garment hoisted up between the legs, a long gold coat, and the warrior's plumed shield-like hat.

He could see long years stretching ahead when he would have to do this for hours, days, weeks and months. Uncle Rangsit told him how to relieve the strain. 'Turn your mind inward, focus on re-arranging your skeleton, root your legs into the ground. Stretch your spine, tailbone in, head back, everything in balance. Make your good eye small and look down into your heart, and send your mind off to deal with other things.'

The rehearsals were merciless. For his first palace procession, he had every facial muscle under control. A court official crouched on the floor, ritually apologising for the Unworthy One Speaking From Beneath the

August Feet, and then delivered instructions: 'Then Your Majesty will advance to the western part of the *Baisala*, preceded by Brahmins and Pundits in the order prescribed, followed by chamberlains and pages bearing the Regalia in the following order. On Your Majesty's *left*, first, the Great White Umbrella and the Brahmin Girdle. On Your Majesty's *right*, first, the Golden Tablet of Style and Title and the Great Crown of Victory . . . Then second, *left*, the Sceptre and the Girdle of Brilliants, and *right*, the Girdle of the Nine Gems and the Sword of Victory . . . ' King Bhumibol tried not to twitch his head from left to right like a metronome as the voice droned on: '*left*, the Fan and the Whisk of the Yak's Tail and *right*, the Whisk of the White Elephant's Tail and the Slippers. Then *left*, the Stick and the Diamond Ring and abreast of it . . . *right*, the Ring and the Personal Sword.'

He imagined the mix-up behind him in the parade if he got slightly out of sequence: 'To *left* and fifth in order of march, the Receptacle and the Betel Nut Set, with abreast of it to the *right*, the Water Urn and the Libation Vessel. Then the sixth pair: *left*, the Hostage Sword and the Discus, and *right*, the Trident and the Diamond Spear. Last of all, *left*, the Long Handled Sword and the Sword and Buckler and *right*, the Bow and the Gun of the Saton.'

He sent his mind back to schooldays when he might have laughed with Elder Brother at all this. The situation wasn't really funny. If he forgot these rituals, Siam would go the way of China, its dynasty ending with the abandonment of ceremony, disorder creating fiefdoms run by a score of warlords, until finally Mao had imposed absolute power. 'While we dusted off the old rites, China mobilised for huge development schemes,' he recalled. 'Young Asians were excited by what seemed a great new experiment in self-development.'

Lek rationalised the use of superstitious ritual. 'I thought, well, the Whisk of the Yak's Tail originally grew out of people's imaginations. The Sceptre was the thunderbolt of Indra and sprang from minds poetic. Our Golden Tablet of Style and Title derived from a creative act of ancient times. I had to restore the old to invent the new. You become a king. The people respond differently. The nobles approach and want to get closer. You take advice but the decisions are yours and you are terribly alone. Everything has changed.'

He disputed with himself while he watched artists, craftsmen and royal clerks sit on the marble floor of the Chapel Royal with a sacred *sincana* thread stretched around them to ward off evil spirits. The work of the Royal Astrologers demanded a thorough knowledge of the stars. The Royal Horoscope was inscribed on gold plate, while monks recited holy stanzas.

Then the gold plates were annointed, placed in gold tubes, each sealed and placed in gold-embroidered bags, gold-boxed into a two-tiered gold receptacle deposited on a gold table, while priests formed a circle and passed from hand to hand tapers, fixed in lenticular holders, the smoke gently fanned toward the centre to drive off evil influences. The Sacred Slippers were of gold, turned up at the toes, a reminder of the incarnation of the god Vishnu, who retired to meditate in the forest and left his slippers to govern in his place. Could this be the foundation for progress?

The most ancient symbol was the White Umbrella. His mother had traced the umbrella all the way back to Egyptian wall pictures and the bas-relief of the Assyrians. The Greeks had borrowed it. Ashoka in the third century BC had used it as a symbol of Buddha's bo tree. The device was, in its way, as slick as anything a New York advertising agency might invent. A royal umbrella's tiers multiplied above a king's head as his dignity was augmented. It represented a tree that shelters colonies of wildlife. It signified a Buddhist king's protection of all who came under it.

Lek had kept a diary in a shorthand of his own invention. Now he drew other symbols as coded signposts for Sirikit alone. These eventually became a different form of calendar. He called it 'Memories'. Only Sirikit knew the meanings. It granted privacy, and became a record of a new Great Game in which he played foreign powers off against each other. He said later: 'The disclosure of the cold war's secrets eventually justified my caution – big decisions were kept from us by foreign powers that directly concerned our survival.'

A return to the old ways seemed in 1950 to be the only defence against foreign interference. King Ananda's murder had followed his ignoring symbols deeply rooted in the national psyche. In 1946, he had gone on foot among the Chinese shopkeepers to reassure them. Once indoctrinated into Siamese ceremonies, Lek could see what a mistake it had been for Nan not to use a palanquin in a properly prescribed Royal Progress. Nan had greeted the Chinese as equals when many were already portrayed as communist subversives. Nan's democratic instincts had deepened the paranoia of anti-communists who suspected anyone with progressive tendencies.

So now Lek again yielded to superstition and submitted to the Royal Progress. He rode in the palanquin around the Chinese settlements, his right shoulder always toward the Grand Palace to ward off evil. He was preceded by the Ancient Bodyguard of Gentlemen-at-Arms and Processional Umbrellas. Years later, he could still recall the units that brought up the rear: 'Silver War Drums, Golden War Drums, Herald Trumpeters, Small Bugles, Brahmins Blowing Conches, Inspector of Instruments, Pages Bearing Royal Weapons, Grand Umbrellas of Ceremony . . . The Monkey

Standard and the Garuda Standard. It was like lyrics in a musical. At the very end, the Royal Golden Palanquin with Seven Lords Lieutenant to the Right and Seven Lords Lieutenant to the Left.'

Later, Lek strolled alone through the Palace of Lotus Ponds and saw an old man under a flame-of-the-forest tree, stuffing fruits and leaves into his *yom*, or shoulder bag, which had become a kind of third arm with age: a *paw-maw*, a man of the mountain. When Lek's father worked among the lepers he would sometimes talk with a *paw-maw* who had spent a lifetime gathering knowledge of natural medications. The neem tree, for instance, was a pharmacy in itself: its twigs made decay-preventing toothbrushes, its leaves, pain-killers, its seeds, antiseptic soap. When Papa found that superstition prevented him from practising modern medicine although the government would still pay him, he had recalled the unpaid services of the old *paw-maw* and wrote: 'My concept of loyalty to His Majesty forbids me merely to occupy a government post as its ornament and draw my pay regularly for so doing.'

His son was not willing to be a salaried ornament, either. Lek thought it over, walking to the temple where Papa's ashes were kept. 'There was an unusual Buddha image,' he said. 'It was crafted in the north by a highly cultivated Laotian tribe of ancient times. Its immaculate beauty, with its smooth and graceful body, its gentle smiling face, and its flame-like halo revealed superb craftsmanship of a tribe at the peak of its artistry.' Lek knelt in silence and felt his father's love for this image of Buddha whose simplicity contrasted with the past week of religious fireworks. He came back through Old Gran's garden jungle. Its vegetation, his father had recorded: 'fried egg tree, variegated-coral and copper pod, sweet-oleander and temple-tree . . . ' The straight-forward names were a relief after convoluted litanies to ward off evil. He stopped at the traveller's tree: a sad reminder of his restless father's short life.

12

Family Versus Duty

EXCLUDED from the wedding ceremony, the press used its imagination. 'In this Wonderland, nobody but nobody was worrying about the cold war or communism,' claimed *Newsweek*. 'Everybody but everybody was humming blues lyrics which the king had written. He had five other songs on the hit parade and consented to let his 'Blue Night' and a royal melody be featured in Michael Todd's forthcoming *Peepshow on Broadway*. He made his lyrics come true by taking Sirikit, his piano-playing cousin, as his queen.'

A cartoon in the *New York Times* showed the multi-tiered umbrella above Thai dancing girls at the Winter Garden and portrayed the king's 'musical collaborator', Mike Todd, along with 'Hi Wilberforce' Conley, Lillie Christine, and drum-beater 'Peanuts' Mann beating out the king's lines, 'In the kingdom of my dreams/ You are my queen.'

Mama need not have feared that Lek would be seduced by grandiosity. He rejected the dozen official pages of portentous titles. Even *Time* magazine, clever at condensing complicated stories, had trouble cramming into a single column the titles that began: 'The Great God On My Head, The Power Coming From the Strength of the Earth ... '

He simply signed the marriage register: 'Ruler of the nation.' 'The Ruler of the Nation hurries home to Mama,' sneered Police-General Phao. But he was wary of Queen Sirikit. He had tested her nerve during the short honeymoon at Far-From-Worry.

Queen Sirikit loved this villa where it seemed Somerset Maugham might show up any second wearing a white linen suit. From their bedroom, she and Lek could watch the purple monsoon thunderheads march across Cambodia from Vietnam. Beaches sloped so gently, it was possible to wade waist-deep far into the sea. Sometimes they had the company of a baby elephant that used its trunk to turn the tap on a beach standpipe where the couple showered. The one-bathroom 'palace' stood near the seaside resort of Hua Hin. Luxury hotels and costly condominiums had not yet crept along the shoreline, and the adjacent jungle-topped islands had yet to be pierced by the abandoned needles of drug addicts.

Police-General Phao Sriyanon had hurried there with gossip that he hoped would destroy Queen Sirikit's trust in her husband. He had heard the queen wanted to go with him to London and wrongly assumed the king had not told her that George VI had declined to receive the king, saying, 'Buckingham Palace does not host murderers.' But Sirikit already knew. Kings of England did not intimidate her. Neither did conspirators like Phao. She sent him packing, aware that he was a dangerous enemy to make; but she had the courage of the very young, reinforced by the romantic vision of herself and Lek as past lovers who had been great warriors at different periods, each pursuing the other through many incarnations until they finally met in the same lifespan. It was a belief born of her lonely wartime childhood listening to family retainers tell the old tales. Sirikit understood the hidden universe of the Siamese mind where, like it or not, Lek had become a divinity.

'Maybe half a million Siamese know who Joe Stalin is,' *Time* remarked. 'But everybody, right out to the remotest borders, knows about the king.'

Everybody also knew and feared Police-General Phao. He had the power of total amorality. He was known as Top-Cop at Phoenix Park, the British intelligence centre in Singapore, where his wartime association with Tsuji was well documented. Tsuji was now back in Japan, after leaving China in the guise of history professor Kenshin Aoki on the faculty of the University of Beijing. Top-Cop Phao's paramilitary forces were now so heavily supplied by US covert-warfare units that they out-weighed Thailand's conventional forces. Phao was not going to tolerate competition from a moralising monarch.

Uncle Rangsit's days were numbered. The monarchy's enemies moved more stealthily than when they had sentenced Rangsit to death before. And Lek sensed this as he returned to Switzerland, knowing if his Regent were to die, he would have to cut short his studies. He found it hard to tell his mother. But he had kept his promise. He was a responsible young man at last. Her doctors told him that her emaciated body had survived mostly on air and hope. Lek assured her that he had shed titles whenever he could in Bangkok. He told her what happened when he began to sign the marriage register. He was going to call himself 'Government Servant'. He had changed his mind. 'I signed myself "Ruler of the nation" because people should know I was ruled by the laws of kingship.'

He knew his mother might never go back. His debates with her were long and subtle. She said simple Buddhist logic must govern his actions, not a muddle of superstitions dating back to the village magicians of animist days. Lek reminded her of passages she had read to him from *The Plague* by Albert Camus in which a doctor says he does what he can in a doomed city because he has been taught by suffering. That was a Buddhist concept. The doctor asks why the writer is there? 'Comprehension,' the writer replies. Lek had comprehended a great deal in Bangkok, and he suggested his mother would too.

She shelved her fears when Queen Sirikit announced she was pregnant. Sirikit gave birth to a daughter on 5th April, 1951, named Ubol, the Thai word for Lotus Blossom. Overjoyed, Lek pampered the baby. Beyond the nursery, he worked on his political science studies but he was sure nothing applied to the Siam he had started to know better.

He was helped by a long-standing classroom friend who understood Lek's forebodings. This was Baudouin, who was called upon in July to be crowned successor to his father Leopold III, King of the Belgians. Leopold was another victim of King George VI's prejudices, for the English King had swallowed tales that Leopold collaborated with the Nazis. Rioters had forced Leopold to abdicate and Baudouin was haunted by his father's view that the English monarchy's interference brought Belgium close to disaster. The abdication of King Leopold impressed upon Marshal Pibul the long reach of an English monarch's displeasure. It fired his renewed campaign to exploit the story of George VI's rejection of Lek as the killer of his brother. It was the kind of lie that, repeated over and over, might unnerve a less tough-minded target.

Young Baudouin was close to Lek's age. Like Lek, he'd had no ambition to be king. Like Lek, he was told the country would split apart without a monarch. No other two schoolboys had so much in common although they came from opposite ends of the earth. They had inherited responsibilities they had never anticipated. Nowhere else could two young men, by shirking duty, thrust such strategically important countries into danger. Belgium had been the invasion route for aggressors in two world wars, and its internal unity was now vital to the North Atlantic alliance blocking further Soviet advances in Europe. Siam had long been on the invasion routes of aggressors like Japan and now it was on the Soviet Union's route into East Asia.

Things that Lek and Baudouin could not discuss with others, they could confide to each other. Baudouin had politically seasoned advisers. For years to come, King Baudouin would pass along wisdom gathered as a devout Catholic who respected Buddhism. King Bhumibol had grown up adhering to Christian ethics and guided by the actions of his famous great-grandfather, King Mongkut, whose close confidant had been a Catholic bishop to whom he had once observed: 'What you teach people to *do* is admirable.

What you teach them to *believe* is foolish.' Lek said he did not want to rely on old beliefs. Baudouin thought that tyrants uprooted them because they were obstacles to absolute control.

Within Lek's family, Mama had the wisdom to say that from all Lek had told her about recent events in Bangkok, she could see that a King of Siam must build on the old ways. Siam had been evolving in its own manner toward order, justice and stability. She told him about an old judge who had started out, as she had, a child with poor prospects. The boy paddled to Bangkok, staying in temples lining a water road that gradually became congested with sampans and boat-shops. The boy rested under a sacred bo tree at Wat Borvoranives, the very temple whose abbot Mongkut had been before he became King Rama the Fourth. The judge had told her, 'I was found by a Grand Abbot whose eyes were neither pious nor pathetic like the eyes of the saints we saw in Christian cathedrals. When I told the abbot I would work all hours in exchange for an education, he took me on. And so, eventually, I read law and worked by way up to a judgeship.' Bhumibol could repair the soul of a nation where a poor child paddles his way from one circle of society to another.

Queen Sirikit told Lek how Thai kingdoms were structured, with concentric circles of monks, bureaucrats and the peasantry. The king was at the core. There had been lateral mobility between the circles, but this was now blocked by corruption. Only a king could change this. Sirikit wanted Lek to start right away, before the ruling generals had time to blunt the impact of his last triumphant visit.

The Princess Mother knew Sirikit was right but it was hard on a woman who had come into the world with nothing and then, for a tragically short term, knew of the joy of a family. Now this was being snatched from her. She had known too much horror to go back.

She encountered more. Police-General Phao led a military delegation to rush the king into signing a new constitution that would give the army control over the electorate. The king rejected the proposal. Phao immediately held press conferences in Europe at which he implied that King Bhumibol's part in the King's Death Case was still unclear. The effects were long-lasting. An intimate friend of Graham Greene, the New York socialite, Beverley Woodner, later said, 'I was led to believe the Central Intelligence Agency saved King Bhumibol from the consequences of killing his brother.' Miss Woodner, a brilliant Hollywood set-designer, had worked on wartime OSS deception mockups and later with high-level CIA officers. She quoted from a State Department policy paper that, if it had not been secret at the time, would have warned Lek of the formidable opposition he faced. It said he lacked qualities of leadership 'whereas Pibul conducts his

Government in a manner friendly to the US and has openly declared himself opposed to communism'.

Phao's role was defined in a Phoenix Park report: 'The United States has planted under loose cover a CIA dirty tricks department, the US Far East Office of Policy Coordination, whose activities are supposedly hidden from the British government.' An intelligence chief in Singapore quoted from the CIA unit's mandate 'to plan in advance the future of Asian societies and not neglect any contingency [nor] the operational effectiveness of assassination'.

A member of the unit covering Siam was Joseph Burkholder Smith, described as 'a covert-action specialist in the CIA Clandestine Service, with special experience in the dissemination of false information'. One conduit of his 'black' propaganda was Police-General Phao whose crooked activities escalated faster than a non-stop elevator heading for the executive suite. Phao now blackmailed brothel-keepers, rigged the gold exchange, collected money from big business, took protection money from slave-traders and the brokers who scoured the countryside to buy children for city vice-dens.

Phao had detained three men as accomplices in King Ananda's murder. Malcolm MacDonald, the British commissioner-general for South East Asia whose intelligence sources reached into China, wrote that the scape-goats 'are tortured. They are threatened with summary execution, and given truth drugs. They are offered deals if they will rat on one another. Their refusal to confess to anything touching the king is astonishing because they are in the hands of an expert torturer. Their real crime is loyalty to the Crown.'

Whenever Malcolm MacDonald visited Bangkok from his Singapore base, Phao would try to compromise him with tours of the notorious sex shows in Patpong. 'He and Pibul do all the preparatory work whenever a military *coup d'etat* is necessary, issue all the secret orders, and reap all the rewards,' MacDonald reported. He noted that the Japanese behind Pibul's wartime activities, Masanobu Tsuji, was now out in the open in Okutama-cho, Tokyo: His war-criminal status had been officially lifted when war in Korea reminded US General MacArthur's intelligence advisers in Tokyo that Tsuji was an expert on that part of Asia too.

Prince Rangsit died, aged sixty-six, on 3rd March, 1951, a month before Ubol's birth. His death was blamed on heart failure. A post-mortem was ruled out by Phao, running the police, and by Pibul controlling the judici-ary. If Uncle Rangsit was poisoned, as rumoured, it was impossible to launch an investigation. The news was another emotional setback for the Princess Mother.

The king was torn between family and duty again. King's Men said the kingdom was run virtually by American generosity, now more open-handed than ever after Thai forces were sent to Korea where the war with communist forces had broken out a month after Lek's coronation. The Korean War had taken an ominous turn with the intervention of Red Chinese 'volunteers'. Similar attacks along China's southern periphery were feared in Washington, and Thailand seemed most vulnerable.

Lek waited until the new baby was eight months old and Sirikit felt ready to travel. Mama clung to what small family she had. When she said goodbye, it was with a feeling she would never see Lek again. He knew her mind well. As he said later, 'Every Siamese woman's highest ambition is to have a son who is ordained a monk.' Mama finally let go when he promised he would diligently study the Buddhist scriptures and for a time discard his kingly robes to enter a monastic cell. It is still common practice for young Thai men to spend a short time as novices, but he proposed to undergo the strict exams and the harsh physical and mental tests that as a king he must expect from Siam's *Sangha*, the community of monks whose moral authority was above even that of the monarch.

The king arrived at Singapore with Sirikit and eight-month-old Ubol in November, 1951 aboard the Danish steamer *Meonia*. Malcolm MacDonald was on hand to pass along a warning of impending political storms. Police-General Phao was plotting a coup – against his old comrade, Field Marshal Pibul. 'Phao is a rather nasty specimen of humanity,' Malcolm MacDonald reported to London. 'But Marshal Pibul is as capable as any man alive of dealing with hostile takeovers.' On one earlier occasion, the British embassy in Bangkok had reported that Pibul was missing during another attempted coup within his own unruly clique. The news reached MacDonald in the middle of a formal dinner: 'I asked my guests to stand for a minute in silence,' said MacDonald. 'When all sat down, I made them get up again and drink a toast "to Field Marshal Pibul who I'm sure is alive and kicking".' MacDonald was right.

Now, Lek received advance notice that the Field Marshal would confront him on arrival in Bangkok with a new constitution giving soldiers and police the right to vote wherever they were stationed. Elections would be staged to persuade the American public that their money supported democracy. Of course the military regime would win. Marshal Pibul won wider support by his declaration that the British had plans to occupy Thailand if they felt Malaya was threatened. It was true that the British needed help in cleaning up the Thai-Malay border, a privileged sanctuary for communists who had ambushed and killed the Governor of Malaya, Sir Henry Gurney, a month before King Bhumibol's arrival.

The king liked the informality of MacDonald. He seemed free from the prejudices that still plagued Singapore. Among the old colonialists there, he was viewed as a dangerous socialist. Lek kept a newspaper cartoon of pot-bellied white men in tuxedos on the veranda of the Malaya Country Club: MacDonald approached in shorts and open shirt as one member said: '*Gad, Sir. We can't have fellers like that saving us from Communism, they have no dinner jackets.*'

Another warning reached Lek from Francis B. Sayre, the son-in-law of US President Woodrow Wilson, and the adviser to earlier Siamese kings. Sayre wrote of 'the sordid ambitions and unworthy motives' of those around King Bhumibol. 'Do not let yourself be discouraged. The Thai people themselves have great qualities . . . Follow the pathway which your father always followed, the pathway of selfless service for the country and its people. Your ideals like his must be kept untarnished . . . Your constant compass if you would avoid shipwreck must be utter goodness and integrity.'

The king replied: 'You know Siam much better than I do. I shall try not to get discouraged, although sometimes I nearly got discouraged even in Switzerland . . . But I know I must hold on [to] what I think is the right thing to do, and I can assure you I shall try my best.'

Sayre had a particular reason just now for recalling how Lek's great-grandfather, King Mongkut, balanced between the great powers. Mongkut had written to his ambassador in Paris:

It is for us to decide what we are going to do; whether to swim upriver to make friends with the crocodile or to swim out to sea and hang on to the whale . . . Being surrounded on two or three sides by powerful nations, as we are now, what can a small nation like us do? Supposing we were to discover a gold mine from which we could obtain many million catis weight of gold, enough to pay for the cost of a hundred warships; even with this we would still be unable to fight against them, because we would have to buy those very same warships and all the armaments from their countries. Even if we have enough money to buy them, they can always stop the sale whenever they feel we are arming ourselves beyond our station. The only weapons that will be of real use to us will be our mouths and hearts, constituted so as to be full of sense and wisdom for the better protection of ourselves.

Mongkut, the Fourth Rama, was now on the brink of worldwide fame, of a sort, as the hero of *The King and I*. Its first performance took place in the year of the Ninth Rama's final return in 1951. The lyrics were sent to Lek from London's Theatre Royal. He paraphrased words put in the mouth of his great-grandfather because they were uncanny in conveying how he himself was feeling. As a boy, he had learned facts about which he was now not so sure. And he echoed the fictional king's cry that his world was now 'a puzzlement!'

13

A New Kingship

On the eve of King Bhumibol's twenty-fourth birthday, the Danish steamship *Meonia* entered the Gulf of Siam and left behind an escort of British warships supporting the savage war fought in near-secrecy in the Malay jungles. Orange-red Jupiter replaced the diamond-bright planet of Venus as the Royal Thai Navy sloop *Meklong* came up alongside. An Associated Press report, relayed from the ship's wireless room, confirmed that Marshal Pibul had pulled off another theatrical coup and again asserted his predominance. He would 'curtail royal influence . . . The king must issue a royal decree and sign a new constitution.' Lek bridled at the word *must*.

He remained on deck most of the final night. He was to transfer to the sloop at dawn. He would leave Sirikit and the baby on board the neutral Danish vessel for safety. Danes had been the first from Europe to 'discover' Siam. Danish seamen had been employed by Siamese kings to sail their ships, and other Danes for a long time ran the police and drilled the army. 'Dependable', great-grandfather Mongkut had said of them. Lek had an infant daughter and a teenage queen whose future now depended on the ship's Danish captain, and on how the king got through the next few hours.

Lek watched the dancing fireflies of passing fishing boats. Bigger ships had to wait outside the river with its treacherously twisting coastline of solid reddish mud. The coast closed in upon the river like a giant crab's claws. Military's claws awaited him. He thought back to when he had arrived here with Nan so long ago. He almost shared A. E. Housman's envy of 'the lads that will die in their glory and never be old'. Elder Brother had died with his illusions intact. Tonight, feeling his presence, Little Brother wondered how Nan would adjust his idealism to the ominous information stitched together during this last voyage.

Lek knew that Marshal Pibul's henchmen were emboldened by the anti-communist jitters gripping their US backers. General MacArthur had proposed to bomb China's industrial centres and lay a 'belt of radiation' along the China-Korea border. President Truman fired him but was branded 'soft on communism' for it. Lek was being asked to choose between the crocodile and the whale. If he went openly against Pibul, he risked American hostility. If he knuckled under, there would be a violent uprising against military rule undiluted by the presence of a king whose hands were tied by restrictions never imposed on any previously reigning monarch.

A loyal general came aboard with details of Field Marshal Pibul's latest performance. He had staged a coup, crushed it with a counter-coup, and now claimed to be the kingdom's saviour: his men were waiting to make the king sign this new constitution. Pibul would claim it restored parliamentary democracy. Without the king's signature, the government was illegal. If the king tried to patch things up, Pibul would take this as surrender. If the king opposed him, Pibul would try again to become uncrowned monarch: *Phaw Khun*, the paternal kinglike figure of tradition. But the people would not be fooled. The King's Man did not mince his words: 'Your Majesty is in danger.'

'And my wife and child?'

'Leave them here for now.'

'That is arranged.'

'Then Your Majesty must be concerned for your own safety.'

'What would you do in my shoes?'

'I would go on,' said the general.

The king had been right to trust him. 'Political science textbooks in Lausanne were no use to me here,' Lek said later. 'I got more out of reading *Romance of the Three Kingdoms*, Miyamoto Musashi's Japanese *Book of Five Rings* and Machiavelli's *The Prince*. They were masters in the art of winning battles without waging open war.'

The general advised, 'Don't make anyone lose face.' The king went below and changed into an ordinary suit. It would not out-shine the glittering regalia worn by Pibul and his men. The people would see a king who, like themselves, dressed in working clothes.

He kissed Sirikit and the sleeping baby goodbye, not sure when he might see them again. The queen held him tight, certain of his invincibility. He told her to be prepared for anything.

He said later, 'I was learning to leave opponents guessing by planning nothing ahead.'

'You must have seemed inscrutable,' I suggested.

'Even to myself,' he replied. 'But my brother was behind me.'

The sun was burning the mist off the river as he boarded the sloop. The long journey upriver recalled a passage in the English nanny's memoirs, now re-published with the success of *The King and I*: 'Thousands of boats glide noiselessly over the silver flood that winds on for ever. In the gloom at the upper end of the river, many a boatman, perched on the prow of his boat, seems like the Angel of Death.' Such a boatman seemed to be at Lek's elbow now.

Army loudspeakers greeted him with the propaganda music of Pibul in place of Lek's own cheerful songs, played the year before. The king took comfort in reminders of a more distant past that were revealed with each bend of the river: the Temple of Dawn, the immense Reclining Buddha, and all the gold structures that pointed their spires defiantly at fighter-bombers circling ominously above. Waiting on the same old Grand Palace river-landing stood a bodyguard of brawny men in dress uniform with gold-and-black helmets, arrow- and bullet-proof leather flaps enclosing neck and sides of faces innocent of any cunning. The king could always rally these simple soldiers to his side. They flanked older men whose ornate uniforms sparkled in the sun, outshining the skinny boylike figure in the linen suit.

'I wish I could spank that spoiled brat,' said Air Chief Marshal Phoen Roanapalart, commander-in-chief of the Royal Thai Airforce. The king had kept them waiting. The words were reported later by a King's Man, Luang Prasert Maitri.

'Of course I kept them waiting,' the king confessed later. 'In one hundred degrees of heat, their backbones were melting.'

The new draft constitution, rolled into a sacred gold tube, was held out by Marshal Pibul. 'Resplendent in his new self-designed uniform of Great Leader, Pibul looked like the Nazi bosses he once cultivated,' recalled the ex-OSS agent who had given his gun to Nan, Alexander MacDonald. 'Pibul's personal bodyguards with Sten guns were reduced to comic-opera because they stood ankle-deep in water due to an abnormally high tide. The king appeared small and insignificant. Pibul delivered an endless speech to tire the king he still regarded as a boy, expecting he would do any-thing to get out of the broiling sun and quickly sign a constitution he had not been allowed to read.'

The king removed his dark glasses. The one good eye glittered in a face rigid as a mask. He took the scroll. Pibul's men were seasoned intriguers but they shifted from foot to foot in the long silence that followed. 'They were plotters [with] an anti-royalist motive behind their coup because the King seeks liberal-democratic changes that threaten military dominance,' Cyrus Peake reported to the US State Department Bureau of Far Eastern Affairs. Peake had so far escaped McCarthy's anti-communist purge. 'They fear what he might do with the countryside behind him.'

'The king cleverly plays the witless fool,' reported Reuter's man, Denys

Corley-Smith, and quoted Britain's commissioner-general, Malcolm MacDonald: 'The masters of deceit boast the existence of a Siamese "Parliament", and now and then hold elections that never yet removed an established team of Ministers from office. That is achieved – when those who arrange such things deem it necessary – by a military *coup d'etat*.' The *New York Times* reported that the committee was 'a merry swindling crew of generals working with crooked drug dealers and muscling into every branch of business'.

The wind off the river blew the king's jacket hard against his spine, damp with sweat. He looked around him and then gave an aide the gold tube with the new constitution still rolled up inside it, and told Pibul, 'I shall consider it.'

Marshal Pibul and his crew knew their legitimacy was in question without the king's signature. Their new political party, Might Is Right, had not yet unsheathed its sword. King Bhumibol said innocently that he wished to visit the major temples immediately. An inner voice whispered that he must show himself to as many people as possible before disappearing into the Grand Palace where he could become the prisoner of ritual duties. He knew now how cleverly these could be piled upon him.

Pibul had again encircled the capital with military forces to keep countryfolk from swarming in. But he could not stop the king from going out. To the surprise of those who thought him frail, Lek slogged from one royal temple to another. Again the crowds appeared from nowhere to cheer him. Again the cheers also came from Pibul's troops. Lek broke away from his military escorts to kneel and touch the prostrate forms of the old and infirm. Perhaps they were the only ones really to sense the famous Chakri temper beginning to boil behind the mask.

Queen Sirikit brought tiny Princess Ubol into Siam for the first time. In the weeks that followed, sacred traditions creaked back into life. Sirikit made the family at home in the Grand Palace, but not for long. Lek wanted to live without ostentation. His power rested upon public respect. He could hold this respect if he escaped from the fortress Field Marshal Pibul had made out of the palace.

Pibul's ace up the sleeve was a conference in Bangkok of US diplomats and intelligence officers from all over Asia, stamped TOP SECRET, a label sure to attract media attention. Nothing was secret about it. The roving US ambassador, Philip C. Jessup, announced that within four weeks of the king's return, '200,000 Chinese are predicted to invade Indochina.' Thailand was the key domino that must stand firm or begin a toppling sequence. 'This is where we must make our stand against international communism and why it is international communism's chief target.'

The king could not very well oppose the considered judgement of the most powerful nation on earth. Nonetheless, he still did not sign Pibul's new constitution because it would give legitimacy to US military control through Pibul. The day touted for the Chinese invasion came and went, and nothing happened; but Pibul and Police-General Phao got more US weapons by providing what they called evidence of widespread insurgency. US suppliers had to pay bribes – twenty per cent of the listed price – to get the regime to buy weapons with the money provided by US taxpayers. The military elite was sitting pretty. Phao seized the lion's share of profits from the CIA's proprietary SEA Supply, a false-front trading company. Field Marshal Pibul kept his most-favoured-strongman position in Washington. He became the main channel for distributing US funds after making himself Supreme Patriot in addition to his earlier self-promotions as National Hero, Extensive Warrior and all the rest of it. Anyone who did not share Pibul's new version of patriotism was subversive. He was careful though, having learned from his incarceration as a war criminal. His political tactics were laid out in the memoirs of his wife, Lady La-iad: 'He'd say, "I support you, even if for the moment I must keep a distance."'

The king fought for time to comb through Pibul's draft of the constitution. 'Save the kingdom from disorder and sign quickly,' urged the Field Marshal.

Lek's answer was to move his family away from where his brother had been killed, to another cavernous residence where he plunged into nocturnal work on the constitution while his opponents were busy in debauchery. He hid his rage at the impudence of randy old men who squandered money on whores and gambling dens, financed by the opium and heroin profits made by Chinese *Teochiu* mobsters with their links to the wartime Northern Command clique. At morning councils, he wore out men exhausted from all-night carousing. Palace Law required the holding of such councils, and even a lawless government was afraid to tamper with tradition. In a small room at night, a loyal and obscure expert on Siamese law sat with the king and went through the draft bill: 'I learned more from a few months on this than I did from years of academic study,' the king said. 'We reworked it and I made sure the word PROVISIONAL would remain at the top whenever and whatever we finished.'

He struck out a passage giving the military the right to declare martial law. Pibul offered to make him Supreme Commander. The title was as empty as Lord High Poo-bah. Lek threw a couple of inkwells in the privacy of the room he had requisitioned as a study, then re-emerged to tell Pibul:

'My brother made me an army lieutenant, and that is good enough for me.'

Pibul tried another kind of flattery. Surely His Majesty's newly acquired Swiss law degree would ensure justice if the king were to be graciously pleased to sit as a judge on the Bangkok district court. Lek found himself listening to minor civil suits and cases of petty larceny. The controlled press fawned upon the king's Solomon-like wisdom. Pibul rubbed his hands. In the last analysis, it was never possible to flatter a king too much.

Then the king took a closer look at a ceremonial appearance arranged for him early in March, 1952. It would have him preside over routine parliamentary business. Cunningly buried in the agenda was a promulgation of Pibul's constitution. He cancelled the engagement, and took Queen Sirikit and their daughter to Far-From-Worry.

Police-General Phao caught up with them there. This time, the withering scorn of a seventeen-year-old queen would not repulse him. Sirikit had an infant daughter now, and again she was pregnant. Phao was confident she would give no trouble; and that like the Seventh Rama when the 1932 revolution caught him at the same little seaside retreat, this king would be intimidated. Paramilitary forces filled the streets of Hua Hin. Phao arrived full of a new swagger, contemptuous of a boy who did not have a string of wives and mistresses. Yet even Phao was superstitious. He had armed himself with amulets to ward off ill-fortune. King Bhumibol sat silent as a statue. Phao dropped to his knees under the blank stare. Keeping his gaze fixed on the floor, Phao hissed an invitation to return to Bangkok. It was an invitation backed by physical force.

'The real struggle began here,' recalled the expert on Thai constitutional law, Thongthang Chandransu. 'The military was stronger than the monarch. He was a child in their eyes. But a lot of ordinary people would eventually see him as being the early incarnation of Buddha, wrestling with demons and resisting seduction. He could only get real democracy by shifting the balance in his favour against the generals. Years of great loneliness were just beginning for him.'

The king left Hua Hin in his own time, avoiding a physical confrontation that could result in civil war. Thinking Phao had succeeded, the US embassy leaked reports that the king was signing the original draft constitution. Joseph Burkholder Smith, the CIA black-propaganda specialist, wrote, 'Any methods were justified to halt the communists in Thailand whose pliant people had instantly become loyal subjects of Japan in 1942. [Now] they were offering us their fullest cooperation.'

But not the king.

His popularity rose in the countryside. He had not agreed even to an amended constitution, despite American pressure to sign away his right to advise any government. So the regime cut funds for his visits into the countryside.

Old Gran was now immensely old. Prince Rangsit had been so much a son to her that his death seemed like the loss of the last of her own children. All had met with tragedy, starting in 1878 when her first baby died. Though she had known so many setbacks over such a long period, the ordeal had served only to sharpen her wits. She was cheered by the news that Queen Sirikit was once more with child. Old Gran was convinced it would be a boy, ensuring the continuation of her personal line of descent into the next generation. At ninety, she was the only direct living link to her father, King Mongkut, whose statecraft now had more meaning for Lek, his great-grandson. It had an astonishing relevance to today. The royal court had changed drastically, and yet so much remained the same. With close to a century's experience to draw upon, Old Gran could see in a flash the right things to do in a crisis. She could still convey with a small gesture and the use of few words, whole volumes of sensible advice. 'Keep out of politics,' she told Lek. No matter how provoked, he must never be seen joining those wallowing in filth.

Similar advice, couched in politer language, came from King Baudouin, Lek's old school friend, writing regularly from the palace at Laeken in Belgium. He believed in Lek and his ability to keep his kingdom intact by staying out of politics and commanding popular respect to deal with enemies. That was the hard voice of experience. Baudouin encouraged the Ninth Rama by paraphrasing from Shakespeare's *Julius Caesar*. Both had acted in the play at school: 'There is no terror in their threats because you are armed so strong in honesty.'

Whenever Lek appeared in public now, arms rose from the crouching crowds to offer sweat-stained notes. The crumpled currency was more trusted by the poor who knew that crisp new notes might be forgeries. People who had no money held out baskets of fruit or vegetables. Accepting the gifts was an act of charity. The poorer the giver, the more merit the king bestowed upon the giver. A scrupulous record was kept, each giver's name inscribed as if in some divine ledger. Rich families suddenly saw a way to win prestige: Lek saw a way to use their donations to carry out social reforms and avoid being charged with interference in government.

'Even among the poor and ignorant, Marshal Pibul is seen as jealous of the king's popularity,' the US embassy was obliged to report.

Lek heard this with caution. 'People consider that the Buddha is the perfect one, but in his life he was attacked,' he said later. 'People think a leader should not have failings and turn him into a super-hero because he tries to do good. And then critics feel entitled to find him fallible. Look at Superman in the comic books! His admirers insist on building him up, and then they start looking for faults. Everyone is Superman and everyone is Bad Man. We are all fallible, but people so often want kings and queens to stay in fairytales where they have no impact on reality.'

14

Ancient or Modern?

Appearing ceremonially and then dissolving from sight, the king and his family did seem part of a fairytale to foreign observers. Out of their view, Lek built up a detailed picture of the kingdom's resources and slipped away privately to interrogate public officials about conditions in the countryside. Queen Sirikit stayed in Bangkok, dreaming of the baby boy she was certain would be born this approaching summer of 1952. She urged Mama to return: the Princess Mother would be enchanted by little Princess Ubol and as a grandmother, she was missing out on family life. Mama was perfectly sure she did not wish to be in Bangkok. She read about the revolution in China and sympathised with the nationalist aspirations of Asians who had suffered humiliation from colonisers and brutality from the Japanese. Siam's response to communism, she thought, should be to find economic freedom through the energy and skills of its own people, and by following simple Buddhist logic. She saw little hope of this under Bangkok's military rulers.

She changed her mind about going back after events beginning with a judgement issued in the King's Death Case. 'In the name of His Majesty the King', three scapegoats were pronounced guilty of conspiring in the murder. This made it seem that the king had approved the judgement.

Lek had taken the rule of law for granted. Now he saw the law subverted to suit the government. Judges' salaries and pensions depended on the regime's approval. The king could try to advise, but adroitly enough to avoid censure for interfering in government affairs. He had to find a way to draw public attention to the need for an independent judiciary. His silence intimidated the covertly hostile regime, unwilling to test its physical strength against his moral authority. The death sentences were delayed.

In a brave reaction that turned out to be suicidal, defence lawyers argued that Marshal Pibul's government was illegal. The king had not signed the new constitution. Judges in an appeals court, waiting to be paid at each month's end by Pibul's men, rejected the pleas with Alice-In-Wonderland logic: 'If, after a successful *coup d'etat*, all administrations are to be held unlawful, when will a country ever be lawfully governed?'

The former wartime British agent and prime minister, Pridi, was por-trayed by the judges as the mastermind behind Nan's murder: 'He formed the notion that the King [Ananda] harmed him or stood in his way.' Pridi was in communist China. That was enough to condemn him.

Arthur Miller, the American playwright, and victim of the Un-American Activities Committee in Washington, was staying at the home of Prince Bhanabhandu Yugala who led the first murder inquiry. Miller thought the smear tactics against Pridi were like the Salem witchcraft trials when dolls' necks were wrung to make a distant enemy's head drop off. 'Here, the real distant enemy is your king,' Miller told his host. 'We Americans who share his unconventional views are denounced as "traitors" after McCarthy's witchcraft trials.'

He thought the king ought to use his role as god-of-gods. This had already occurred to Lek. 'Fresh appeals against the sentences were in the works,' he said later. 'I couldn't undermine the position of honest uphold-ers of our written laws by intervening until a final appeal for clemency reached me.' But that was to wait five years; and when it did come, it was too late.

Miller's host explained that by remaining aloof, the king touched a deep chord. Even those controlling the case were afraid to bring it to a bloody close, so long as a majority of people saw him as a god.

This led Arthur Miller to sketch the theme of a play in which 'the gods ask if they exist because humans think they exist'. Prince Bhanabhandu Yugala responded: 'The king is god-of-gods because the people say so!' Later, Yugala asked me, 'Did we make up the play? Or did the gods cause us to write it?'

This deep-rooted uneasiness about tampering with a king who could be truly a god made even the most worldly Siamese careful. Arthur Miller had said, 'The king can't escape playing a god when he's in a land of gods and demons.' And this was the role Lek felt pushed into performing more and more.

Great-grandfather Mongkut had purged Siam of superstitious knavery but some beliefs were interwoven with Buddhism. He had written volumes on Buddhism and its origins, of which the sacred White Elephants were part. Pibul and his fellow revolutionaries in 1932 had removed the White Elephants from the Grand Palace to destroy the foundations of superstition that sustained the monarchy. Why shouldn't the Ninth Rama bring the sacred elephants back? They were cheerful and harmless symbols of authority. 'There is a National Guardian Spirit that needs to be nourished,' Mongkut had written. A National Guardian Spirit would have once seemed to Lek, as an American-born schoolboy, to belong to some other cosmology. Queen Sirikit got him to accept it as part of the hidden universe in which she was born. And so to nourish it, Lek reconstructed ceremonies like the Speeding of the Outflow in which the king would play the role of magician to disperse flood waters in the first lunar month of each year. In a grand parade of state barges, a king would wave a long-handled fan toward the sea to summon flood-demons to drain the waters and save the rice crops. The imagery, thought Lek, would make countryfolk more receptive to the construction of dams and reservoirs. He would pay for them through more royal foundations like the one named for his father which had paid for Mama's schooling in America.

Sirikit salvaged a *Treatise on the Royal Ceremonies of the Twelve Months* by their shared grandfather, King Chulalongkorn. He had collected the details from Court Brahmins and Vedic texts. There were hundreds of rituals and forbiddances that made it difficult to get the most commonplace things done. Sirikit understood the need for a certain amount of deviousness and why the use of a special palace language preserved a magical secrecy. Her visits to the Palace at Versailles had taught her how a King of France was undone once the magic was lost because the public saw each detail of his daily life.

Lek wanted to use magic to educate people away from magic. He remembered Radio Lausanne, the pioneering Swiss station that brought education to people in their homes; and on 25th September, 1952, he completed his own 150-watt transmitter and began broadcasting as Radio Anporn, named after Anporn Villa which he used as a temporary family residence in the complex of Grand Palace buildings before settling for good a further distance away. Radio Anporn made the ruling strongmen chuckle unkindly: 'the spoiled brat' was indulging himself. The king, though, was shrewder than they guessed. Every coup-maker first seized the state-run radio because until now, Thais automatically submitted to official government statements. Lek learned to do all the technical jobs required to run a radio station. In an emergency, he could override government broadcasts and speak directly to the people.

Queen Sirikit gave birth to a healthy boy, Vajiralongkorn, just as Old Gran had predicted. Sirikit wanted to settle into a real home just as much as Lek. She found a suitable site, four kilometres from the Grand Palace and on the other side of the Royal Turf Club racecourse. It was also beside the Dusit

Zoo to which the 1932 revolutionaries had consigned the sacred White Elephants. Opposite the site was the old Samsen railway station on the Northern Line, and also the Opium Department which exercised nominal control over the illegal opium trade. The area is marked on 1932 Royal Survey Department maps as Chitlada but like so many Siamese names it changed over the years in transliteration. Now it was Chitralada. There were a few acres of land, some old teakwood barns filled with rotting farm implements and oxcarts with canopies made from woven vine. An adjoining canal ran from here for two kilometres to the Lords of Life River, which would supply water for Lek's proposed experiments to modernise and diversify agriculture; and nearby were barracks housing infantrymen likely to be more loyal to the king than to tyrants in any major showdown.

Chitralada Villa was called a palace for formal occasions, as custom dictated. The king began to muster modern farming experts, from Japan for fish-farming, but mostly from the United States or men who had trained there, to help modernise a kingdom which had always relied on its rural population. Agrarian reforms in China were going horribly wrong because the central communist government exercised administrative control and dictated policies that were unworkable in many regions. Lek was not going to make the same mistake. He quietly examined each part of Siam. Local materials differed hugely from one place to another. Farmers in some regions were idle for months when floods swamped their fields. Elsewhere, drought caused famine. Large amounts of coastal land were unused because of sea-water. He had to find ways to balance all this out, and show villagers how to make their own machinery from whatever was at hand.

It was a relief to focus his attention on practical matters, and steer clear of politics. The law, in his mind, was a practical tool. The King's Death Case judgement had shown him how naive he had been to let the regime manoeuvre him into sitting as a judge in local courts. It told the public that the king approved of the present Ministry of Justice whose judges did as they were told. He surprised Marshal Pibul by resuming his court appearances, but now he made sure to use them to come into direct contact with countryfolk. He judged the case of neighbours quarrelling over a piece of land. 'Who benefits if one of you wins?' he asked. 'Does the winner gain merit for his victory? Does the loser win greater merit by forgiving the winner?' People saw this as an allegory: there would be no real winners if the conflict between king and strongmen ended with one side on top. A growing number of older generals remembered that Buddha had spoken with the same kind of apparent simplicity. But Lek was well aware that people listened because he had the aura of majesty. Time and again, he was called upon to look into cases that arose from blind superstition. And what was disconcerting for him was that sometimes he could find no scientific explanation for events.

A lady-in-waiting reported to Queen Sirikit that she had seen a ghost known to Great-grandfather Mongkut. It appeared as a woman waiting in an ante-room to the Throne Hall. The Fourth Rama had become so curious about this ghost that he changed the tradition of taking a palanquin to the Throne Hall by way of a robe-changing pavilion built upon an eminence. Kings were not supposed to walk at ground level in their role of gods but Mongkut walked over to see for himself. He encountered in the small chamber what appeared to a disappointed consort from an earlier reign and, opposed to superstition though he was, he ordered a painting of the lady to be imprinted on the wall in the hope that this would allow her spirit to find rest.

Lek found the painting, dimmed by age, deep in shadow. People said the unhappy woman was still seeking her lover, and he decided that if people believed certain things, then these things were real to them. No king could totally ignore their influence upon the public mind. He recalled the words of Malinowski, the American anthropologist: 'Magic is not just something invented to tease the mind, but from the dawn of human history has been part of humankind's survival.'

Sometimes, as Lek-the-western-student, he wondered if he was straying too far into superstition. He knew it was time to enter a monk's cell when the King's Death Case delivered another shock.

Eight years after his brother's murder, Lek still felt he was king on sufferance. One false move, and powerful and wealthy groups might remove the symbol, and the subsequent fight for supremacy could lead to the chaos more and more characteristic of the world immediately around Thailand. 'I tried to perform like a carpenter's spirit-level,' he recalled, showing me the carpenter's shop where he built his wooden sailing boats. 'I had to keep the balance but I wasn't sure how.'

He regularly tested how far he could go, but always by careful indirection. He spoke publicly about '*M'sieu le Patron* . . . It brings back memories of school and French for The Boss, as in *Le patron de bistro*, the pub-owner . . . [but] also evokes for me the ancient Roman interpretation of an influential person with clients under his protection.' Few listeners could miss his meaning. What passed for democracy was patronage. *M'sieu le Patron* was not Rome but Washington.

He had it in mind that the big powers still did pretty much as they liked in certain small countries. A king in Africa had been hauled off, kicking and screaming, and flown from Buganda to Britain with a blanket over his head because he was judged a threat to western security. That was in November 1953 when Thais were secretly hired as mercenaries and took a verbal oath to serve in US Special Forces covert operations. In theory, they could be ordered to help if Lek had to be hauled off under a blanket.

He did not believe any loyal Thai would do this so long as he was seen as a king on the way to Buddhahood. He challenged the ruling generals at the most significant moment in the Buddhist calendar: the full moon of the third lunar month, on the holiest of Buddhist holy days. He announced that he wanted his own revisions in Marshal Pibul's proposed constitution and demanded 'a strong and independent judiciary on the American model'.

He still had no real power to stop a new judiciary being controlled by militarists, secretly financed in the secret warfare waged by the CIA. His coronation oath, though, was a sacred bond with his people. 'Breaking it would mean letting them down,' he said when King Baudouin of the Belgians expressed concern for his safety.

Baudouin had gone through some testing times himself. He had modelled his actions on the British system which deprived kings of tyrannical powers – but kept the monarchy to deny absolute power to anyone else. Baudouin wrote: 'The Crown possesses, *first,* the right to be consulted, *second,* the right to encourage, and *third,* the right to warn. And these rights may lead to a very important influence on the course of politics, especially as under a system of party government, the monarch alone possesses a *continuous political experience.*'

The Ninth Rama was in a world where this continuous political experience was officially beyond his reach. The time had come for him to add to the aura of majesty the authority of a king fully ordained as a Buddhist monk.

'I used to think it was not possible to live with one foot in modern times and the other in the Middle Ages,' he recalled. 'Then I felt my brother's spirit with me and I accepted this because I remembered that walking spirits are common to both worlds and that it was the English poet John Milton who wrote: "Millions of spiritual creatures walk the earth/ Unseen both when we wake and when we sleep."'

Before he could enter King Mongkut's old cell, though, he was faced with a *fait accompli,* a slaughter that appeared to end the mystery of his brother's death, but only complicated it.

15

Execution

DURING the dry season when the winter monsoon brings a flow of air from land to sea, the citizens of Bangkok reach for their warm clothes, although the temperature may be no more than that of a mild oven. By late afternoon on 16th February, 1955, it was 85°F in Bang-Kwang Central Prison. Five thousand inmates were told there was to be a special meeting for the prison staff and filed obediently from workshops, vegetable plots and pigsties. By the end of the day, locked in their cells, the prisoners sensed that something secretive and dreadful was about to happen.

Near midnight, Police-General Phao got ready to show the king who was boss. He decked himself out in a spotless white linen suit at the most splendid of his several houses, was chauffeured in his Royal Lancer custom-built Dodge to the prison, and waddled into the governor's office.

In the cells were the three former Grand Palace retainers accused of conspiring in King Ananda's murder. For 2,650 days they had been interrogated, released, re-arrested, set free and hauled in again as if caught in a revolving door. Death sentences had been announced in October. Then came more delays while Field Marshal Pibul looked for official business to keep him out of the country for the executions. Police-General Phao, with US dollars and military hardware, could challenge the mythical powers of a god-king on his own.

King Bhumibol was at Far-From-Worry with Queen Sirikit, now twenty-two and resting in expectation of a third child. Lek had spent most of that day on the beach making tiny waterways for Princess Ubol – little Lotus Blossom – aged three, and Prince Vajiralongkorn, aged two. He retired to the small room where he worked at night. Standing at a tall wooden desk, he re-read technical manuals, then transferred onto maps his plans to prepare nearby marshland for the resettlement of refugees fleeing from communist Vietnamese armies in Laos. The French garrison at Dien Bien Phu had fallen ten months before. Lek regarded Laos as his responsibility:

a part of Old Siam. Through the floodgates of Laos, the US National Security Council had predicted, communism would pour into East Asia and pose a new threat to Europe, already divided by an Iron Curtain. Thailand must stand firm as the Key Domino. The king had his own ideas about relying on guns alone.

His great-grandfather, King Mongkut, had banned the death penalty. But Phao felt he could break laws he was sworn to protect. He had been provided by the CIA with an armoured division, an airforce and navy. He had Nationalist China's 93rd Division which claimed periodically to invade Red China, although an earlier CIA director, US General Walter Bedell Smith, who had a distinguished World War Two record and knew more than most about well-conducted military operations, complained, 'They only skate up and down the border.'

Phao put on the red beret of an executioner. He had learned the uses of secrecy from Tsuji during the Japanese war. Tsuji was now campaigning openly for election as a conservative member of the Japanese Diet, and congratulated Phao on his new device: abattoirs for the secret disposal of humans whose squeals were indistinguishable from pigs when slaughtered.

Nobody told the three prisoners that by next morning they would be dead. They were the senior royal page, Nai Chit; a page of the royal bedchamber, Butr Paramasrin; and a Senator, Chaleo Patoomros, King Ananda's personal private secretary. There had been some hesitation about condemning Senator Chaleo; but anti-communists said he must be guilty of complicity because he was a crony of the mastermind, Pridi, now in China. As for Pridi's former fellow-Promoter, Field Marshal Pibul, he was making a speech in New York on the theme: 'The Third World War is inevitable between communism and the Free World.' For this, he was awarded a Congressional medal and more US defense money.

At one in the morning, Senator Chaleo heard the rasp of iron shackles outside his cell. Sympathetic warders let him make notes which he addressed to the king. Chaleo's running diary would continue almost to the moment of his death. The uncertainties he had suffered were grotesque. During giddy bouts of liberty, he was offered inducements to implicate King Bhumibol in King Ananda's death. Each time he refused, and was flung back into the cells. He had been re-arrested again only the previous week. His family had a record of long and faithful service to the monarchy. He had a fearless daughter who, at the age of twenty-three, was graduating in law. She believed that two of her father's lawyers had been murdered by Police-General Phao. The two defence lawyers were among cabinet ministers and deputies who had once served in the Pridi government. Such men had been tried for treason because they were alleged to have distributed propaganda against dictatorship. They were freed by two tribunals but six of the suspects were later taken from their homes by Phao's secret police who were listed on US payrolls as 'special riot police'. The six were never seen again. Chaleo's two lawyers continued to defend him. 'They ended up in one of the abattoirs,' his daughter said later.

Chaleo scribbled with pencil and paper provided by the warders whose eyes were veiled and whose mouths stayed shut. Even now, he retained the punctilious habits of a king's private secretary. This direct link was enough to make the guards treat him gently. It was a question of which power they feared most; that of a king they never saw, or Phao whose spies were everywhere. They took a chance on the king.

Chaleo glimpsed the other two men. One was carried like a sack of rice between jailors, the other shuffled as if a cannonball hung from his scrotum. Chaleo followed through an underground passageway, shielded by his guards while he recorded his last hours. The fearful realisation had sunk home that the door on this life would soon close and another would open to reveal the next incarnation. A monk stood by to deliver a sermon on this subtle matter. At 3 a.m. the three men were led past a Buddha without a head. A terrifying sight, the image was more pagan than Buddhist. The monk told the condemned that if they were innocent, they must have committed wrongs in some previous life. If their earlier incarnations had no history of wrongdoing, then their premature departure from this life paid for the sins of others, and they would be reborn higher up the ladder, happy as skylarks.

Chaleo had a burst of adrenaline, the kind that caused aristocrats during the French Revolution to jump up and run after their heads had been axed from their shoulders. He wrote furiously, hand shaking, while his sympathetic guards looked the other way, and the monk droned on.

Senator Chaleo went out first, shortly before five o'clock. Searchlights flamed along the top of high walls around the yard. He was brought to a wooden cross. He slipped his last notes to one of the guards before his feet were lashed to the foot of the cross, his hands tied to the cross-bars. Other jailors jammed joss-sticks between his crabbed fingers for good luck, and a lotus flower for peace of soul.

The murdered king's last private secretary was placed with his back to a dark blue curtain. On the other side was a machine gun. The curtain had a bull's-eye which created for the Buddhist gunner the useful illusion that this was target practise: he was not really taking away life and would not be tormented in his next incarnation. To be on the safe side, he walked over to ask forgiveness from Chaleo who gave it on condition that the executioner make sure the king heard of this, for he could not believe the king knew of it.

The gunner returned and squinted at a red flag held aloft by Phao who stubbed out a cigarette and dropped the flag. The executioner fired a burst from his machine gun. The sharp clatter drowned out Chaleo's last spoken words. It did not matter. His written testimony was on its way to the prison governor who stayed in his office, being the kind of Buddhist for whom to see no evil was to do no evil.

Phao strolled over to hear a prison doctor confirm Chaleo was dead and then retired to light another cigarette. Guards spreadeagled each royal page on his individual cross. Phao lowered his little red flag for stout Nai and then for stubby Butr. The last of the royal pages groaned after the burst of fire sprayed around him. The gunner's hand had shaken. Phao sauntered over, scowled at the nervous gunner, wrote down his name, paused for another smoke, remounted his tower, lifted his red flag one more time, dropped it, and nodded approvingly when the last bullets finished off Butr. The King's Death Case was over. For now.

King Bhumibol woke with a jolt from a dream in which a black sun struggled to get out of the aerial roots of a Buddha bo tree and the White Raven's wings glinted like metal as they flapped across the pond toward the study where, when he was in residence at Chitralada, he had been lately preparing for his ordination as a monk and pondering Buddhist laws. He remembered the law that every action generates a force of energy that returns to us in like kind. He had been told nothing about the executions.

The public heard first through marketplace gossip. This allowed Phao a final touch of cruelty. The unsuspecting families continued their usual early morning routine of making the rounds to plead for their men's lives. The dragged-out fight had beggared them. The bureaucratic processes required them to go on foot or bicycle from office to office. Finally they made their way to revisit the prisoners.

The man at the gate said, 'It's too early to pick them up.' Senator Chaleo's daughter misunderstood. She thought she had come too early to escort her father once more to freedom. The man corrected her: 'You're too early to pick up the bodies.' Then she knew that all morning she had been trying to save the lives of the already dead. No official notification was issued. The king hurried back from Far-From-Worry when the rumours reached him. He had let the months pass without interfering with the due process of law, thinking he had won his demand for a strong and independent judiciary. In his silent rage, he saw how powerless he really was. He had insisted that every citizen had the right to petition him directly. Now he discovered that attempts to reach him by the scapegoats' families had been stopped by courtiers subverted by Phao's police.

Phao circulated reports that the king had approved the executions because he wanted to end speculation about his part in the murder. On Phao's desk remained the last written appeals from the dead men for a king's pardon.

Queen Sirikit gave birth to Princess Sirindhorn seven weeks later, a daughter who would later swear never to marry and who remained nun-like and dedicated to serving the oppressed. The executions were never discussed within the family, she said later, but everyone knew the victims had come from a long line of utterly devoted palace officials. This deeply affected her.

The woman lawyer who tried to save the life of her father, Chaleo, was still using another name when she said later, 'The king had to stay to protect us. But if he could not protect us from what happened, then could he protect us from anything? I was angry at the time and thought he should have hit back at his opponents even if they faked evidence of communist sympathies against him, which they tried to do whenever he directly confronted them. This was done against businessmen because they did not pay enough bribes. Many took refuge in China. Among them was the chairman of the Chinese Chamber of Commerce whose daughter and I kept asking questions and were denounced as communists too. To get out of this sick atmosphere, I applied for a British Council scholarship. I was interrogated by a little British embassy clerk-ish fellow. He kept asking trick questions. I felt so humiliated I said, "The police told you I'm a communist, didn't they?" Before he could answer, I said, "Well, I am!" I was not. But I saw no reason to answer such stupid questions from an English popinjay.'

Lek had appealed to the departing US ambassador, Ed Stanton: 'Please be careful about the kind of Americans sent to this country.' What he got was a new ambassador, General 'Wild Bill' Donovan, the former chief of wartime OSS covert operations. He came back to Bangkok with an assistant, William J. vanden Heuvel, who called Donovan's undercover staff 'a miniature OSS'. There were 200 advisers from the CIA's South East Asia SEA-Supply Company of Miami, Florida, and seventy-six US military advisers from a new Special Operations Group, in addition to some 500 members of other clandestine services. 'You have a tough and dirty job,' Donovan had been told by Bedell Smith, the former CIA director who became US under-secretary of state. Ambassador Donovan was recalled when his health failed, but he left in Bangkok a base for secret warfare. The king had to match this with secrecy of his own. If Phao got away with murder because he had American protection, then the king had to expand the protection he got from King's Men whose identities he did not reveal.

The news of the executions reached Mama in Lausanne. She pleaded again with Lek to give up the throne. He wrote that he had to get rid of injustice. 'Buddhism is a philosophy of life and requires an earthy logic,' she replied. The judiciary was run by an illegal regime. How was he to change that? He said he was going to enter the monastic cell where King Mongkut meditated during his fourteen years as a bishop. Mongkut had left voluminous notes, more useful than the thoughts voiced in *The King and I* which was now a movie. But some lines, put in the mouth of Great-Grandfather Mongkut, were summarised by Lek as applying to his own dilemma: 'Should I join with other nations in alliance? If allies are weak, am I not best alone? If allies are strong with power to protect me, might they not protect me out of all I own?'

Life magazine ran a cover story on the new movie depicting Yul Brynner as 'the tempestuous monarch tamed by Deborah Kerr as the English governess'. The text, like the film, reinforced the notion that Siam's kingship was hopelessly out-dated. This wasn't quite the case. Lek had read Rebecca West's *Meaning of Treason* and now understood her warning: 'In modern espionage there is being used, day in and day out, a weapon which inflicts on society considerable spiritual and material devastation.'

He had to prevent the moral devastation. Communist Chinese broadcasts called Thailand 'a colony of American militarists'. He was accustomed to this kind of verbal belligerence, the daily denunciations, the name-calling and threats. Lek needed to know ahead of time if China were to be provoked into going beyond mere propaganda.

His King's Men collected information through unorthodox channels. Within two months of the executions, they learned of a provocation that could have led to hostilities. An attempt had been made to kill Chairman Mao's right-hand man, China's Premier Zhou Enlai, on his way to the first Afro-Asian conference of under-developed countries, being held in Indonesia. Zhou chartered an Indian airliner, the *Kashmir Princess*, to fly him there from Hong Kong. But then he warned the British that the plane was to be sabotaged in Hong Kong. His warning was dismissed as typical Chinese paranoia. Zhou switched to another plane. The *Kashmir Princess* blew up over the sea, killing Zhou's colleagues. Flying by another route, Zhou was asked by the British commissioner-general, Malcolm MacDonald to fake engine trouble and land in Singapore; and they had an unprecedented, secret meeting at the airport. Malcolm MacDonald promised that the British would find who was responsible. British navy divers later recovered from the sea-bed proof that the airliner had been destroyed by a sophisticated device from the CIA proprietary company, Western Enterprises.

MacDonald shared his unorthodox link to Premier Zhou Enlai with the king. Lek began expanding his own network, independent of allies whose secret operations served their own interests. He wanted no more nasty surprises. He advised the families of the executed men to seal the bodies in stone coffins. Cremation now would only release their spirits to roam in torment. The king would bring peace to their souls in his own way. He was keeping the promise he'd made his mother. He would become a monk. In Mongkut's cell, he learned from the real king behind *Life*'s picture of a comic King of Siam.

16

Monk Kings

Old Gran was in her ninety-third year. Dowager Queen Sawang had been all the Ninth Rama had left of the few advisers who watched over his parents, his brother and himself. She never got over her horror at Phao's gloating public celebration of his new power based on fear. She died twelve days after Lek's twenty-eighth birthday in December 1955. She was his last living link to King Mongkut, her father.

After the months of intensive scriptural studies, Lek removed his kingly robes in a public ceremony on 22nd October, 1956, to put on the single rust-coloured robe of poverty. His head was shaven to the scalp. He moved into the cell occupied on the very same day 138 years earlier by King Mongkut at Number 7, King Street, which then as now is Wat Bovoranives. The temple lanes are inhabited even now by dogs that never bark, and monks move silently over cobblestones polished by the passage of generations of unshod feet. High walls and thick tropical vegetation shut out Bangkok's traffic.

Each morning Lek's cell door was unlocked and he came out in the robe that left one shoulder bare. He got to know the trees and shrubs his great-grandfather had once tended as abbot before he became king: the scented frangipani, the monkey-flower tree, feathery bamboo, weeping fig and fishtail palm. Mongkut had lovingly noted each one: nutmeg, quince, mango, myrtle, golden dewdrop, cannonball and sacred *bodhi*. Lek was a monk among monks. Here were no nobles nor serfs. Title, rank and privilege were surrendered. All were members of one brotherhood.

He was required to take to the streets when there was just enough morning light to read the lines on the palm of the hand. With his wooden bowl, he seemed childlike and defenceless, his polished skull rising above the large protruding ears in a pixyish dome. Millions were familiar with the impersonal pictures of their king on a golden throne. Millions abroad had seen a king with a bald pate and bare-legged in the Hollywood movie that the regime banned – it portrayed a monarch whose authority was supreme.

Now, people saw Lek face to face. They knew who he was but respected his right to be treated as a simple monk, his possessions reduced to the cotton winding sheet, an umbrella, a toothbrush and his bowl that was not for begging. He was a *bhikku*, a monk who lives off alms. On his rounds, he could not make any sign of request for food. 'A *bikkhu* only makes himself available to accept whatever is offered,' I was told by Lek's former teacher who became Supreme Patriarch. Lek ate only two meals of gruel, early and late. He was locked in his cell after midday, when the humidity began its climb to saturation and condensed out in afternoon downpours. He was untroubled by royal duties: Queen Sirikit acted as his Regent.

King Mongkut's huge collection of papers were written for the most part in his idiosyncratic English. The rest, like the scriptural texts, had to be translated. Lek, in the cell Mongkut once occupied, felt as if he was at one with this man whose 'pilgrimages were made in the way of Jesus Christ: "Carry no purse, no wallet, no shoes . . . And into whatsoever house ye shall enter, first say, Peace . . ."' the Ninth Rama said later. He found an old book by a British army officer, Colonel H. Fielding Hall, who wrote: 'Even the king himself takes a lower seat than a monk in the palace . . . Such a king believes in the Buddhist admonition, "Never in the world does hatred cease by hatred. Hatred ceases by love." . . . [but] only three Siamese kings have ever taken holy orders. There is a potential for violence when Buddhism becomes an institution used by the state to camouflage its excesses.'

King Mongkut had foreseen this danger. He reformed Siamese Buddhism. His disciples then formed a new order, with a stricter interpretation of the disciplinary code. Lek felt the code certainly needed enforcement now.

'It was my duty to lock my king in the same cell that was occupied by King Mongkut when he wrote six thick volumes on Buddhism, as reason and philosophy, not as a muddle of silly superstitions,' said His Serene Highness Prasertsri Sayomgura, a self-effacing old prince and ex-soldier, a King's Man, willing to confide after almost forty years. 'Both kings had to study the original Tripitaka texts of forty volumes. The cell had not changed. Very small and dark, tiny grilled window, heavy teakwood door, a mat of reeds to sleep on. My king, long before daybreak, rattled the bars and bombarded me with questions that I could not always answer . . . Bhumibol, Lord of the Sky, became Bhumibol the Beggar.'

King Mongkut had written about classical Chinese concepts of war. 'Hard' weapons were used for hand-to-hand combat. But 'soft' disciplines of mind and body were the most effective protection. As a boy of twelve, Mongkut

had led an army astride the neck of his own war-elephant. Old temple pictures showed caparisoned elephants rearing back to engage the enemy with
huge sharp tusks, forelegs raised like the fists of boxers. It hadn't been easy
for Mongkut to reconcile the martial arts with non-violence, either.

Born in 1804, Mongkut had been the forty-third son of the Second
Rama. An older half-brother was a general whose exploits won him the
position of Third Rama which meant Mongkut was suddenly next in line.
The new king might see Mongkut as a rival and have him killed. So
Mongkut took to the safety of monkhood. At fourteen he lived in a monastic cell. At twenty he was ordained as a full monk. For ten years, he walked
all over Old Siam. 'This is the only way to know the people, a pauper
sharing whatever other paupers have to offer,' he wrote. He saw monks who
'became naughty and played on the people's credulity'. A Buddhist refor-
mation was the best defence against all forms of wickedness. At thirty-three
he became abbot at the monastery where Lek now studied. Mongkut was
forty-seven when the Accession Council invited him to become king after
his half-brother died. European colonisers were grabbing land all around
Siam and another Great Game had been foreshadowed in the Communist
Manifesto beginning, 'A spectre is haunting Europe . . . '

Queen Victoria's curiosity about Mongkut had been piqued already,
when in 1862 Lord John Hay reported on a singular reception given his
English men-o'war. They had moved on Bangkok, having bombarded
Malay sultans into submission. The Queen-Empress sent letters 'To the
King of Siam from Your Affectionate Sister, Victoria'. Many of these
letters only came to light through Manich Jumsai, a scholarly aristocrat-
publisher who also salvaged certified copies of Mongkut's replies from the
basement of the old Thai Embassy at 23 Ashburn Place in London. 'There
were heaps of papers about to be carried away in several lorries for
burning,' Manich told me later. 'The landlord had given our embassy a
month's notice and it moved into new premises at 30 Queen's Gate in such
haste that a great many records were lost.' He deposited his findings with
the Royal Thai Historical Document Commission whose archives were
opened to me although normally they are difficult to access. Manich recovered 200 letters to Victoria signed by Mongkut as, 'Your Affectionate
Brother'. The two had confided to each other problems that only monarchs
share. 'King Mongkut's English style, considering he had to learn English
mostly from American missionaries, is most ravishing and sometimes
strange,' Manich noted. 'This was because he was also conditioned by Thai
expressions, Thai way of thinking and traditions. The discovery of these
files shows his character in true light, not as portrayed in *The King and I*
where the King is reduced to an unreasonable and funny tyrant.'

Lord Hay had signalled his intention to sail to the river-gates of the Grand Palace. Mongkut wrote to his own ministers: 'If the British force an entry, they might spike and dismantle our guns in a manner similar to what they have done in China and elsewhere.' So he invited Hay and his officers to be his guests. They arrived by pilot-boat and were escorted to the Throne Hall, smoky from hundreds of flickering candles. Gold curtains rose from the flagstoned floor to a flat ceiling segmented into gilt-edged red square pictures of blue angels.

Mongkut feared the English might misconstrue Siam's humility. He had cleansed Buddhism of its efflorescent displays of superstition. Now he reverted to the old magic. Three sharp claps of ivory blocks and the gold curtains parted. Lord Hay gazed up at the galleon-like Golden Hibiscus Throne on a tiered pyramid carved with mythical undersea figures. Oil lamps threw a spotlight on what seemed a statue that slowly resolved into King Mongkut wearing the Great Crown of Victory, topped by a diamond as big as an ostrich egg. Above the king was the white nine-tiered *chatra* – 'A stylised tree whose tiers represented layers of leaves sheltering protective genies,' wrote Hay. 'The sacred circles are like the halo with which Christians endow saints. When the king came down from the throne, he turned into a genial host. He had taught himself a quaint English, translating from Siamese to Sanskrit to Pali to Latin and finally arriving at English.'

The visitors were shown Siam's royal regalia. Hay thought the legendary ruby in the helmet of Henry V at Agincourt dimmed by comparison with the rubies here. 'Where had Edward the Confessor found the sapphire to put in the Crown of State, unless in the leather bag of a Portuguese navigator returned from Siam?' asked Hay. 'All the gold, precious alloys and gemstones we hoard in England as great treasure, for Siamese kings may be had for the taking.' He reported that a concealed universe of the mind was made visible in Grand Palace effigies, the eye descending from higher divinities to 'fantastic beasts and hominoids, arabesques, simians and pachyderms . . . overwhelming the senses with white fish-tailed monkey, green crocodile-bird, violet elephant-lion, purple rhino, the yellow-Tonkin-cock of Indo-China.'

Siam was more valuable as England's friend. Colonies were costly to overwhelm and hold. Letters and gifts flowed between the two monarchs. 'Pair of Royal Pantaloons of varied colours ornamented with gold,' were included in one shipment to Victoria after Mongkut took a cartoon of her in oversize bloomers as being an accurate portrayal. He sent fruit whose name sounded to the untutored ear like *mongkut*. This, he pointed out helpfully, would cure dysentery. Inside the tannin-rich purple rind were pearly-white segments, melting sweetly on the tongue, with a tingling acidic touch that so excited Victoria, she offered to reward anyone who knew the secret of how Mongkut kept the fruit from going rotten at sea. Her cargoes to him included models of locomotives to open up Siam, globes in recognition of his reputation as a geographer, charts and 'Philosophical apparatus, illustrative of astronomy, electricity, optics, an arithmometer . . . with books of great proficiency in Science'.

These exchanges intensified Anglo-American commercial rivalry. In 1856, Harry Parkes, a British consul, had already accused Americans of sabotaging British trade. Presents from Victoria to the Fourth Rama were sometimes delayed or sunk at sea, or misappropriated by what Parkes called 'sulky royal courtiers' who had been bribed. He hand-delivered one of Victoria's letters and wrote that: 'I had the pleasure of observing the genuine satisfaction that its contents afforded the King at a moment when *in the absence of his Ministers and courtiers he had no need to hide that it touched his heart.*' The italicised words touched a nerve for Lek. So did words about Victoria written in another context by her favourite prime minister, Benjamin Disraeli: 'The sovereign has no friends – at best they are suspected of jumping over their official superiors to their Great Friend (the monarch): at worst, they are regarded as royal spies . . . They can enrich themselves by quoting their Great Friend who remains unconscious of having been quoted.'

All this echoed Lek's own experience.

Victoria sent Sir John Bowring to report on the Siamese court. He wrote that the king's study 'might be that of any opulent philosopher· in Europe . . . he discoursed on stars, space and time . . . He had discovered monolithic stones in Laos defying explanation [until] he found them to be sandstone markers with carved symbols that, decoded, told of long-vanished communities, perhaps part of a Lost Golden Continent of *Suwannaphum* that became submerged by rising seas.'

In other writings, Mongkut expressed misgivings about loyalty. He seemed again to be speaking directly to Lek: 'Anyone on our throne must search for hidden motives in those professing blind devotion.' This warning was prompted by a near-fatal accident that involved Old Gran when she was a small girl. On a children's outing, Mongkut had been trapped when their carriage overturned. He freed Sawang by lifting an axle but badly injured himself. He wrote: 'There was conjecture in court circles about the effect of my death on future careers. We need insight into the blackness or whiteness of people's hearts, for in the royal court, all true feelings are concealed.'

Mongkut started a palace school. Teachers recruited from the American missions tried to convert his children to Christianity. In 1862, the king replaced them with the English governess Anna, instructing her to teach anything but religion. Despite this, Anna later planted the belief that every virtue the Siamese royal family displayed came from her tactful inculcation of Christian ideals. When Anna's *Romance of the Harem* was republished during Lek's reign, Freya Stark wrote in a foreword: 'She [Anna] achieved so much single-handed! Harrassed and indomitable . . . she loved the women in this royal slavery and trained a new and happier generation of children to carry light into the future . . . Few people can have wielded a stronger influence in that corner of Asia.'

'Ah, well,' said Lek later. 'I suppose she put us on the map.'

His great-grandfather died on 18th August, 1868, after predicting all too accurately where an eclipse of the sun could be best observed in coastal wetlands. His eclipse-watching party drew scientists from all over the world to a small city in the jungle that sprang up literally overnight, for the Thais had been prefabricating houses for centuries, the pieces transported by water. Mongkut consulted his own books on global cooking to make fourteen different kinds of sandwich for his guests, and French chefs did the rest of the catering with ingredients floated, like everything else, along the waterways. Visitors stood on a special platform built of unique bricks fired in the old capital of Ayudhya. And the sun went out on schedule. At this high point in his reign, Mongkut was struck by the blackwater fever that killed him.

Lek beheld in his cell scenes he had never seen before, with a king he had never known. His monastic retreat was brief, but he discovered the mind could travel great distances in what he would have previously called the short span of a month. The phenomenon was explained by the Supreme Patriarch who had been the king's Teacher: 'The king was born out of his due place and found it here.' Lek could live whole lifetimes in his cell, said his old Teacher, and he told me the story of a monk who sent a boy to fetch water: 'The boy crossed the river, wandered far afield, met a girl, married, had children, lost his family in a storm, and came back to the monk who was astonished to hear the boy's saga and said, "But you've only been gone for the afternoon."'

Lek returned to a world that, however strange, he now felt Mongkut would have known how to handle. 'His Majesty studied for many months and passed the most diligent examinations to become a full monk,' said the Supreme Patriarch. 'This does not demand celibacy. He was a father and husband. But . . . he was also Father of the Nation. It was hard to combine the roles . . . He continued to revisit the monastery for further meditation.'

Marshal Pibul was persuaded by his American sponsors to prove himself the expert on Buddhism. Pibul, without inviting the Ninth Rama, took sole charge of celebrating the start of the twenty-fifth century of the Buddhist Era and proclaimed the mass ordination of 2,500 new monks and the casting of 2,500 golden Buddha images at the old capital of Ayudhya. He invited the Burmese leader, U Nu. It was the Burmese who had ravaged Ayudhya in 1767 so that the capital had to be moved to what is now Bangkok. In the 416 years prior to that date, thirty-three kings of four dynasties had ruled Ayudhya and developed it into a powerful maritime centre whose trade was worth more than that of any single major port in Europe. Its citizens now regarded Queen Sirikit as the reincarnation of the most renowned of its women defenders: a queen who in 1549 drove her war-elephant across an advancing Burmese army, was cut down, and plunged a dagger into her heart to save herself from being raped and her husband from being dishonoured. But neither Sirikit nor her king were present when the modern-day Burmese leader attended Marshal Pibul's marking of the most auspicious anniversary in the Buddhist calendar. 'The Nation's Guardian Spirit showed thunderous disapproval,' reported the local newspaper. 'Winds howled through the ruins of the old capital under black skies that turned days into nights . . . We heard the wailings of out-raged ancestors even before the celebrations began.'

Pibul had arranged a travesty of a general election to follow, expecting to win. Superstition intervened. Popular feeling was against him. Hoping to deflect blame for these signs of divine displeasure, he quickly invited the king to see the rest of the ceremonies. The king made no reply, but stayed away until they were over.

People knew the king was putting together an oral history to make up for Burma's destruction of all the great libraries. The seriousness of the gap in knowledge was described later by Dennis Duncanson, a former British diplomat who became vice-president of the Royal Asiatic Society: 'One of the less considered, but grievous misfortunes that befell old Siam when the Burmese sacked Ayuthia [sic] was the destruction of Thai records.' All that remained of written accounts were those of foreigners like the Jesuit priest Guy Tahard who in 1688 recaptured the superb spectacle of the royal court reached 'through glittering squares filled with gold-laden elephants and fierce soldiers on foot backed up by giant Moors on horseback and hundreds of Persian bodyguards . . . The King wore a long pointed helmet of gold ending in a spire brilliant with jewels on a huge throne of solid gold within three circles of solid gold bricks. On his fingers many huge diamonds sparkled greattly [sic]; his jacket was red and fringed with gold and over it a cloak of chain mail made from gold with large diamonds for buttons.' But such stories gave only a tantalising glimpse of centuries of lost history.

Lek, gathering whatever old people had been told about those days, found inside the palace at Ayudhya a forest of *putsa* trees. The fruit was a kind of crab-apple, never grown in Siam. Seeing her king's puzzlement, an old woman said, 'Sit down. There's no hurry. I want to tell you a story . . . The day before the Burmese attack, the general ordered all cooking pots to be destroyed. The Burmese soldiers would carry this fruit in the knot of their sarongs. In the day's fighting, they ate the fruit. It is hard to digest. They climbed the walls, destroyed everything inside, Buddha images and all, and took away the gold. Their bowels passed the *putsa* seeds inside the palace and that's why you see a forest of *putsa* here now.'

The Americans who backed Marshal Pibul had not known Siam's history well enough. The animosity he had aroused came to the boil when soldiers later followed his orders and cast their votes for their commander-in-chief. As a result, Pibul was returned as prime minister. The public rebelled against this blatant manipulation. Protesters took to the streets. Police-General Phao arrested them as communists. Some, he had cremated alive. Others, seeing no alternative, joined communists in the jungle: 'It was what I feared would happen,' Lek said later. 'Later on, I spoke to these youngsters in the jungle, and coaxed them out. I said there was another and better way to change things.'

Great-grandfather Mongkut had issued a proclamation that those who deceived the superstitious and the ignorant 'will be visited by the pain of Heinous Demerit'. Marshal Pibul had attempted such a deception. But was it entirely his fault? Lek saw the text of a despatch to Washington from the US embassy claiming, 'The local CIA chief can get the Thai Prime Minister to do anything we ask.'

The king controlled his temper, helped by news from Lausanne that his ordination as a monk had decided Mama to come home at last.

17

Mama Comes Home

THE Princess Mother arrived back in January, 1957 at the airport from which she had left as a seemingly broken woman more than ten years previously. A remarkable photograph in the royal archives shows her reunion with the Ninth Rama. She is standing on the tarmac in a simple lace-collared cotton blouse and homespun skirt. Her head and arms are bare under the fierce sunlight. Her long, loose hair still has the bluish-black look of raven wings although she is in her fifty-seventh year. Her face shines with childlike delight. She rises on tiptoe, clasping her son's neck. She is thin as a stick. Her back is cradled by Lek's large hands. He looks like a schoolboy on holiday. Neither of them seems to have aged, although it is more than five years since they have seen each other. So much has happened, though, that when he looks again at this picture, he remembers the story of the boy who left the temple, had many adventures, and returned to relate all the many things he had done, only to hear the monk say, 'But you've only been gone for the afternoon.'

In Lausanne, she had suffered from what would now be called extreme trauma, causing chemical changes in the body. Unaware that her illness was physical, not mental, and impatient with what she thought was her own weakness, she had submerged deeper into academic studies.

'Now she was a flower that opens up again,' the king said later.

Two of her grandchildren she had never seen: Crown Prince Vajiralongkorn and Crown Princess Sirindhorn. As for Princess Ubol, now six, the Princess Mother had last held her as a baby. A fourth grandchild was due in July.

'Mama' she remained, a woman who had never known an untroubled family life, with neither a father to sustain her childhood nor a husband at her side when she had to surmount tragedy. Some royal courtiers thought of her as an intruder still. Nothing would make her move back into the Grand Palace. Only the Palace of Lotus Ponds could give her the same freedom enjoyed by its former sturdy occupant, Dowager Queen Sawang, Old Gran. Mama had not lived in the modest villa on Rama One Road since those few months after Papa died twenty-eight years ago. Over it now loomed the first of the concrete towers that would soon consume the fields of jasmine rice. Across the road was Siam Square, a growing maze of indoor markets and crooked little alleyways soon to be crowded with one-room typing and language schools, and bookstores for students from Chulalongkorn University which was expanding rapidly with help from the king's growing numbers of foundations circumventing government control, and therefore discreetly administered. Even the poorest inhabitants of Siam Square were possessed of a cheerfulness that took her back to childhood and the supreme confidence of an orphan who mercifully had no notion of the awful things that lie in wait for us.

Inside the Palace of Lotus Ponds, the roof continued to leak. The gardens remained a cultivated jungle. The canal had not been touched by the road-makers. Their zeal paved many *klongs* but created new problems for a capital whose lifelines had always been its waterways. *Klong* Bang Kapi still ran straight as a die along one side, but the quiet splash of oars had been replaced by the clatter of longtail boats, marvels of ingenuity, driven by old Volkswagen engines geared to long propeller shafts that tilted to clear the weeds. Boatmen throttled back when they passed. She heard only the calming hum of activity from the temple containing her husband's ashes. The most humble people approached her with the same mixture of familiarity and awe they showed when they worshipped at the little wooden spirit houses among the trees. She did not have a king for a father and so she could never be Queen Mother nor Her Royal Highness. Yet people turned to her as a natural aristocrat in their private pantheon of gods.

In her theological studies, she had found no conflict between western and oriental wisdoms. 'I understood the essential pattern and flow set forth in the Chinese *Book of Changes* – the *I Ching*,' she recalled. 'I saw how we can influence change by accepting and opening ourselves to it, rather than blocking our senses with hatred or remorse.'

The ruling military strongmen saw no reason to fear her increasing popularity. Her staff became intensely loyal. A detective, assigned by the king to keep her from harm, knew Phao ran the Golden Triangle opium fields. He also knew what happened to honest policemen. 'I told the king's mother, "Each time I am called out in the middle of the night, my wife never knows if I'm going to come home alive." She asked if I wanted her to talk to the king about it. I said His Majesty had too many petitioners demanding his time – but . . . perhaps she could speak to the White Monkey at Chitralada, the silent listener who knows everything, and he would tell the White Raven who carries information to the sacred White Elephants.'

Mama did speak to her son about the power of illegal drug traffickers. He said much was concealed and much he still had to learn. He played now by the cardinal rule of Asia's martial arts: 'Stay still as a mountain/ Move like a mighty river.' He faced forces intertwined with a corrupting Chinese *Teochiu* underworld that reached right into royal circles and into the military clique, once supported by Japan and now by the United States. He needed her help.

She saw that within the two square miles of moat around the flat-roofed three-storey Chitralada Villa, he was building an inner kingdom. Some day it would show the rest of the country how to become self-sustaining. He took technical information from modern Japan and the west, and his philosophy from monks like Buddhadasa Buddha who had a temple deep in the forests and taught that Buddhism was a socialist religion. 'It's not "socialism" of a kind that frightens Americans,' Lek told her. 'It's like Jesus feeding thousands with a few loaves and fish. If we conserve resources, there's enough to go round.'

Lek showed her how the people exercised their own form of democratic protest. In the middle of the night, crowds would gather around the statue of King Chulalongkorn, close to where she had once gone to school. Now, paper coffins appeared there, containing effigies of Pibul and Phao, to be sprinkled with black pepper and salt and burned in the presence of Chulalongkorn's 'free soul', or *kwhan*. The Ninth Rama had to move at the pace of a country where superstition gripped the popular imagination even while modern technology was changing its future.

Foreign newspapers sometimes said the Ninth Rama encouraged these magical beliefs. The London *Observer*, under the headline of MASTER AND SLAVE OF TRADITION, still emphasised the 'suspicious circumstances' in which Lek found his murdered brother. The newspaper championed Pridi as 'the wartime resistance leader against the Japanese, the nearest person the Siamese have ever had to a democratic leader', even though Pridi was now in China. It added: 'Pridi's family believes that the palace is hiding a secret about the death of King Ananda, which is still the most extraordinary unsolved crime story.' Hints that the solution was in Lek's own hands were still circulating. They were inspired by his enemies to keep the king in line, wrote Murray Fromson of Associated Press: '[He is] a powerless figurehead who does what he is told . . . directed by Marshal Pibul. The king seems content to stay within the palace walls playing jazz records.'

In Lausanne, Mama would have read such reports with deeper concern than she now felt. Here, she saw how Lek worked out of sight to break up the old hierarchical system, avoiding any showdown with military rulers that might lead to civil war. To train his own cadres of technically proficient youngsters, he built laboratories and experimented with new kinds of crops in Chitralada's fields. 'We don't want to do for people what they can do for themselves,' he told his trainees, selected on the basis of talent rather than birth. He could say what he liked here; break all the taboos.

She was more worried that he might apply to his children the same rigid standards she had imposed upon her own. It was harder on his young family because they could not escape into anonymity and play in the streets like her own children when they all lived in Lausanne. Behind Lek's delighted smile at their first meeting, Mama gradually perceived the turmoil. When she came for supper, she found him showing the children how to cook his favourite Mongol hot-pots; and as they grew older, laughing with them over American comics. His worries he kept to himself, but he freely showed his love for Sirikit; photographing her and painting her portrait in striking colours. His creative work made up for the strain when he was on ritual display. Some of his oils on canvas betrayed frustration at the need to conceal his feelings from those who would use them against him. Mama wondered if his self-control might cut him off from domestic life. Lek, with no memory of the living presence of Papa, had to feel his way into being a good father while he felt his way into being a good king.

The Princess Mother, through charitable foundations financed by Lek and Queen Sirikit, utilising donations proferred to the king when he walked among the crowds on official occasions, and then through her own charities, began to launch projects in the impoverished north. She built medical clinics for hill tribes and found alternative crops to opium. 'She was not too popular among certain descendants from other reigns,' said a titled woman, Kanitha Vichienchuen, who later became a Buddhist nun and ran shelters and homes to educate battered women and prostitutes. 'These relics of the past squabbled over property rights, and thought she would destroy the old system.'

Other parts of the old system, Mama encouraged Lek to endorse. The celebration of Buddha's birthday became an important ritual at the royal chapel in the Grand Palace. Soldiers carried lotus flowers instead of guns. The king walked unprotected around the home of the Emerald Buddha, carrying a flickering candle. Under the full moon, king, queen, senior politicians, generals and court officials chanted the complicated sutras in Pali, the language that like Latin threads together co-religionists in all parts of the world. Nobody dared offend tradition by being absent. Watching this later, I thought it was like seeing members of the British royal family and dignitaries circumambulate Westminster Abbey singing in Latin all night while unarmed guardsmen clasped flowers. But in the Grand Palace, King Ananda had been shot dead. It took a great deal of faith to dispense here with any physical security measures.

The kingdom itself faced larger security problems, though, that made Mama suggest the king and Queen Sirikit might soon travel abroad to show other countries that the old Siamese way of doing things was valid in a time when the United States preached democracy but lavished money and weapons on a repressive regime. These were the years when the west still spoke of 'backward nations'. Lek should talk to world leaders. Sirikit had poise, beauty and a flair for setting fashion. The couple would demonstrate that Siam was not backward. The Princess Mother would take over as Regent, ruling in the absence of the king: this proposal sent a shudder through the court. Mama, though, already had the people's vote. She was a nobody who had worked for her high estate. No propaganda machine spread the notion. Market gossip re-told the stories of how she had suffered from the contempt of courtiers, and how she had risen above worse things.

She went to Chiang Mei where Mahidol had died while working among lepers. The northern provincial capital was a place where all the senses could be gratified. Mama soon discovered the hidden sources of its growing wealth. Small girls were locked in the permanent darkness of brothels. Nobody ever admitted seeing drug transactions. She started her own clean-up campaign, relying entirely on an appeal to Buddhist morality. It attracted scorn, of course, and some wealthier crooks took to making extravagant gestures of support for the local temples while burying the sleaze from casual observation. Drugs still moved through here at 2,600 tons of opium a year, generating billions of dollars for the big dealers abroad whose chief customers were in America. Anything was on offer: girls, guns, smuggled gems. Papa would have been appalled by this moral squalor where he had worked to bring an earlier American style of progress. Mama was no fool and she made use of the title that growing numbers of countryfolk gave her – Mother from Heaven – to do what her husband would have wished. She selected the nearby sacred mountain of Doi Suthep as the site of a working-base which she called Phu Ping which means 'Up Top'. Thousands of local villagers donated their labour in constructing a long and winding road through what was called 'a veritable paradise' by the English botanist, Dr A.F.G. Kerr, who had spent many years exploring the mountain environs and documented 'one of the world's most magnificent assemblies of rare creatures and plants': 326 species of birds, 275 species of plants, another 250 species of orchid, flying lizards, barking deer, leopard cats and fifty other kinds of mammal within a total area of 261 square miles. In the entire British Isles, there were fewer varieties of flowering plants and ferns than the 1,961 different species he discovered here. But now the forests were being destroyed by illegal logging and the wildlife was dwindling. Her part of the mountain was not entirely poisoned by greed, although worldlier observers doubted her good intentions would scare off the gangsters. Still, there were well-educated civil servants who said that the spirits of girls who died in the brothels came back in the form of the marvellously colourful butterflies that fluttered around Phu Ping in hundreds of varieties and that these butterflies would prevail over the wicked demons below. Mama simply thought that by concentrating on her own Buddhist path, others might think it was not so impossible to follow.

One day she saw men in black berets at Doi Suthep. Innocently, she asked one of them what his uniform represented. 'The Border Patrol Police,' he replied. The Princess Mother then asked the BPP man if he would mind climbing a ghost tree to pick one of its flowers she had never seen before: the blossoms were globose inflorescences, creamy white and pendulous, like tiny ghosts. He was a country boy who believed birds were the souls of the dead and that this kind of tree harboured them. He carried an automatic weapon, yet he did not believe in taking life and was steeped in the old myths. Mama appeared as a frail woman, sensibly dressed in loose trousers and top, but when she spoke, he responded. He climbed the tree and returned with an armful of the flowers. Then he answered her questions, unaware of who she was, but captivated.

'She could charm young soldiers into doing what she wanted,' the king said later, laughing when I asked him about this story. 'They led dangerous lives but they wanted to do good.'

Queen Sirikit had given birth to another child, Princess Chulabhorn, in July, 1957. The growing brood drew the Princess Mother to Chitralada more often, but she was careful not to encroach upon their mother's authority, and went north as often as she could. The city below Phu Ping had lost its main water supply from the mountain when the illegal loggers destroyed evergreen forests whose deep roots retained the rainy-season water in times of drought. Mama led a local rebellion against the mountain's enemies. How did she do it?

She explained later, 'I asked the people to remove the cause of their suffering by concentrating on their own inner development.'

I had tried to comprehend this Buddhist rule and asked somewhat diffidently how it avoided the charge of being self-centred.

'Isn't it what Jesus Christ did?' she countered. 'If you turn yourself into a good person, isn't it the way society changes?'

Her passion for English detective stories had grown, although she had overcome the pain that first made her use them to get through sleepless nights. Her favourite fictional detective was The Saint, created by Leslie Charteris. She knew something about Charteris that millions of his readers may never have found out: that he was the son of a Chinese doctor who claimed descent from one of the great teachers of *I Ching*. The Saint helped the underdog, and tracked down criminals by looking for motives. She wasted no time wondering *who* killed Nan, but she still wished she knew the *motive*.

One evening she sat among the aerial roots of a pagoda tree, the species of *bhodi* made holy by Buddha. She'd always had the habit of combing through newspapers for items that she drew to the attention of King Ananda, and later to King Bhumibol. She peered through her spectacles at a newspaper report she had overlooked, taken from the Associated Press wire, and published under the headline: WAS SIAM'S BOY KING SLAIN LEST HE UPSET THE APPLE CART?

The AP correspondent, Milton Marmor, had asked if King Ananda was killed because he spoke openly of starting a kingship that would lead to a Buddhist socialist republic. Nan had talked of running for election as premier, and quoted George Bernard Shaw's play *The Apple Cart*. 'Did the king meet his death because Shaw inspired in him a desire to reform his own country?' asked the AP correspondent. There had been speculation that a foreign power feared any reforms that weakened its own ideological influence.

Here was a clue to motive. Elder Brother Nan had indeed talked of Buddhist-style socialism. If Lek made too many advances in that direction too dramatically, he must stand in the same danger.

'Buddhism spreads like the *bhodi*,' Lek told his mother. 'The roots burrow into the ground and form new trunks and the entire tree shelters every form of life.' The king, too, burrowed out of sight, his advances small. He had to learn how to be a good father, how to modernise his country, and how to protect it from foreign predators. He spoke of the *bhodi* roots spreading slowly. In fact he had little time. He had quickly to master current world affairs which could have serious consequences for the kingdom.

Mama showed him an old letter in which his father recalled Ho Chi Minh speaking in Paris about the 1919 Versailles peace talks after the First World War. Ho Chi Minh had said: 'Everyone wanted to shape a new world, but did not include in that visionary world any suggestion of freeing the west's colonies, nor of Vietnam freedom, nor the dissolution of white empires.'

This sense of western bias, it seemed to Lek, had pushed Ho Chi Minh deeper into the arms of the Soviet Union. But then Ho's Vietnamese communist guerrillas had fought the Japanese in World War Two and received

US aid through OSS covert operations. After the war's end, in 1945, Ho Chi Minh looked to the American model for a new society and wrote letters to US President Harry Truman asking for help in establishing Vietnamese independence, in the way Americans had helped the Philippines. Truman never replied.

Instead, the United States government had been told it should 'cease to talk about vague – and for the Far East – unreal objectives such as human rights, the raising of living standards and democratization'. The advice came from George Kennan when he was director of the US State Department policy-planning staff. He called for 'straight power concepts' to stop the Soviet Union's expansion.

The Ninth Rama underlined the words for his mother. More than one foreign power feared that his social reforms would undermine its ideology. At the very least, the words explained why the United States government backed military strongmen it could control, rather than having to listen to a physically powerless king.

Part Three

18

Civil War

Lek thought of the United States 'as my other motherland'. It had reduced him, ironically, to a figurehead. Thirty years after his birth there, he had to consider going back as Ninth Rama to remind Americans that what he called Siam had never been colonised because of the monarchy's role. It was a tricky proposition. He could not go abroad while there was any chance of civil war breaking out. Yet the danger of civil war was growing because of widespread anger against CIA support for Field Marshal Pibul and Police-General Phao. In 1957 US President Dwight D. Eisenhower ran for re-election and reports leaked from the CIA's SEA Supply Company's office in Bangkok that its senior US paramilitary officers were anxious to see Eisenhower win. Eisenhower was on record as saying 'Let Asians fight Asians.' The CIA employed Thais to fight clandestine wars. Such mercenaries swore allegiance to the United States, not the king. American covert warfare was being directed from his soil. If things went disastrously wrong, he was sure there would be a total withdrawal of American involvement. And yet he needed the generous US technical help so freely offered so long as the kingdom provided a base against communism.

He wanted to go to Washington to say that the country valued US aid but intended to pay all of it back; that it would stand on its own feet. He had to wait, though, until he could be certain that others would not replace him: Marshal Pibul's cronies from the old days of collaboration with the Japanese had tried in the past to create a surrogate monarch; and right now, they confined Lek to ritual duties and what they called his Chitralada playpen.

Then Phao made a foolish move with the same insolence that supposedly ended the King's Death Case. He called upon Lek to dismiss a former member of the Northern Command group that once collaborated with the Japanese, Sarit Thanarat.

Sarit had fallen out with his old comrades in Northern Command, cosy in World War Two with the Japanese, and with Tsuji, the God of Strategy; a clique loyal to Marshal Pibul so long as he supported the hugely profitable postwar traffic in drugs that nobody openly talked about. Sarit was forty-nine and the regular army's commander-in-chief. Shrewder than the others, Sarit saw that the king was no stammering fool. He glimpsed a better future if the Ninth Rama was allowed to pursue social reforms behind a shield of western military strength. In a wicked world, it was better for Lek to have Sarit on his side.

Sarit had been born in the same Bangkok slums as Mama. Later he went to temple school in the impoverished north east and then entered a preparatory school for army officers. He had led a Japanese-supervised battalion in Burma, believing the Japanese really were restoring Old Siam to its former glory, until he watched how they dealt with poor families like his own. He had felt disgraced after Japan's defeat. All the talk of 'Asian liberation' had proved to be camouflage for Japan's own imperialist ambitions. Then he discovered that the United States, in pursuit of 'straight power concepts', was buying up self-styled nationalists who might otherwise turn to the Soviet Union for help. He vented his nationalism through his own newspaper. The US embassy had labelled it 'anti-American'.

The king called him to Chitralada for a private chat. Sarit claimed to be a monarchist. Rumours of an ultimatum requiring the king to fire Sarit spread during September, 1957. Crowds appeared on the streets, calling instead for the dismissal of Field Marshal Pibul. Phao again rolled out his paramilitary forces against 'communist mobs'. It was no longer safe for Sarit to be seen going to Chitralada. Early one morning at a royal temple ceremony, Sarit quietly told the king, 'Tanks encircle their homes,' referring to Pibul and Phao. 'Order and consent,' replied Bhumibol. Sarit withdrew. The ancient Thai phrase meant social order was a priority. The people could always withdraw consent to the rule of tyrants, even kings.

Sarit did not have total control of all army units. The king later recalled: 'Pibul started to strafe demonstrators with American military planes, saying the noise would be enough to end mob rule. I warned him that "strafing students will *cause* mob rule".' Pibul and Phao retreated to their city homes, ringed by what they thought were tanks to protect them.

The king went to the Thammasat University of Moral and Political Sciences, UMPS, founded by Pridi in the old days when he and Pibul were fellow Promoters of Political Change. The university rector told Bhumibol that communist literature had been planted in the university library. 'Tell the students,' said King Bhumibol, 'they will not be shot, as communists or as anything else.'

Within the hour, student demonstrators marched to General Sarit's office and called on him to get rid of Pibul and Phao. General Sarit replied in two sentences carefully crafted by the king: 'I have conducted my activities based upon the common will and the interests of the people . . . Your coming here gives me moral support to continue.'

The paramilitary police tanks had their guns facing toward the crowds assembling outside the homes of Pibul and Phao. So far as anyone knew, the tanks were under Phao's control. There was a hush of expectancy when Sarit appeared. The protesters made way for him. They had got the message from the UMPS rector, a devout Buddhist, that the king guaranteed their safety. Sarit put himself between the students and the tanks. The crews swivelled their tanks through half a circle. The two strongmen found themselves staring into their own guns.

'Sarit's courage turned things around,' the king said later. 'He walked ahead of the socalled "mob" so that if any tanks had fired, they would have killed him. Pibul accused me of being sly because I was supposed to have encouraged Sarit's "counter-coup".'

Police-General Phao had banked a fortune in Switzerland, skimmed from CIA payments and drug smugglers. This had been the cause of General Sarit's first major quarrel with Phao seven years earlier. Sarit's army trucks had been delivering a drug shipment to Bangkok and Phao's police confronted them and won possession of the illegal cargo.

Drug money was used for 'self-sustaining' American covert activities. A man of Sarit's poverty-stricken origins grabbed what he could. He was a curious mixture, about whom Lek had no illusions: a general on the take who could support the king's work for the poor. Lek was not yet strong enough to move against the drug barons, but several hundred Americans working for the CIA were asked to leave. Later, Joseph Burkholder Smith of the CIA caught their mood. He reported upon their reaction to Eisenhower's November, 1957 re-election: 'One of the senior paramilitary officers from the SEA Supply Company in Thailand ran through the offices shouting, "Now we'll finish off the fuckin' pinkos."'

Phao vanished into Swiss exile and the king began to bring Phao's paramilitary forces under his own control. Field Marshal Pibul, who had been courted by every big power since Nazi Germany, spent his sixtieth birthday driving to Cambodia. There he was provided with military transport to the United States but he had lost his usefulness. His claims to be an anti-communist hero no longer earned US medals and subsidies. He went to India to become to monk. Finally he was invited to reside in Japan by Tsuji, the self-proclaimed God of Strategy who had conspired with Pibul's fellow army officers during World War Two in the opium fields of Upper Burma.

General Sarit made himself a Field Marshal. He put in a caretaker premier for a few months. Then he bared his knuckles and had an unknown number of 'suspected communists' put in jail. An era began, known within the US embassy as Despotic Paternalism, justified in many minds by events in the neighbourhood. In 1959, the communist assassination programme in South Vietnam escalated massively. In neighbouring Cambodia, a bomb exploded in the royal palace and King Norodom Suramarit and his queen narrowly escaped with their lives. In Laos, one king died and his successor, King Savang Vatthana, faced a communist insurgency which would eventually lead to his disappearance. Clandestine wars were intensifying.

The domestic consequences were that Chinese banks got richer on a drug trade protected by the need to finance anti-communist mercenaries in secret US-run operations. These operations could not risk being exposed through leaks from the Congressional oversight committee in Washington. Field Marshal Sarit kept the bankers happy by saying the country needed discipline. A president of the Bangkok Bank, a Chinese family affair that was on its way to becoming one of the world's five most profitable banks, told me later, 'The Sarit years were the best for us. They brought prosperity and order.' With this kind of approval, Sarit could solicit financial support for the king's reforms. 'It was a small price, a fraction of one per cent, but a lot for the royal projects,' said one banker. 'The opium problem began with the west and the later market was created by the west.'

The Ninth Rama concentrated on his children and Chitralada's inner kingdom. He still believed that economic reforms were the best answer to the communist threat but he had to face the immediate dangers of insurgency. He and Sirikit became proficient in the use of hand-held weapons. Lek had been interested in military arms since his World War Two schooldays and now he studied everything there was to be known about the arsenals and tactics of both the communist and western blocs.

The impression abroad was that the king had shut himself away. One misconception still hampered his efforts to counterbalance American dominance with other benign allies. The old canard in Buckingham Palace that he had killed his brother needed to be rectified. King Baudouin of the Belgians wrote that his old schoolfriend *must* speak up for his people. Baudouin had been told by his father King Leopold not to attend King George VI's funeral in 1952 because Leopold was still bitter at being pushed into abdication by George's unfair charges against him. After Elizabeth became queen, though, she had apologised for the false accusation that Leopold collaborated with the Nazis. Baudouin thought it would set matters right publicly if Lek accepted an invitation from Elizabeth.

'All royal courts are sluggish, timid, bureaucratic, amateurish,' wrote Baudouin, commenting on the absence of any apology to the Ninth Rama from Queen Elizabeth. 'For me, trying to get things done is like swimming in treacle and takes years of absurd negotiations.' But Elizabeth II was immensely popular and in a position to undo the harm caused by past mistakes. And the British, ending the war in Malaya against the communists, faced a new threat from another of Thailand's neighbours, Indonesia, whose government was infiltrated by communist Chinese and whose defence forces were being reinforced with Soviet weapons. The British needed the Ninth Rama's goodwill.

19

Revisiting the West

THE lie that Lek killed his brother could be laid to rest if Queen Elizabeth II welcomed him to London. He had less reason to fear being replaced while out of the country now Field Marshal Sarit was in power.

Reconciliation between Lek and the British monarch began with an experiment by a British commander of the South East Asia Treaty Organisation whose headquarters were in Bangkok. Rear-Admiral E.H. Shattock saw how communist propaganda swayed many Asians with allegations that western colonial contempt still prevailed. He said publicly, 'It's arrogant to say we protect the region if we know nothing of its cultures.' He was invited to Chitralada for an informal talk. The admiral was a very modern professional warrior: a jet fighter pilot, a former commander of nuclear submarines and aircraft carriers. 'The king talked about modern warfare, about which he knew a great deal,' he said later. 'Then he got me interested in things of the spirit – "Without these," the king said, "none of us has any armour."'

The British admiral entered a monastery for several months. 'Humankind seemed to have evolved in two totally different directions,' he said later. 'Buddhist monks have explored far out into the spaces of the mind, while we pushed technical progress. As a novice monk, I could never empty my consciousness to pass even to the first level of *mindfulness*. I understood what the Ninth Rama had gone through to become ordained. He came out of the west and could now look at us through eastern eyes.'

This intrigued Queen Elizabeth's cousin Princess Alexandra who was daughter of the Duke of Kent, King George VI's brother, killed during World War Two. She flew to Bangkok in October, 1959, and the king took her to the jungles on his side of the border with Malaya where British forces were fighting terrorism. Lek had heard that some British officers believed the Thais sheltered the communists. 'The Thais are the real bastards,' a CIA officer quoted one frustrated Special Air Service commando as saying.

'There's a small Thai village where we've seen the Commies dressed in uniform, buying food and enjoying a spot of beer. Yet the Thais claim they haven't been able to find a single guerrilla in the area . . . American aid for the suppression of these border activities sticks to someone's hands in Bangkok.'

Lek showed her the difficulty of pursuing insurgents into the wilderness where Malay Moslem sultans were jealous of their sovereignty and where hard-core communists were not 'dressed in uniform' but blended with the local populace. He was king-protector of all religions. His own southern provinces, all the way to the border, were Moslem. He had to be careful not to offend Moslem feelings on either side of the border. But there was in fact close cooperation between British and Thai security forces.

He introduced Alexandra to some of his King's Men. One was Vasit Dejkunjorn, a young and ascetic policeman who would later become immensely popular as a writer of Thai novels exposing drug traffickers. Speaking later of Lek and Queen Sirikit, he said, 'At first I thought Their Majesties' forays into the countryside were a public relations stunt, but I often saw them perform genuine acts of heroism under insurgent fire.' Vasit refuted the CIA's allegations against the Thais, with the authority of someone who risked his life as an agent in communist-dominated borderlands.

Alexandra was invited to one of the king's all-night jazz sessions. The band was made up of members of his staff. A round-faced general played trumpet.

'Do you like the trumpet?' asked Alexandra, making polite conversation.

'No,' said the general with disarming honesty. 'His Majesty ordered me to learn.' The general was a King's Man, and loyally tried his best to like jazz, but it was obvious he had no ear for it. Nonetheless, Lek told her anyone could learn to play an instrument. Music was a form of thought: 'If a nuclear war wiped out human capacity to communicate through language, music could reconnect us. Buddhist chants link the minds of the past to the minds of today.' It was a concept clearly beyond Princess Alexandra's comprehension.

This face-to-face encounter taught the king that he was now so far removed from his western upbringing that he would have to take care he was not misunderstood, in the way Thais were generally misunderstood when they attempted to put their ideas into English. Nonetheless, Queen Elizabeth's cousin thought the king should come to London in 1960. There were objections in Bangkok to his mother acting as Regent. Mama paid no heed. She was occupied with new possibilities opened up by Princess Alexandra's visit. It was not just that her son and Queen Sirikit could enlighten the west about Siam. Foreign visitors should be received with oldfashioned Siamese warmth and modern sophistication. Mama turned the mansion where King Ananda had been killed into a residence for over-seas guests. The mansion no longer held any terror for her, though the wall paintings were still dominated by Shiva the Destroyer and Yama the God of the Dead. Kala continued to dangle the hangman's rope from the high rotunda like some hovering god of Evil.

Mama did not want to censor Grand Palace imagery. All should be restored to remind the kingdom of its unique heritage. She won over the old man who held the purse-strings as Crown Property chamberlain by quoting from *Records of Spring and Autumn*, one of China's Five Ancient Classics: 'Ceremonies are founded in the procedures of Heaven and Earth. When these are out of balance, obscurity and confusion follow and the people lose their proper way. The rules of ceremony are framed to support the natural order of things.' The one-time orphan girl who had once resided in the forbidden quarters now laid out rules for receiving dignitar-ies in a Grand Palace ceremony: the state banquet. She had come a long way from the slums. She knew the Crown Properties managed private busi-nesses founded by earlier kings, from which the money could be drawn that legitimately kept up the kingdom's royal image abroad. This was a tradi-tion she could use for many purposes.

The Royal Household Bureau was taught specific tasks. Mama drew up a guide, reproducing menus collected by earlier kings; including such gems as *Menu de la Cour de Russie, 29 Janvier 1912* . . . *Menu de la Cour d'Angleterre: Buckingham Palace, 19 Juin 1911*. She listed European wines and their suitabil-ity for each dish. She charmed the French ambassador into donating vintage wines. The labels from some of the bottles remain in the royal archives: *Clas de la Republique 'Pour celebrer l'Independence du Canton de Vaud 1798'* . . . *Bordeaux de Haut Medoc 1943* . . . with tiny maps of famous wine-growing regions from Germany to Dijon. She described the appropriate drinks for each course from the '*Aperitif* all the way to champagnes suitable for each kind of cheese. She wrote out appropriate meals: for potatoes alone she had twenty different methods of preparation, from *Pommes Alsacienne* to *Pommes Pont-Neuf*. She illustrated how tables should be laid and decorated for special occasions and wrote out the definitions for French cuisine, from *baron d'agneau*, 'Double sirloin of mutton served at banquet', to *vol-au-vent*, 'a light pastry case made of puff pastry'. These seeming extravagances were not as costly as they might seem. Foreigners seldom understood a society in which people gave their time to enhance royal activities; within the kingdom were resources that would allow King Bhumibol to pursue his goals of self-sufficiency at a price which was modest when translated into western currency. His mother used her experience of the world to make sure foreign visitors would be disabused of the idea that this was a backward backwater whose people could be pushed around.

The dark old mansion and the adjacent royal halls needed to be livened up. In the Back Palace where she had once lived, girls of poor backgrounds were taught to stitch together curtains of brilliant flower-petals to sway once again in the unshuttered, obelisk-shaped windows. Once upon a time, the Princess Mother's mother had been a humble worker in the art described by the English physician at the court, Malcolm Smith: 'Flowers are taken to pieces petal by petal, and with stitch and fine wire put together again to make new flowers, even dosed with scent to heighten the effect.' Now, the daughter of that humble worker wrote: 'Foreign dignitaries are entitled to a display of good manners. Every gesture, every word, every thought produces, in addition to its visible effect, another effect which is not immediately perceptible. This applies to the kingdom's reputation abroad.'

Consulting some old records, Mama found that relatives of Emperor Hirohito had been received politely, even in wartime, by Siamese princes who were serving in the anti-Japanese resistance. The Americans had kept Emperor Hirohito separate from the war-crime trials. By renouncing war, Japan had escaped costly postwar commitments and was in a position to help Thailand now. She thought Lek ought to see the emperor.

In the musty palace papers, though, was a fragment from the orders circulated to Japanese forces before they invaded Siam in 1941–2: 'On confronting each enemy, regard yourself as the avenger come at last face to face with his father's murderer. Here before you is the man whose death will lighten your heart of brooding anger.'

The words briefly chilled Mama's heart. Their author was Masanobu Tsuji. The name meant little to her, although Tsuji was making newspaper headlines with a world tour to meet leaders of non-aligned nations. 'Nonalignment' in reality meant alignment with the Soviet Union. Tsuji even had himself photographed with China's communist leaders. His self-glorifying memoirs were now being published in England as those of a military genius: the general who commanded Australian forces opposing the Japanese advance from Siam, Gordon Bennett, wrote: 'Every soldier worthy of the name pays ungrudging tribute to his outstanding opponents. I have not hesitation in recognizing Tsuji as one of the ablest of mine.' It seemed strange to endorse a man who had been driven by such hatred that he urged individual Japanese soldiers to deal with each enemy as if he was their father's murderer.

Mama pushed this small mystery out of her mind. Japan today seemed the only country able to understand Lek's search for a fresh approach to economic problems. The Ninth Rama told a group of Japanese business-men in Bangkok: 'What seems *"impossible"* to people who only count numbers is possible if good results are felt by everyone, and that is why I do things in what seems at first an unbusinesslike way. Our Buddhist philosophy can be blended with the new science . . . as European innovators like Isaac Newton blended their sciences with religious beliefs.' He submitted a theory: '"Our Loss Is Our Gain" – meaning each development project serves the human spirit and we cannot count the cost in money alone. No matter how cash-poor a country might be, the people are its real resource and can create their own wealth.'

The king applied the results of experiments in his Chitralada citadel to the countryside outside. About his private land-reform projects, he said:

Our budget is rather unbalanced. Expenditure greatly exceeds revenue. Our returns do not look good. That isn't the purpose . . . rural folk contribute their labour freely on projects they see as beneficial. Small enterprises can go wrong but the penalties are also small. If a project goes well, the more funds are invested. The key is no red tape, doing things small, no big schemes that might end in big disasters. No formal committees. We do our consulting in the field. Men and women come from all walks of life to help. An economist who was once minister of state, a police constable who is also a teacher (we train them that way) . . . They volunteer their own time, often to remote and difficult regions, exposed to danger. Our pilots often fly the volunteer experts into the hills. The pilots are those who rest from combat.

His projects were outside the government's reach and escaped political opposition and red tape. Japanese industrialists who had climbed out of a war-ravaged economy understood his unconventional philosophy and encouraged Lek to visit Tokyo. He was careful, though. Some rich Japanese were scouring Asia for cheap labour to be employed in factories built on the spot, regardless of the local environment. He foresaw a wave of outside money carelessly despoiling the countryside. He had come to love the sacred spires amid the gold of the rice paddies, the sheen when the sun rose, the fragile herons and dancing dragonflies, the old abbots on their platforms waiting for the morning swarm of children for temple school. He feared those Japanese who might create a new version of the old Asian Co-Prosperity Sphere they once tried to build by violence.

The Princess Mother had a deeper purpose in preparing to show the world the best side of Siam. By taking the king's place as Regent during his absence abroad, a woman for the first time would be openly responsible for the kingdom while the king was abroad. During centuries of overt repression, women had learned to exercise indirect power. It was a reaction to the sexual bullying techniques described in the *Artha Sastra*, an ancient Sanskrit classic that instructed men on how to wield power through women, using them as spies, *agents provocateurs*, and psychological manipulators. It advised on 'How to make this woman my sexual ally so I can ruin my enemies'. The passion for making sly trouble that possessed some women in the royal court derived from this; and Mama saw the potential danger to Lek's gradual acquisition of moral influence, not least among womenfolk who lacked youth, beauty or wealth.

'Conspiring, passing on information, such things give a kind of power,' said a disapproving lady-in-waiting. One woman who played the game later told me: 'The king's *hand* is so strong, *sanft* as the Germans say – velvet soft on the outside but hard within.' She let me assume she knew the king in physically intimate ways. Other ladies of the court sympathised with the king and said he was like the prince who became Buddha. 'Attempts to seduce him were an inevitable part of that journey,' said Queen Sirikit, confident she was dearly and exclusively loved.

Lek wanted women to take open responsibility. He had made Sirikit the Queen Regent, and if they went abroad together, then his mother as Regent would underline his point. He knew many men thought he was strange not to share their regular indulgence in what they called recreational sex. Yet there were also men who were glad his example freed them from an institutional view of women. The appointment of his mother showed a respect that put a damper on the stories told abroad about Siamese princes with brutal sexual appetites who, in the ferocity of copulating with virgins, were said to kill and bury them at Ghosts' Gate in the Grand Palace.

Lek had to go to Washington first. Americans spoke of 'the free world' and democracy but backed governments of right-wing strongmen who had made the profitable discovery that disorder enlivened US fears of communism. By fabricating 'protests', local politicians could count on more financial subsidies. Lek remembered Graham Greene's description of *The Quiet American*: 'Nobody had more good intentions and did more harm.'

Despite a huge presence in Lek's kingdom, Americans at home still saw it as somehow comic. He read a hefty book on US and world affairs by the popular American historian, William Manchester, who had only this to say about Thailand: 'It has a king who writes songs for Broadway, a prime minister who is the Coca-Cola concessionaire, and a police chief with the Pepsi-Cola franchise in an Ice Cold War.'

The real cold war filled Field Marshal Sarit's pockets with US dollars. It was a price the king had to pay. Sarit could hold the fort politically while the Ninth Rama was abroad, try to prevent any coups, and frustrate Soviet bloc embassies that were said in Bangkok to run the widest networks of spies anywhere.

The king was impartial in dealing with foreign intervention. He tweaked the Russian ambassador's nose and asked him, 'How much do we owe you for the Russian arms exported here?' Lek said later, 'I wanted the Russians to know that we knew they were arming insurgents. I drew a line through the map. One side showed the weapons reaching guerrillas from Russia, and the other side showed those from China.'

He revived a medieval oath of absolute loyalty. An Englishman in the Lord Chamberlain's department of the Court of Siam in 1923, Quaritch Wales, had advised the Sixth Rama: 'Drinking the Water of Allegiance is a powerful instrument for the support of the established form of government, and so long as a considerable percentage of the superstitious and half-educated officials remain in the service, some not entirely disposed to turn a deaf ear to the slogans of communism, so long will Siam be wise to refrain from attempting to substitute a simpler and nobler form of Oath.'

Nothing in western Oaths of Secrecy came so close to striking fear in the participants, nor threatened more dire penalties. The ancient oath took an hour to intone. One passage went: 'If any person here among us fails to keep this oath of allegiance, we ask that His Majesty may inflict punishments of all sorts, and may we be reborn in the thirty-two hells as long as there is sun and moon.'

The oath-taking took place in the royal chapel under the gaze of the Emerald Buddha. Years later, the king let me witness such a ceremony. The massive teakwood doors were shut tight. The air was oppressively humid, and thick with incense. Men of power stood along three walls painted with scenes from the life of Buddha and older beliefs. Through the smokey gloom appeared a panel that showed demons surrounding a foreigner, a *farang* intruder, white with large red nose, fat as a sack of flour. The king lit candles in a cabalistic order, and then watched stony-faced as each notable drank from consecrated water into which the royal weapons were dipped one by one after each man vowed: 'If there should be one among us accused of betrayal, let the presiding priest bathe the weapons and give him to drink three handfuls of it. He to whom no calamity happens within a week, to himself or to his wife or family or property, is innocent beyond doubt.'

This additional warning was the king's idea. He had become tougher after events in Buddhist Tibet, a country so similar to his in its beliefs and in its proximity to China. Busy with their inner-world, and 'voyaging into the soul of mindfulness' in a monastic culture, Tibetans were unready for China's military takeover. He had to guard against innocence as well as betrayal, and he invoked old demonic fears.

He went to America in July 1960 after President Eisenhower had been asked by the Japanese cabinet to scrap plans to visit Japan. Moscow had threatened reprisals against Japan for allowing U-2 spy-planes to operate from secret Japanese bases. Lek knew through his own sources that U-2s also flew from secret US bases in Thailand. Japan was protected from invasion by surrounding seas, but punitive communist armies could easily pour over Lek's land borders. He wanted to be consulted when covert US activities were launched that might provoke massive retaliation.

President Eisenhower wined and dined the royal couple at the White House. Lek and Ike swapped recipes for Thai hot noodle soup and Ike's ice cream. The US Marine Band played selections from the king's jazz compositions. There was little opportunity for serious talk. The Ninth Rama had a captive audience next day, though. He told a joint session of the US Congress: 'Mighty military empires rise through conquest and subjection of alien peoples. They decline and fall when the subject peoples throw off their yolk.'

Vice-President Richard Nixon recognised that the king was talking of American military imperialism as well as the Soviet empire. Nixon had already said, after his first Asian tour, that local leaders ought to be heard; Americans might learn the lesson too late in Vietnam. He wrote, 'The British were not making [our] mistake. They tried to convince local leaders this was *their* war, they were fighting for *their* independence . . . face to face with the new kind of Communist warfare.'

The king saw that voices of moderation were overwhelmed by domestic US politics. There was a fear of losing elections if politicians were not vociferously anti-communist. 'There was no percentage for them in weighing the first-hand experience of any Asian leader who did not strike the same bellicose postures,' he said later. He saw that he must still follow his own course under the cover of US-supported military regimes, and salvage what he could from US military spending in Thailand to help his own reforms.

He was tantalised by the contrast between Washington politics and the rest of America where there was nothing but goodwill. He was already expert in computers, long before they became a part of everyone's life, and his foresight was praised by Arthur K. Watson, the president of IBM World Trade, when the king was shown every corner of IBM's California plant, including its research-and-development divisions. 'I know Mr Watson's remarks must be true,' joked the Ninth Rama. 'They tell me all the facts put into an IBM computer come out true the same way.'

In the US media, he was seen mostly as the Siamese Cat. 'I'm the jolly kid with trumpet and oriental crown,' he said after *Time* magazine on 18th July, 1960, reported: 'King Bhumibol, who looks half his age, and his almond-eyed Queen Sirikit, who looks like mandolins sound . . . went to dinner with the King of Swing, Benny Goodman [in New York]. For 90 minutes after dinner, Bhumibol and Benny led a foot-stomping starch-melting jam session. Next day, the king toted a sax up to the 22nd-story roof garden above Benny's Manhattan House apartment for the fulfilment of a jazzman's dream.' The king was depicted 'toe-to-toe with Gene Krupa on the skins, Teddy Wilson on the piano, Urbie Green on the trombone, Jonah Jones on trumpet, Red Norvo on vibes.' No journalist could possibly have guessed that the session made the king feel close again to Elder Brother.

Lek read, 'Bhumibol is monogamous, unlike most of his celebrated ancestors . . . "He doesn't need any more wives," Queen Sirikit once said with a smile. "For him, the orchestra is one big concubine."'

Queen Sirikit had said nothing of the sort. She had no wiles in dealing with the American media. She spoke her mind and afterwards felt gauche when misquoted. At twenty-seven, she had the same Queen of Hearts appeal as Princess Diana, and she could make clothes as well as wear them, using her popularity with magazine picture editors to advertise the best of Siamese silks because she was saving the old crafts through her own SUPPORT foundation, in need of markets overseas. There was no artifice in her seductively soft-spoken replies to reporters' questions. Since infancy, she had been taught to speak in the low tones that make Thai conversation a soothing and musical whisper. Somehow the idea spread that the king was besieged by women who studied the *Kama Sutra*, the Hindu guide to all kinds of sex, as well as the *Artha Sastra* textbook on female power. Sirikit was seen against this tapestry. She was accused by left-wing journalists of being as manipulative as other 'dragon ladies from Asia'. She captured editorial interest at the cost of significant sections in Lek's speech on Capitol Hill.

He spoke of great-grandfather Mongkut's offer of elephants to US President James Buchanan in the Civil War. That, he said, was a time when roles were reversed and Siam could help America. He believed Americans would repeat in Vietnam the mistake of the French who lost their Indochina empire by ignoring 'primitive' Asian weapons like the use of elephants. His words went over the heads of politicians who were jumpy about being called soft on communism in an election year. They preferred to talk about technological superiority to crush communist campaigns. Nobody was interested in war elephants. Lek already knew elephant-borne artillery had defeated the French in Indochina and he feared their use on the Ho Chi Minh Trail would defeat America's reliance on high-tech weaponry.

Nobody reported his speech on a self-help approach to stabilising small countries where poverty led people to seek communist solutions. 'The average income of a Thai is only about one hundred dollars a year . . . Thais need to achieve a better life *through their own efforts* . . . consistent with a precept of Lord Buddha which says: "Thou art thine own refuge." We are grateful for American aid; but we intend one day to do without it.'

Time merely concluded that: 'The King of Siam, as any heart-wrung fan of *The King and I* knows, is likely to be a fellow whose love for Thailand is matched by a thirst for the best of the West.'

He was invited to the Beverly Hills Tennis Club by Jack L. Warner, studio boss of Warner Bros. His partner, Merv Griffin, was shocked when a hard volley headed toward him from the king and Warner yelled at the top of his voice, 'Hit the Chink!'

In the musical, the King of Siam asks Anna how to react to being called a barbarian abroad. Anna replies, 'If someone were telling a big lie about me in England I should do my best to send the truth to England.'

Lek went on to England to clear up the big lie about the murder of his brother. Queen Elizabeth II had instructed the band waiting for him on a railway platform on 19th July under no circumstances to play excerpts from *The King and I*. In Buckingham Palace, which King George had closed to Lek because it did not 'play host to murderers', Lek and Queen Sirikit were guests at a banquet where he spoke of 'the sense of fair play in the British character'. It was his simple way of burying the hatchet. The irony was that England, after an unrelieved diet of Anna's stories about the harems kept by the King of Siam, saw the Ninth Rama as a puritan in a new age when, reported the *Bangkok Post*, 'short skirts in London are now at breath-taking heights. The wraparound skirt is celebrated – all you have to do is open it to have sexual intercourse.' In contrast to the king's popularity at home, commented the *Post*, the British 'are asking awkward questions about Elizabeth's personal wealth and the behaviour of her family . . . scandals are just beginning.'

Bangkok newspapers could now voice pride in their royal family without fear of angering the jealous rivalry of men like Marshal Pibul. Their reporting of the Ninth Rama's stately progress around the globe, though, was so worshipful that readers were unaware of the *sanuk*, the fun, that characterises the Siamese character: and the fun that Lek, Queen Sirikit and the entourage were having behind the scenes. They were looking forward to more fun in Paris, thirteen years after the king and queen had first met there.

They had to deal with French President Charles de Gaulle, though. It was three centuries since a Siamese king sent the first embassy to the court of Louis XIV. De Gaulle regarded this as an unprecedented bit of oriental enterprise in a distant time when a sea voyage was long and perilous; the first Siamese embassy had been lost at sea with all hands. The Siamese, said General de Gaulle, had always had a special affinity with France. He spoke majestically about 'the coming disaster' if Americans continued the war France had lost in South East Asia. 'There is no chance the people of Asia will subject themselves to the law of the foreigner who comes from the other side of the world, whatever his intentions, however powerful his weapons,' intoned the former leader of Free French forces who, when World War Two had ended, decided France must withdraw from Indochina. Now, he vociferously opposed the replacement of the French colonial presence by the Americans.

Lek had found a counterbalance to the near-hysterical fear of communism he had seen in Washington. He said later: 'General de Gaulle was one of the world's great leaders. He had courage.'

In continental Europe, the royal couple could relax, too. This was where they had grown up. This was where they recaptured a sense of freedom from tension and feudal ceremony. Bits of the royal uniforms got mislaid and there were mix-ups in the heavy schedules. Minutes before an audience with the Pope, it was found that the appropriate Siamese sashes worn on formal occasions had been left at the hotel and a king's aide raced back to retrieve them – on the handiest and most flexible vehicle, a bicycle; everyone dissolved into gales of laughter. The innate good nature of the entourage won over leaders whose characters Lek was weighing up as he flew from capital to capital.

Queen Sirikit likened him to Narai, the king who sent the first Siamese embassy to France. Narai had the great good sense to open up Siam to foreigners who could help the country. He had guarded against such advisers trying to take over by bringing them from places as far apart as Genoa and Persia so no single foreign state could dominate. Lek's version of this strategy was to cultivate personalities who continued to provide him with information to measure against the America interpretation of events. He found that majesty still exercised a curious kind of magic in unexpected places. Tito, the Yugoslav communist president who defied Stalin, had developed a strong relationship with China to counter the Soviet Union; and Tito's men gave the king details of China's rebellion against Kremlin oversight at a time when the chief of CIA counter-intelligence, James Jesus

Angleton, insisted that the Sino-Soviet split was faked to break down resistance to Moscow's monolithic power. The Ninth Rama began work on a textbook on Tito for the guidance of young Thai military cadets. The king did not include a riddle credited to Tito: 'In Siam, who is His Majesty's Secret Service? Why, the king himself.'

Many years later, I remarked that the king's own, unofficial secret-service, his King's Men, had provided him with an emergency radio call-sign: Double-O-Seven. He corrected me. The number had been changed to Double-O-Nine. 'I don't want to be known,' he joked, 'as King James Bond.'

When the couple returned to Bangkok, Mama reverted from the role of Regent to that of a grandmother, worrying over children who were never free from scrutiny. She felt that Lek needed to spend more time with youngsters whose lives were made unnatural enough by a court that never forgot they represented the next generation of the dynasty. Mama, as a single-mother in Lausanne, had never known pressure like this. She had no experience in protecting children from so much undivided attention. Each was expected to make marriages from within a very small and select circle and a good deal of royal court intrigue went into manoeuvring them into friendships with other high-born children. When her grandchildren did venture beyond Chitralada's moat, they rode in chauffeured limousines, accompanied by an entourage. Inside the grounds, workers humbled themselves in their presence. Some would fall flat on the ground. It was impossible to replicate Lausanne here. The Crown Prince and the princesses could not earn pocket money by cutting neighbours' lawns. Here, servants insisted on performing the simplest tasks. No amount of lecturing would stop them from undertaking tasks that Lek had done himself when a boy.

Lek was preoccupied with the realities about the outside world which had been hidden from him before he went abroad. Now he had new sources of information. His armed forces were easily out-numbered by the hostile armies around him and he knew one thing was certain: Nobody would come to Siam's rescue if things were to go badly wrong. He had to think like the Chinese sage Sun Tzu who had written in *The Use of Spies*: 'Raising a host of a hundred thousand men and marching them great distances entails a heavy loss on the people and a drain on the resources of the state . . . Hostile armies may face each other for years, striving for the victory that is decided in a single day. This being so – *to remain in ignorance of the enemy's condition . . . is the height of inhumanity* . . . What enables *the wise sovereign* to achieve things beyond the reach of ordinary men is foreknowledge.'

His foreign sources of foreknowledge had grown since his journeys abroad. Premier Zhou Enlai of China reassured him that Chinese troops, occupying India's disputed borders in 1962, would withdraw ten kilometres and return prisoners. Lek saw this as a re-enactment of a *Three Kingdoms* engagement: 'An invader was seven times captured by China and seven times released until his heart was touched and at last he swore eternal friendship.' But the king's Yugoslav contacts reported that Zhou was struggling to keep control over Soviet-trained forces; and the question remained: if Chinese troops occupy parts of Thailand, would Zhou still have the power to withdraw them? The only real restraint was the American military presence: and this was reflected in the bellicose daily broadcasts from Beijing Radio claiming Thailand was nothing more than an American base for aggression. General de Gaulle warned him that French intelligence said Chinese forces were moving toward Lek's northern borders in reaction to American talk of 'squeezing China between the giant pincers of Korea and Thailand'.

Americans informed him that China secretly exploded seven of its own atomic bombs, and there was a risk of radiation fallout drifting south. The Chinese had made a film of their own soldiers riding into the fallout from the mushroom clouds: the film was propaganda to reassure the Chinese armed forces. It gave no hint of the long-range consequences of exposure to radiation.

Political assassinations multiplied. Elder Brother's death seemed to Lek like the first in an era of evil. A confidential report in 1963 claimed that US President John F. Kennedy tacticly approved the murder of President Diem in South Vietnam. Three weeks after Diem's death, Kennedy was shot dead. Lek's sources said Kennedy had voiced a superstitious fear that he would be assassinated for allowing Diem to be killed.

Lek still disliked the use of superstition, but his restoration of the Oath of Allegiance seemed more than ever like a sensible precaution. He took to heart Sun Tzu's advice: 'Knowledge of the spirit world is to be obtained by divinition . . . but the dispositions of the enemy are ascertainable through spies and spies alone.'

20

American Good Intentions

THREADS of intelligence came into Lek's hands. Past events took on deeper meaning. The attempt by Japanese militarists and their wartime collaborators to make Elder Brother Nan remain in Siam as the Eighth Rama fell into perspective once Lek learned more about the fate of the last Emperor of China, Pu Yi, who in the 1960s was protected by Premier Zhou Enlai against Chinese zealots. As a boy, Pu Yi was cut off from everyday life, virtually a prisoner of Forbidden City ritual. Pu Yi became even more isolated as Emperor of Manchukuo under Japanese militarists who treated him abominably when he was not on public display. Then Chinese communists grabbed and brainwashed him.

Because Mama was half-Chinese, Lek had some understanding of China. It made him less panicky than Americans. He appreciated more than ever the tenacity of his mother and Old Gran in preventing Elder Brother Nan from sinking into a quagmire of feudal ritual which once would have made it easier for the Japanese to manipulate the Siamese monarchy, and would have provided ammunition for the first wave of communist revolutionaries. Premier Zhou Enlai, with his mandarin background, valued the Ninth Rama as a stabilising influence on China's vulnerable southwest borders.

But Lek could become paralysed by royal ritual, as Emperor Pu Yi had once been, or neutered by those who professed to protect him from communist aggression. Lek's strength lay in the countryside, and here again his Chinese heritage and his mother's humble origins allowed him to look for lessons in China's peasant revolution that were mostly now ignored in the west. He saw how military generals in China had become the means of imposing fear, not order. Only as a good Buddhist king could Lek bring about peaceful reforms. Instead of the Japanese, though, it was now the Americans who wanted to keep the monarchy in its ritualistic place.

He heard from his King's Men in 1964 that US President Lyndon B. Johnson regarded the Vietnam War as pointless and would pull out his troops, except that he feared impeachment. 'Americans might relinquish power and territory without much thought about the consequences for us. That makes America dangerous,' said Kukrit Pramoj who, since he wept with his brother Seni on the eve of Nan's murder, had discovered he could accomplish more as a journalist than as a prime minister. As a descendant of earlier kings, Kukrit kept his king informed in this period when so much was still hidden.

Field Marshal Sarit had died the previous year and in his place ruled the Three Tyrants. They had once collaborated with Japan's imperial armies. Now they did as Americans told them. They were Thanom Kittikachorn and Praphas Charusathien, together with the son of the first, who was also son-in-law of the second, Narong Kittikachorn. In defence of the trio's submission to American policy, the Three Tyrants revealed that Sarit had already endorsed the US State Department's 'subtle, carefully unstated exchange by which US military bases have been secretly sanctioned, allowing the US government to run the nation'.

US servicemen flooded through an unobserved corner of Bangkok's Don Muang airport, their passage unrecorded by Thai officials. Other American forces flew directly to Thai bases from which secret American Air Commando units and the newly formed Special Operations Group (SOG) launched covert operations in neighbouring countries.

China retaliated indirectly through Indonesia which in 1964 declared a war of confrontation against 'neocolonialism'. The Indonesian forces were equipped with Russian warplanes and submarines that roamed the seas and skies around Thailand. Their target was Malaysia, a federation formed from former British colonies. Lek watched how the British handled the challenge. He remembered the advice of his great-grandfather, Mongkut: 'The only weapons of real use to us will be our mouths and our hearts, constituted so as to be full of sense and wisdom.' Lek had no visible means of preventing these unilaterally declared wars. His physical weapons were under American control. He had no wish to let them control his moral weaponry, but it was not easy for a king to keep his ascendancy when communist psychological warfare was waged to convince his own people that white imperialists still ruled in a new guise. The Chinese propaganda, he was certain, came from the zealots eager to please Chairman Mao, and was not authorised by Premier Zhou. The divisions within China were recognised by the British, and Lek had quietly arranged for King's Men to work with British Special Air Service commandos in the Malay peninsula, and to learn a very special kind of response which would encourage dissident forces to turn against the communists.

Indonesia had been 'liberated' by the Japanese when it consisted of Dutch colonies. Its current leaders had been groomed by Tsuji, Japan's God of Strategy, to continue fighting after the Japanese defeat. Indonesia's President Sukarno had been Tsuji's prize pupil and he now governed 200 million people in a 4,000-kilometre arc of islands covering three time zones. He accused tiny Thailand of bullying the neighbourhood as a pawn of American imperialists.

The British put on Malay uniforms and with local forces, absorbed the punches without openly striking back at Indonesia itself. Their tactics required stern self-discipline. A King's Man reported that when nut-brown Gurkha soldiers from Nepal saw their English captain, Richard Haddow, killed in a Borneo ambush, the Gurkhas swarmed through the jungle after the Indonesian infiltrators and beheaded each one with their curved *kukri* knives. They were recalled to Singapore and severely reprimanded for killing the enemy in the Gurkhas' own time-honoured way. 'In this war we take prisoners alive for what they can tell us – *and heads without bodies can't talk!*' roared a frustrated commander. The British helped rebel Indonesian generals to overthrow Sukarno. The war came to an abrupt halt. By 1967, the British had gone back to their misty islands in a secrecy that was never broken.

'Some think Siam might have been better off if we'd tasted this kind of imperialism,' the king said later. He had seen the British learning from the mistakes they first made in leaving other colonies too abruptly. In Malaysia they had fought under Malay command until sure of its capacity to survive, and then left again. The fate of his neighbours in what had been French Indochina was in the hands of Americans who launched undeclared and covert wars that everyone but the American taxpayer knew about, and who preached democracy and human rights but propped up the Three Tyrants.

Lek would like to discover the magic formula that now allowed the Japanese to keep their freedom and still enjoy American protection. The trouble with Japan was that, with American approval, it threatened to dominate commercially some areas it had previously conquered by force. He needed to be sure he had public support before he ventured abroad again, and he said in a rare speech: 'The highly industrial powers have nowhere to go but down, and down in a very dangerous way unless they pay attention to "the Poor Man's Way".' The words were meant for the Japanese and Americans as much as for the Soviet bloc and China. But they were also addressed to the audience whose backing the king most needed. He made his first open and direct reference to his poor man's revolution, making best use of Thai talents and resources without terrorising the population: a dream shared with Elder Brother Nan. 'Greed,' Lek said, 'is more dangerous than the publicised danger of communism. If we clash among ourselves, it will destroy us and we shall become slaves of what I call this New Imperialism.'

He could not risk being forced to abandon this Poor Man's Way by the authoritarian Bangkok regime and its US backers. So he disguised his land reform projects as 'royal initiatives' and made use of American generosity in sharing technology. He encouraged the former American OSS agent, Jim Thompson, who had revived the Thai silk industry. Thompson was initially funded by the World Commerce Corporation, WCC, started by Sir William Stephenson and a post-World War Two group of Anglo-American intelligence allies to help economic development in poor countries under communist pressure. Thompson vanished without trace in the Malay jungle one Easter Sunday afternoon in 1967. Later that summer, his sister, Katherine Thompson Wood, was discovered savagely battered to death in her Pennsylvania home. There was never an explanation but many theories. The whole business was as much wrapped in mystery as the death of Lek's brother.

There was a sense of danger about everything Lek initiated. Queen Sirikit had a robust reaction to this. She had read how the first Queen Elizabeth of England used a private intelligence service to inform her of traitors. Sirikit still returned in her dreams to what she believed was her earlier incarnation as a warrior queen. She consulted her own informants who were full of stories about plots to bring down her husband. She shot at cardboard targets, saying bluntly that Buddha sanctioned the destruction of evil. Her targets represented live enemies. She was not squeamish like the executioner who fooled himself that there were no scapegoats behind the targets in the King's Death Case. Photographs show her with lustrous black hair tied back, bracing herself against the sandbags, her long slim fingers supporting the rifle or curled around the trigger. She looks like a legendary Siamese woman warrior with a white ribbon around her head. These are not publicity pictures. They were snapped by a king deeply in love, and aware of how his wife was giving up so many things she had enjoyed in cosmopolitan Paris for this life of constant anxiety.

'The king wanted Queen Sirikit to replace him if he died during this period,' a noblewoman said later. 'There was a lot of speculation about the succession anyway, and opinion was mostly on the side of the heir to the throne being a male. In any case, *she* would have to become "*he*". The ruler has to be a god – not a goddess. As a god, Queen Sirikit would have had the strength to strike fast and hard at enemies.'

Sirikit had no intention of letting anything harm the Ninth Rama. 'He only had to sneeze,' she said later, 'and we hear anxious inquiries about his health from all over the country.' Symbolism, Sirikit had taught the king, was always the key to Siam's leadership. If the public continued to see him as the symbol of their own welfare, he would have the moral ascendancy needed to win the respect of his own soldiers. He had to be better than they were.

He had handled guns since his youth, and he found that the M-16 could be fired laterally so that exhaust gases gave impetus in sweeping a confined space. He challenged army instructors to hit three targets with the rifle in one burst from a five-bullet clip. 'They said it couldn't be done and I took a big chance,' he said later. 'I hit all three in ten seconds. Our soldiers got it down to hitting all three targets in one five-second burst. I made it more difficult and made the men run to another position and crouch, and so on.' In a border battle, one of his soldiers was killed when a gun jammed. 'I took the gun he was still clutching and stripped it down. The faulty part was a tiny spring and I fixed it and contacted the manufacturers and said, "This gun killed one of my men." The gun from the dying soldier, I keep to remind me.'

He used symbols in the unique calendar he kept for Sirikit alone. His graceful lines are astonishingly reminiscent of the Siamese seals that appear in documents left in Paris by King Narai's embassy in 1686, and of seals salvaged from much earlier centuries. Lek's calendar – 'It is not a diary,' he told me firmly – is a shorthand record of the perilous times shared with the queen, typified by his simplified silhouette of the M-16. It covers a period when he shuttled between meditative talks with wise old abbots, and discussions with his own soldiers fighting in contested borderlands. 'I tried to live by Buddhist rules,' he said later. He paused and added, 'Fate presented me with questions I couldn't always answer. I took things one step at a time.'

He took no special precautions in going with the queen to observe hit-and-run battles against communist insurgents. Countryfolk believed he was protected by the very magic of majesty, and it gave them heart. 'People had to see us share the same dangers,' he said. 'In the long run, the way to disarm the communists was to relieve poverty. Terrorism was used by a few highly-trained insurgents to cow villagers, and we devised ways to help the villagers stand up to the terror. Our soldiers in the endangered areas became farmers. They were settled in the troubled zones, in mountains and jungle, in salt marshes of winding coastlines, and were always available to fight.'

He knew his approach was regarded with skepticism by the Americans.

They tolerated his interference so long as it kept the people passive. He was appealing, though, to the complicated traditions which Uncle Rangsit and Old Gran had first taught him, and that Sirikit helped him further to master. His mother, representing the non-violence of Buddhism, worked among hill-tribes that since the mid-1950s had been targets of China's communist 'National Minority Institutions'. These army-run institutions indoctrinated young people along the Himalayan borders with the notion that communism originally came from the practices of Stone Age societies. One graduate was Pol Pot whose fanatical leadership of the Khmer Rouge in Cambodia would lead to the slaughter of a generation of educated persons in an attempt to drive the country back into this idealised Stone Age. The Princess Mother followed her own gentle policy of absorbing physical aggression without striking back. Near Laos, a small girl had been carried to her, clinging to the back of a soldier. The child had been injured by a bomb jettisoned from an American aircraft. Mama took in the child as if she were one of her own family, and arranged for the soldier to work on rural reforms. She showed no hostility to either side. She said later that in one year alone, eighty per cent of the American bombing raids on North Vietnam originated from bases in Thailand.

The Ninth Rama needed more alternative allies. He had already broken his own promise to himself not to leave Thailand again in order to meet leaders in the region, from Singapore to Australia. He flew to Tokyo to get more technical equipment and to see the progress that young Japanese were making in diversifying crops. The Japanese were only too ready to cooperate, and to erase bad memories. Lek had no illusions. He had seen the reports on Japanese businessmen who were once again being inspired by the cunning of the sixteenth-century warlord Hideyoshi Toyotomi, the great master of secret-intelligence who set the example for that later God of Strategy, Tsuji.

Lek heard in Tokyo another version of why Siam's leadership had become so dangerously reliant upon Japan during Marshal Pibul's days of glory. Pibul, now in Japanese exile, begged the Ninth Rama to let his body be cremated in his homeland when he died. Lek had found little time to learn Siam's history of the recent past. The argument now presented by Marshal Pibul was that in 1941–2, with Japanese invasion forces already on their way, he had been a victim of American hesitation and British obfuscation. He had been promised American aircraft that never came, and British support that boiled down to Winston Churchill's message that 'we shall regard an attack on Thailand as an attack upon ourselves.' Churchill had always claimed Pibul got the offer to help *before* Japan's invasion. Pibul insisted that in fact, he received it *after* the Japanese already surrounded him with their troops. He said he had wanted only to secure Siam against all foreign imperialists. He cited a broadcast he made in 1942, alleging 'Winston Churchill was keenly disappointed when the Siamese refused to be killed in order that Britain should survive.' He had been shown, through the then ambassador in Washington, Seni Pramoj, a US State Department note that influential Britons wanted to take over Thailand and 'think in terms of a revival of Thailand's absolute monarchy'. The American note went on to say that the British 'would like to elevate a member of the [Thai] royal family to the throne who would be so dependent on British support that Thailand would virtually become a British protectorate'.

The Ninth Rama concluded that it was wise to bury such a murky past along with Marshal Pibul's ashes. The family was told, when he died, that his body was to be transported from Tokyo back to Bangkok for cremation.

Lek could no longer postpone revisiting the heart of American power. He had heard that President Johnson thought the US Joint Chiefs of Staff were warmongers out to destroy Johnson's Great Society. Before flying to Washington in 1967, the king wanted to see the consequences of American interference in Iran. The Shah had replaced the prime minister, Dr Mohammed Mossadeqh, in a coup for which credit was claimed by the CIA. The Shah suppressed dissent with US-trained secret police. Lek concluded that this ruthless use of power would provoke a massive uprising; and once the Shah became a liability, he would be rejected by the United States, and his subjects would be left to suffer the consequences. The Ninth Rama had no wish to find himself in the same situation.

Lek arrived in Washington that June to tell President Johnson a line had to be drawn between US aid and US control. They talked together in the Oval office. Encouraged by LBJ's apparent concern for the American underdog, the king spoke of his own quiet revolution. He needed two or three small helicopters, 'where rural reforms are most needed and the terrain is difficult'. The fact was that the latest Bangkok clique of old pro-Japanese wartime cronies kept an eagle-eye on Crown Property expenditures that might strengthen the king's ability to win over 'communists' with his own methods and thereby weaken their case for more weapons through a system of US defence-procurement loans and the large bribes paid to persuade recipients to take the weapons offered by rival manufacturers.

The king said later, 'The president called defence-secretary Robert McNamara on the phone and said something like, "Give this king his choppers." I heard nothing more, and never saw the helicopters.'

McNamara was busy running a cost-efficient weapons assembly-line into Vietnam. He was not interested in a king's non-violent solutions for a defence nightmare involving 120 different ethnic groups inside borders that twisted through mountains and along stretches of water that made infiltration easy. There was no propaganda material in a king who, without fanfare, compassionately drew into soldier-settlements those villagers intimidated by terrorists, and separated them from die-hard communists.

Listening to him later tell the story, I could imagine the stoney silence in which he was heard at the White House. Through McNamara's pipelines poured billions of dollars' worth of high-tech weaponry. Along came a fugitive from *The King and I* to speak about moral authority and tolerance for uneducated peasants who were terrorised into cooperating with communist guerrillas. The king reckoned he could bolster resistance more effectively if he could fly into the endangered areas, not with American permission but in response to what he knew from his own experts about local problems. In Vietnam, a secret American programme of assassination made no distinctions and razed villages suspected of concealing the enemy. 'If I had worn monk's robes instead of a business suit and declared myself to be Lord Buddha, I would not have made less of a dent,' he recalled. 'Their Secret Service pushed my people around. So we said, "Okay, we'll do things our way and you do your things your way." And we pushed their security men around our way. Five months later McNamara resigned without telling us that the overt and covert wars were already lost. Thousands continued to be killed in action.'

After his return, America's clients, the Three Tyrants, Praphas Charusathien and the father and son, Thanom and Narong Kittikachorn, made the first overt move against him. They tried to ban the Ninth Rama's work-bases which were said to subvert their military objectives. They had tumbled to the way the king was pursuing his own revolution and why he wanted a few American helicopters that they would not let him buy through the Crown Property Office. The Three Tyrants could only get all the helicopters they wanted, and the payoffs, by portraying a huge military threat and the need for even more weapons.

21

The Royal Children

PRINCESS Ubol, Lotus Blossom, was sixteen when she began asking questions about life in America. She was already kicking against the confines of the court. Her younger siblings would have liked to see more of their father. The Ninth Rama told them to study hard for the time when they could pay the people back for their privileged existence. He was conscious of preaching like an uninspired headmaster. He tried to break down the walls of isolation by making it easier for them to find friends outside Chitralada through the school he had built within the grounds which was open to the children of commoners. But some courtiers said the royal children should not play with ordinary folk and undermined the king's efforts to break down class divisions. The children of household staff and of workers on the king's experimental projects were accepted into the school but the habits of centuries made them shy and the royal pupils became isolated.

The king was distracted by political leaders who needed him as a symbol but were afraid he was becoming more. And he was distracted by the need to use the symbolism without becoming a pawn. All through too many nights, cross-legged and barefoot on the floor of his Chitralada study, Lek fretted alone amid a clutter of technical manuals, notebooks and maps. His enemies wanted to stop him using his work-bases under the guise of palaces. He argued that palaces had been dotted at strategic points to unite Old Siam in the old days. He rejected the American dismissal of his workbases as an echo of the *ateliers de charité* in France where the poor were trained in useful arts like wool-carding, spinning and weaving until their frustrations produced the French Revolution. He and Queen Sirikit had another purpose. They rescued the old crafts by hiring the few remaining masters of traditional skills to pass their knowledge along to youngsters in remote villages. Other countryfolk were trained in huge open-sided *sala* pavilions to make a living from the new ideas flowing from Chitralada. The projects no longer looked like toys invented by a king in his playpen, as the military bosses had jeered. Chitralada was beginning to alter the very nature of a feudalistic society.

Lek and the queen told villagers that prostration was a thing of the past. Countryfolk insisted on squatting: nobody should ever rise above the level of the royal head. So husband and wife walked on their knees to keep their heads below those of the villagers. Foreign outsiders seldom observed this painful knee-walking. Sirikit told the children: 'It is to make everyone feel equal.' The queen showed poor villagers how the vines that choked canals and rivers could be turned into profit through the ancient crafts of weaving the dried vines into wickerlike furniture or expensive gold-laced neilloware handbags; and she had a score of similar projects.

But Palace Law and its special language dictated that every part of the royal person, from head to toe, must be revered and given a special royal word. The children, mostly limited to this insular world, found it more and more difficult to enjoy relaxed moments with a king whose efforts to end the linguistic embellishments had to be pursued in the countryside. Crown Prince Vajiralongkorn had been ear-marked for schooling in England. But not Eton; he was to be packed off to another English public school, whose traditional aim was to prepare pupils for service in the British Empire. A distinguished noblewoman later lamented: 'A lot of pain might have been avoided if the Crown Prince had gone to Eton.'

Lek's second daughter, Princess Sirindhorn, had a baby elephant as a pet and this started a lifelong love affair with elephants. She plagued the king to tell her about Auspiciously Significant Elephants. He promised her that the next time an elephant was found with auspicious characteristics, she should compose a eulogy for the Court Brahmins to recite and a lullaby to welcome the newcomer to the Royal Stables. 'The first of the sacred elephants in the present reign became my close friend,' Sirindhorn later said, showing a photograph of herself at the age of twelve, in a loose white summer dress, one bare arm around her pet elephant. 'When he was smaller, he would sit on a mat and play with me, practically in my lap, so I had to keep moving away. He loved football and blind-man's bluff. We would hold hands – well, he put his trunk in my hand – when we took a stroll. If I wasn't alert, my hand would be suddenly sucked into his mouth. When I took my school friends to see him, he would pick me out with his trunk and lead me away to play only with him. Even if I was in school uniform, he always knew me.'

The youngest child, Princess Chulabhorn, was enchanted by the stories told by retainers known officially as Royal Nannies. She heard how birds could talk and bats could sing, how trees could fuss and orchids squabble. She was told how the first Royal Elephant, White Monkey and White Raven debated which was the most venerable: 'The honour would go to whoever had the earliest memory of Buddha's sacred bo tree. The monkey said his first memory was the upper leaves brushing his stomach. The elephant's was the sapling tickling his tummy. The raven said he carried the tree as a seed, and all agreed this had the greater merit, and so the raven taught the morality of life.' Later, Queen Sirikit explained: 'When we acknowledge higher rank, it is to show respect. We kneel for the Supreme Patriarch and address him as Father. We kneel to the farmer and call him Father too because his experience comes from a long collective memory.'

The Princess Mother was uneasy about the strange isolation in which her grandchildren were growing up. She did not want to interfere; and there was nothing she could do to change tradition. Each royal child was inevitably treated as special. The Crown Prince was regarded as the sole male heir closest to the throne, followed in the male line by his first cousin-once-removed, Prince Bhanabhandu Yugala, already old when he was first to investigate Elder Brother Nan's murder. But the law of succession was in confusion. There had been seventeen constitutions since the Sixth Reign in 1924 abolished polygamy and provided for an order of succession by pure Siamese male relatives in order of seniority. The rule in modern Thailand was that if the constitution got in the way, write a new one. In matters touching upon the succession, constitutional law could be changed and there was always a possibility that if Lek's only son showed himself to be unfit, the king might decide that the next sovereign need not be a male. And so the focus of public interest was as much upon his three daughters as upon the son.

Lek's mother spent more time among children of the streets and villages. In Siam Square she listened to the chatter of Chulalongkorn University students. Young girls from poor homes stayed crisp and clean in blue pleated skirts and white blouses. She knew how hard their mothers worked to keep them that way when it would have been easier to make them earn a living. In the countryside, she talked with parents suspended between poverty and the seduction of child-buyers. A village headman with five daughters later told me, 'I worked hard to give each a good education after speaking with the Princess Mother. Every other family in my village used to sell one girl to the brothels.'

Mama watched her son attempt to bring up his own children to uphold the dignity of royalty while also expecting them to live like other children who had little or nothing and to practice the same frugality she had taught him. In the US magazine *Look*, Gereon Zimmerman wrote,

'The king was stretched between his own values and evil realities. In Bangkok massage parlours GIs paid for sex and in financial boardrooms American officials drew up guaranteed loans to corn farmers.'

As a child herself, Queen Sirikit had enjoyed the freedom of Paris. She was now as much a prisoner of tradition as her children. She had few outsiders to confide in. Americans like Clare Booth Luce, the wife of the founder-publisher of *Time-Life*, were prominent enough to gain access to the queen. 'Clare reported that the queen wore the pants and wanted her son to become the next king, but the king favours one of his daughters,' Lieutenant General Eugene Tighe, a chief of the US defence-intelligence agency, said later. Clare was also an adviser to the US president on intelligence matters. Such little betrayals by friends got back to the king. Caution crept into his meetings with foreigners. It was impossible to discuss the children in privacy. Neither Sirikit nor Lek was ever entirely alone, waking or sleeping. The family bedrooms at Chitralada Villa were modest, joined by a corridor where courtiers and staff were to be found at all hours. Every word overheard was certain to be repeated, often with a malicious twist.

The king could always clear his mind with jazz. The queen, though, was not a lusty tragic blues diva, nor a sultry melancholic torch singer, a role that would have at least allowed her to release her feelings. She still captured magazine covers as a model of fashion, but that was a passive role, only made exciting when she was given some credit: courtiers were proud to say 'The Queen of Thailand made the pill-box hat popular before Jacqueline Kennedy.' She was not pictured abroad, plodding through marshlands with farmers and soldiers, as she so often did, wearing sneakers and loose pants and a light blouse in the tropical heat. Since Sirikit and the king could not spontaneously translate feeling into spoken words without the risk of having them broadcast, he improvised a kind of scatting for her, a jazz form of nonsense poetry. That, and his coded calendar with its symbols for the difficult passages in their lives, took the place of those intimate conversations parents have in seeking to do the best for their children.

Lotus Blossom thought it was all very well for people to call him the Father of the Nation. She and the other children wanted more of him simply as their own father. 'It was impossible to live in a golden cage,' she said later. 'I could not live by palace rules.'

The second daughter, Sirindhorn, rebelled against her mother's fashion-plate perfection and arranged her hair in the plainest way possible. Chulabhorn, the youngest, took the opposite tack and modelled herself on her stylish mother, while also planning to compete with her father as a scholar. Crown Prince Vajiralongkorn, a handsome boy, showed an imperious sense of destiny. He defied a reprimand from a courtier by saying, 'Don't talk like that to your future king!' King Bhumibol tanned his son's backside with the reminder: 'You're not the Tenth Rama yet.' The boy pulled faces behind the backs of teachers or in solemn ceremonies, until the king begged a favour from a palace attendant who had the peculiarity that he could seem to stand still as stone during long rituals while, with his hands behind his back, he modelled clay heads in the likeness of those around him. The courtier made six sculptures of the Crown Prince. The king lined them up along the foot of his sleeping son's bed one night and the boy woke up to see his own grotesquely ugly faces.

Lotus Blossom, Princess Ubol, was close to the king because he could never forget the joy she had brought him when she was born in Europe, coming at a time when her mother had helped him forget the awful prospect of returning to the royal court. The girl cherished the rare, carefree moments on the waters of the Gulf when they sailed together in the two-handed dinghies he designed and built. At sea, he became boyish again. 'He taught her the dynamics of a well-shaped hull skimming the crest of a wave and the lift to be got from sailing properly angled to the wind,' said a high-born prince who had served as an air-force pilot and as an army commando. At an age when her mother fell in love with her father, Princess Ubol could not go out on dates. If she made a friend, his parents might use this to advance their own interests. If word leaked back of a breach of confidence, the princess would have to drop the friend. A day's sailing near the coastal palace of Far-From-Worry became her only escape. The king justified these escapes as a sporting way to get the support of naval officers who might be needed in any fresh clash with army politicians. The two raced their dinghy against naval seamen. Father and daughter won a gold medal in the December 1967 South East Asia Peninsular Games. Princess Ubol said later, 'He got better all the time at balancing forces – wind, tidal currents, optimum forward momentum on the crest of a big wave. It was an allegory for pursuit of his real goals.' Out on the water, the king would be granted some sudden illumination, as if the gods did exist. He had stumbled forward through kingship, guessing the way, yet lately he felt as if the gods had been leading him. It was a disquieting thought: he did not want to retreat into old beliefs: perhaps, he thought, Elder Brother's spirit was part of some great movement toward a predestined end: perhaps life simply began with the sunrise of birth and ended in the sunset of death. On a flat calm sea, the sails flapping while the sun burned off the dawn mist and slowly arc'd to its predetermined setting, he debated if he was part of the old Siamese universe where good and evil turned in a never-ending cycle. Those who believed in such things would say that only within this cycle could he make any changes.

Lotus Blossom felt she was suffocating, trapped by the stubborn old concepts. Anti-war protests in the United States made her even more restless. American students could openly question their government's actions. Why couldn't Thai students? The king explained that Siam was unique, and governed by an age-old passion for order and harmony. The monarchy played a role different to that of any other. To modernise Siam, he was obliged to use its old beliefs. He said. 'I go three times a year to bathe the Emerald Buddha and change his raiment according to the seasons. I then sprinkle water on officials. It makes them feel blessed. When you were about nine years old, I decided to sprinkle this holy water on passers-by. If they believe it will do them good, it will do them good. The first time the driver of a *tuk-tuk* taxi told his friend I had given him holy water, the friend would not believe a king would do such a thing! But I did, and he was happy. It is a small thing for me, but it means happiness for many. You see how the people come into the Grand Palace at these ceremonies? They want to touch me, they want me to take their donations, small to you, very big for them. In their Buddhist way, they want to help my work on their behalf. They trust me and I need their trust . . . In America, if a president goes to church, the FBI, the Secret Service, are all around. Here, if I came to the temple in that way, I would be separated from my people. Anyone can petition me. They are not chosen by the FBI. The people are my FBI, my Secret Service.'

But the eldest princess grew to dislike Siamese docility intensely. In American colleges, students did not feel they had to wait for some pre-destined turn in the cycle of good and evil. They protested against the war in Vietnam. She questioned the American journalist, Gereon Zimmerman, about this. He said later, 'I told her that I had talked with Thai students . . . and they had seemed shy, quite different from the vol-ubles I interviewed on US campuses. And I said the young women in the US have more freedom than in Thailand. I criticised the lack of dissent in Thai academic life and told her, "The US experiences much noisy rattle and debate on campus. Our government does not fret about it." But then came the disclosure of CIA manipulations within the US National Student Association . . . She was either too polite or amused to comment on these revelations.'

Lotus Blossom said later: 'For me, America still meant freedom. I was stifled. Royals live with so many restrictions from early childhood. It's unnatural for children, keeping a lid on their own personality. And I could never answer the things that were invented by courtiers or whispered against me – that I was a drug addict, a sex fiend with lots of boy friends . . . They seemed to have all the right to say whatever came into their heads, yet I had no right to respond, no right to be angry.'

The king let Lotus Blossom go. She had been accepted at a private school in New England and he expected she would return. A preppy young Bermudian student took her out a few times and said later, 'She was hell-bent on letting off steam and I couldn't keep up with her, nor could any of the other guys who dated her.' She thought they were spoiled and indolent, judged by Thai standards. She was so far ahead in mathematics and science, she was asked to sit exams a second time because her teachers were skeptical of the first results. Students would pester her about White Elephants. She said she finally told them, 'Yes, I lived with elephants in Bangkok all the time, and magic monkeys . . . I gave fantastic descriptions of what it was like to be part of a real *King and I*.'

She was too loyal to talk about the dark underside. Like the king, she had managed to escape through the bars erected around the court to see things that others wanted to hide. The hypocrisies were typified by the rich brothel-keepers who hired monks to bless their whorehouses. She knew about the special relationships between prominent people and criminals who, if caught, gave large donations to temples or put on monk's garb. She knew about the repressed conditions in which most women lived, and the Princess Mother's feminist ardour did not seem to Lotus Blossom sufficient by itself to change anything much. She did not wish to marry within the small circle of Thai males of suitable rank. None measured up to her father. Like him, she had been enmeshed in Palace Law. Unlike the king, she could disentangle herself. But she had recognised she could never hope to follow his mother's example.

Some immensely rich Chinese women in Bangkok regarded the Princess Mother's feminism as a joke. The worst exploiters of other women as prostitutes made big donations to temples to atone. These women had a hard quality. Lotus Blossom had seen how such women examined others with shrewd eyes, measuring value in personal wealth or in connections with the powerful. The princess had not fallen for the romanticised version of the gentleman crook – the *nakleng* – said to be kind to friends, ruthless to enemies. The worst gangsters could arrange a murder for prices fixed on a sliding scale, and some had palace allies.

One reformed *nakleng*, Nia, knew the princess, and told her about the underworld. His words came back to her when she decided she was never going to return. At twenty, while studying nuclear physics at Massachusetts Institute of Technology, she announced she would marry a young American, Peter Jensen. She renounced all her titles and privileges within the Chakri dynasty, and took the name Julie.

The blow fell hardest on the king. He had trusted her judgement because he felt the young see things clearly. Had he lost his daughter because he had lost his own clarity of childlike but sensible vision? He stopped sailing. His eldest daughter did not return for eight years. Even then, she made it clear that she would be forever Mrs Julie Jensen, an American resident in California.

Nia, the reformed *nakleng*, said later, 'Princess Ubol was mistaken to think the king could not change evil people. I changed because I wanted to help him. Fortunes were being made in stolen American weapons. Gems were mined in regions controlled by mercenary armies. Trees from the war zones were smuggled out, but wouldn't go through the sawmills because there was so much shrapnel embedded in the wood. The king declared the royal forests to be protected but illegal lumbering had destroyed two-thirds of forestland during his reign. He could not directly stop the banditry. Smugglers brought in the rubies and diamonds and sapphires that stretched through the ground beyond our borders. The frontier guards were so poorly paid, it was easy to bribe them. The only way the king could act was to speak as a monk.'

Nia had been a schoolteacher paid what was then worth about two dollars a week. He said, 'The king understood the temptations, and had compassion for those who did bad things. I needed money when I became a *nakleng*. I saw nothing wrong with smuggling opium. The British developed the opium fields. In the school where I taught, there was a collection of Second World War broadcasts by the British writer, George Orwell, warning us against cooperating with the Japanese in growing opium. Marshal Pibul had pointed out that Orwell's own father was a British collector of opium money!'

Nia groped for rimless spectacles held together with dirty white tape: 'These days an informer's reward is twice the value of the opium he uncovers. Some police officers inform, collect the reward, confiscate the opium and sell it to other traffickers. Along the trail of dealers, a smuggler never knows who his client really is: police agent, courier, or a police officer using his inside knowledge to make money.'

Nia had been helped by the Princess Mother. She took risks in challenging the Chinese *teochiu* underworld whose opium dealers had always exercised power in the royal Siamese court. She put Nia to work at a temple with drug addicts. 'I serve in the way of my king,' he said. 'The big guys buy gold leaf sold by the temples to raise funds, and they stick the gold where everyone can see, on the front of the Buddha. My king puts the gold behind the Buddha . . . '

Lotus Blossom had felt that putting gold behind the Buddha was never going to be enough to stop these evils. One woman who did not give up trying was Kanitha Vichienchuen who knew Queen Sirikit when they were both girls in Paris and who became a Buddhist nun. Support for her work on behalf of exploited women came from a Japanese shipping magnate. Kanitta later said, 'When the princess left, it broke the king's heart.'

His second daughter Sirindhorn became his confidante. She learned the Chinese language, wrote children's stories for Chinese magazines, and refused to go west for further education. She studied the Chinese classical literature from which Chairman Mao Zedung took phrases for his '*Little Red Book*' for young communists. Mao's earlier ideas about using peasant armies for 'agrarian reform' were not unlike the king's. She wondered what had gone wrong in China since then to produce the terrible famines that were killing millions. She asked the king if she could become involved in teaching cadets of the Royal Thai armed forces: the single large body of young men and women whose training might speed up rural development that avoided communist mistakes of authoritarian central planning. It was a tricky proposition. Her father was the fountainhead of spiritual forces in conflict with army generals who wanted to keep authoritarian power.

Second Daughter Sirindhorn grew into a sensitive young woman who preferred to be in the countryside consulting poor farmers in their own dialects about local conditions, something Mao's central planners failed to do. She made it known she would never marry. That put a stop to royal court intrigues. She traced Siam's past through its ancient temple paintings. She saw humankind interlocked with the rest of nature, a view that went back to animism and to Brahminical rites and Buddhist legends and the Master of Tao's path to harmonisation with the universe. She got charts from the cartographic staff of the US Strategic Air Command revealing a continental coastline frozen over in another ice age which, when it melted, caused seas to rise and to break up a Golden Continent. She made archaeological discoveries that seemed to reinforce a theory suggesting Thai people had lived at the continent's heart. They became sea-kings when the vast land mass broke up. She could find no other explanation for the traces in the ancient Thai language of mathematical and nautical terms. Wherever she went, people responded to her gentle ways reflecting her attachment to her father's philosophy. She kept away from politics. She believed the country's salvation was to be found in its own past. She disliked the blind adoption of western ways, although she studied western languages, history, technology. She visited King Baudouin regularly in Belgium and he treated her as one of the family, but she said European self-government had evolved during many centuries along a different path. She drew witty cartoons and wrote pithy stories.

She seemed almost inarticulate when I first met her. Then I understood. She was a victim of royal privilege, which was not really privilege at all, but a loss of privacy. Since childhood, she had learned not to blurt her thoughts out loud because they could be so easily distorted. She had to be on guard constantly. When she was in her thirties, I saw her trapped in embarrassment when the wife of a Fourth Army general fell prostrate to the floor, pleading that her husband be saved from an unwelcome transfer because he belonged to the wrong class of graduates from the military academy: a new group of cronies had taken over. Sirindhorn told the grovelling general's wife that it was a matter for senior commanders. She wished I had not witnessed this servility, yet the scene was commonplace and one she could only change by using the position she found herself in. Liberal democracy was what her father believed in, but progress had to be made by way of this traditional reverence. She quoted George Orwell's *Animal Farm* to me, showing she knew the way to change things was not by a bloody rebellion which only ends with the start of a new fight for power.

She finally got her wish and became a regular lecturer at the Royal Thai military academy where she emphasised that social progress could be made by taking the best from Siam's past and adapting western technology to local conditions. 'Cadets took to slipping me notes about things they felt were bad about the system,' she said later. 'Jobs were shuffled between cronies in business and government. Bemedalled nincompoops posed as experts on subjects about which they knew nothing. There were parallel bureaucracies with overlapping power that stonewalled each other. The lines of administration were clogged with poisonous fears of the whims of dictators.'

Lek's only son, Vajiralongkorn, was formally invested with the title of Crown Prince in 1972. The rites coincided with Palestinian terrorists seizing the Israeli embassy in Bangkok on 28th December. The coincidence seemed to be an ill-omen. Buddhist texts were read over the umbilical cords of all four royal children. Each cord had been buried just after birth, according to ancient custom, under coconut trees at the temple where Lek had stayed as a monk. The Palestinians had been trained in Vietnam. If terrorists from Hanoi could strike one target in Bangkok, they could strike others.

A question mark hovered over the Crown Prince's future. Queen Sirikit said later, 'He's a little bit of a Don Juan. Women find him interesting and he finds women even more interesting. So his family life is not so smooth . . . If the people do not approve his behaviour, he must either change or resign from the royal family.' He was compared to Charles, Prince of Wales, emotionally crippled by an artificial life, but he had his defenders, among them Narisa, a strikingly beautiful daughter of Prince Chula Chakrabongse, once favoured by the British monarchy. Narisa said the Crown Prince was diligent, and 'not a wimp like Charles'. The Crown Prince nonetheless aroused public hostility. 'Why is he giving you the Evil Eye?' a lovely young member of the Royal Household Bureau asked me years later, when he presided over the casting of Buddha images. I suggested he was looking at her, not me. She shivered: 'I hope not – it's fatal for a woman.'

He had proved his competence as a paratrooper and fighter pilot, trained in Australia and the United States. Somehow, none of this won public respect. The presence of the Crown Prince's personal commandos alarmed people when he used them to sweep the neighbourhood around a work-base, apparently to clear it of terrorists before taking up temporary residence. The work-bases became, when he was there, royal palaces in the oldfashioned sense. Those close to him, though, were sorry for someone who had expected since infancy to be the next king. 'Queen Sirikit stopped him from marrying a girl with whom he was very much in love. He was a victim of the whole rotten, age-old system of the royal court,' recalled a descendant of the Fourth Rama. 'He would come to see me and bare his heart. He could not understand why his mother interfered. He became bitter and difficult.'

The Palestinian terrorists had been coaxed out of the Israeli embassy by Thai mediators who believed they had worked with Vietnam troops occupying Laos. The Crown Prince saw Laos as a former part of the old Siam. It was now abandoned by the entire American staff of the US Agency for International Development, USAID, described by the *Washington Post* of 16th June, 1972 as operating 'what amounted to a parallel government . . . a handy front for the CIA'.

The Crown Prince was angered that the Thai monarchy had not been consulted about American operations which could have serious repercussions for Thailand. The United States had been uselessly dropping one payload of bombs on Laos every eight minutes, day and night. The US 'bomblets' were scattered like explosive tennis-balls over a wide area and would harvest casualties among the peasants for decades to come. The Ninth Rama shared his son's view and told reporters, 'If there is any struggle in the world, people want to get or use Siam because it is strategic. And there's always a struggle in this world.' The nature of the struggle changed with the sudden journey of Richard Nixon, now US president, to China. The king prepared for a realignment. 'Silently treasure up knowledge and turn it over in your mind,' was a Taoist rule he had learned from the writings of his great-grandfather, Mongkut. 'Then gradually you can do as you like.'

He taught the Crown Prince to meditate on practical matters during royal ceremonies. The ritual transformation into an icon provided the opportunity to consider information acquired from King's Men, and Lek was able 'to let my mind leave my body, free to roam'. The technique was later described by Vasit, a quintessential King's Man who would play a key role in dealing with the domestic violence now brewing: Americans were going to pull out of Vietnam. Roy Heinecke, a distinguished US Marine pilot and then a war correspondent, said later, 'Americans began sending their families home after the embassy passed the word round that "Thailand will be next to fall". That caused local panic.'

Vasit had to deal with the panic. He was the young police officer first spotted by Queen Sirikit. Now he was widely known and celebrated as an honest cop – Police-General Vasit Dejkunjorn. 'The king taught me the Buddhist power of correct breathing,' he said. 'It sharpens concentration.' Vasit had become responsible for the security of the royal family: 'I was very often worried because they were always going into regions under communist attack,' he said later. 'There was one night of continuous shelling from Laos on a village the king and queen were to visit next day. I called to say it was obvious the communists would keep up the shelling and advised against them coming. But they came anyway, ignored the shelling, and sat talking to the villagers. I was forty years old when I joined the palace staff and by forty-one, I was completely grey with worry.'

The royal family's nerves, and those of Vasit, were about to be tested again. The trouble began when a letter reached a Bangkok newspaper signed by a communist guerrilla leader offering a ceasefire in exchange for a People's Government in the north east. Skeptical reporters went to the northern post office where the original letter had been registered. Incredibly, hilariously, the messenger for an American CIA officer had recorded in the postal registration book the name of the CIA officer who had forged the letter in some complicated scheme of his own. When the forgery was exposed, student activists blamed all US diplomats and demanded the expulsion of 'the American ambassador of espionage', William Kintner, who was indeed a former CIA officer. John le Carré, the English writer, was later shown 'spy equipment' in the abandoned CIA office. It amused the author of spy novels, but it was not so amusing for the king who knew CIA dossiers on himself and his children had been taken to Saigon by an embassy compiler, Albert A. Francis. The files fell into the hands of Vietnam's communist leadership.

22

Uprising

He had been king for twenty-seven years. He had outlasted seven constitutions, eleven prime ministers and a series of military coups. He had won over young soldiers. Now, in 1973, the Three Tyrants told him to abandon his work-base 'palaces' and suspended all constitutions. There were so many constitutions, each introduced after yet another coup, that they no longer meant much. But a new generation of university students thought them important and rose up in protest. The uprising was represented as communist-inspired.

To pre-empt the ruling junta, the First Army Commander, Krit Sivara, had been planning a coup of his own. The Ninth Rama knew of this and called Krit in for what the general later described as 'a monk-like sermon'. The sermon and Krit's loyalty to the king helped defeat a plot to topple the throne by Japan's old wartime collaborators.

Student anger had been building up for some time. The largest demonstration anyone could remember paralysed the capital in June 1973. Nine students were expelled for producing an underground newspaper. Thousands of city workers joined the demand for their reinstatement. During a night of heavy monsoon rains, the king put on old clothes and mingled with youngsters near the Grand Palace. Girls and boys sat in growing puddles of rain, huddled under sheets of plastic, while a spectacular thunderstorm lit up the sky. The jagged flashes of tropical lightning illuminated tense faces, but nobody recognised the king. What he heard did not confirm the reports from the Communist Suppression Operations Command (CSOC) that an uprising had been timed for the arrival of regular communist Vietnamese armies sweeping across Cambodia.

He asked university professors if the students were responding to communist direction from outside? They said communist literature had been planted in the classrooms and libraries to smear the students.

Lek invited the Three Tyrants to come one by one to Chitralada. Each

arrived alone and separately. Each, crawling into the presence of the intim-
idatingly erect king, found himself remembering the dreadful punishments
inflicted on anyone who broke the Oath of Allegiance. The king's face was
expressionless. He fixed each with his one good eye. After a long silence, he
suggested to each man that to avoid bloodshed, the nine expelled students
should be reinstated. Each man agreed and withdrew backward on hands
and knees.

The king told student leaders that if they returned to the campus, the
nine who had been expelled would be re-admitted.

But the generals, their courage bolstered by each other's company away
from the king, forgot the mythical penalties for treachery. The nine students
were arrested when they tried to return to their classrooms. The king was
made to look as if he had betrayed the students. By the first week of
October, it was rumoured that other protesters had disappeared. Crowds
moved to the plaza in front of the National Assembly. The honest policeman, Vasit, said later, 'More student leaders were arrested on army orders
as "communists". They were not.' More students assembled half-a-mile
from the university at the Monument to Democracy and painted across its
base: 'Democracy is locked up inside this vault.'

By Friday, 12th October, demonstrators were pouring into Bangkok from
far afield, enraged by the detention of thirteen students who had issued
pamphlets calling for a proper constitution. Another honest Police-
General, Sa-nga Kittikachorn, advised the king that the thirteen should be
released. 'If their demands are interpreted as treason,' said Sa-nga, 'then
there must be in Thailand traitors to the number of thirty-eight million.'
That was then the total population. General Sa-nga was the brother of one
of the Three Tyrants, and if he protested against tar-brushing innocent
young people, he must have known something.

'On Saturday the thirteenth, I took a look at this huge and growing
crowd and I was quite frightened,' recalled Vasit. 'They were heading for
the king's residence.'

'Stick with us,' the crowd was told by a student leader brandishing a bullhorn. 'You're not safe on your own. You might get charged with treason.'

'His Majesty's life is guaranteed only by the constitution,' shouted a
student. 'Where is the constitution?'

'Buried in the Democracy Monument!' roared the crowd.

A frightened government spokesman promised to release the thirteen
detainees and work out a new constitution – within twenty months, maybe.
The offer was ludicrous and came too late.

'As darkness approached, there were 200,000 people swirling around
Chitralada,' said Vasit. 'It was surrounded by a broad moat. There was

such a crush of excited young people that many fell into the muddy waters. Mass hysteria took over. People imagined they saw dead bodies.'

Regiments of country-bred troops outside Bangkok were ordered by the Three Tyrants to move into the capital. These were semi-literate youths recruited from remote villages at an early age, drilled to obey the regime, and to beat up and kill. They were told the students were attacking the king.

'The king gave instructions to keep the gates open,' said Vasit. 'No violence was to be used to keep anyone out. His Majesty gave a very clear instruction for all guards to remove the magazines from their rifles to make it clear there was no threat from the palace.'

Lek had been up all night, monitoring police and army channels to sort truth from propaganda. Many of the student activists were well organised. Some carried burlap bags to throw over barbed wire barricades, and home-made gas masks to guard against tear gas. Some carried iron bars and wooden clubs. The Communist Suppression CSOC chiefs formed a 'Committee to Restore Law and Order' and portrayed the rebels as akin to American student protesters alleged to be Moscow's dupes or agents.

But the mood of the protesters was not, as the regime tried to make out, anti-monarchist. Tearful young girls in school uniforms, holding huge portraits of the king and Queen Sirikit, led the swelling procession to Chitralada. Inside the villa, the Crown Prince and two of his sisters were ready to go out and talk with the students: the youngest princess, Chulabhorn, was now sixteen. She felt sure the demonstrators' motives were not being fairly reported on the government-controlled radio. The others agreed, although it was hard to make sense of the tales brought in by the royal household staff. The family felt that the student leaders were honest in saying they only wanted to see the king and ask his help. If this was not true, then the king would be in danger and perhaps the entire family. The children said they should all stick together. Their father seemed to know better than anyone what was really going on.

So, perhaps, did Field Marshal Praphas, the current leader of the Three Tyrants. He began to fear for his own life and turned his residence into an armed fortress with outer barricades guarded by heavily armed troops and tanks.

The king's reaction was strikingly different. As more marchers advanced upon Chitralada, he personally checked that all guards had emptied their weapons. Putrie Viravaidya, a descendant of King Mongkut, and the attractive young director of the king's personal affairs, hurried to Chitralada from home. 'Inside the grounds,' she recalled, 'I saw the security chief sitting on a rock clutching his head.

'"What's the matter?" I asked.

'The man responsible for the king's life replied: "I shall have to fight with broken bottles if His Majesty's made the wrong decision."'

Demonstrators were pouring through the open gates. 'Some students had been protesting on the streets for seven days without sleep,' said Vasit. 'I was mentally prepared for irrational acts, caused by exhaustion and wild rumours, but the king was steadfast in saying they should be welcomed inside.'

The massacre of the royal family became the stuff of rumour. Nobody in Bangkok believed the official bulletins any more, and on the streets, the rumour passed from mouth to mouth until it reached the Palace of Lotus Ponds. Mama, now in her seventy-third year, had returned from an upcountry clinic she had just opened. She had been listening, on her mobile radio, to the official broadcasts and the excited chatter of palace drivers, traffic police and firemen. Not for a second did she believe the family would be attacked, although somebody was inciting the people to violence with other stories that students were beaten and killed under the direct orders of her son, the king. Her detectives cautioned her that the crowds were too thick for her to drive through to Chitralada. She recognised the radio patter of ultra-right-wing groups trained to provoke violent reaction – 'The Red Gaurs', 'Lightning Bird', 'Thai Bat', 'Guardians of the Chakri Dynasty'. Sixteen sub-groups of what she considered to be fascistic paramilitary divisions were being called out in government broadcasts that became more and more inflammatory, with reports of burned-out police stations, roads blocked by overturned and burning vehicles, and public buildings smashed and looted by communists. She was well able to drive herself but she yielded a little and accepted an unarmed police driver who was willing to thread a path to Chitralada through a city falling under a premature twilight caused by the rising smoke from fires. Then she waited to speak by radio with Lek.

The king sent word to prime minister Thanom, the original chief of the Three Tyrants, that 'there is nothing to stop you requesting a royal audience'. This was the kind of upside-down instruction he had taught himself to issue, giving no offence, designed to offer enemies an exit if they had boxed themselves in. Thanom needed an exit now, feeling he was, after all, likely to pay some awful penalty for breaking his loyalty oath. So back he went to Chitralada. His own troop convoy escorted his limousine and forced a path through the crowds. He was led to Dusit Palace, the formal part of Chitralada. In the small audience chamber there was an uncanny quiet. The room was furnished in bourgeois western style, with silver-framed photographs of friends and family. No images of gods and demons. No pomp and circumstance. Just Lek in casual clothes.

Thanom prostrated himself. The king asked the prime minister to consider the consequences of his actions, adding, 'If you don't defuse a bomb, it will blow up.' Thanom crawled back out.

Bhumibol spoke over the private radio channel to his mother. Everything was under control. She should get a good night's rest. He walked through the Chitralada grounds, still in his open-neck shirt and slacks, looking astonishingly like his father when the doctor-prince shed formality and scorned Palace Law. The contrast between this casual king and the bombast of the unapproachable Thanom reassured a small group of students who had been chosen to speak for the rest. The evening sky was red from the light of fires reflected by a pall of smoke capping the city. The nine students walked along the main path through Chitralada, seeing no reason to crawl, and gathered around the slight figure of their king. They spoke in the hushed tones used by ordinary people showing mutual respect. They said repression made it impossible to pursue studies at the university founded by Pridi to teach the moral and political sciences.

The king said a Royal Household Bureau bulletin would be issued this time. Then everything would be on record. It would confirm that the government intended to act upon the call for a democratic constitution. Privately, he fumed over the stupidity which had pushed the students to these extremes. 'We were,' he said later, 'supposed to be part of the free world.' But his face showed nothing. 'It was the face,' said one emotional student delegate, 'of the Buddha.'

The youngsters were weeping as they moved back to join the main column of students. 'They had never encountered the king before, and were left in a state of high emotion. They said things like, "The king consoled us," as if he were the Deity,' said Vasit later.

They tried to send runners through the frenzied streets to the Democracy Monument. 'We wanted our colleagues to know the king was on our side,' recalled Tak Chai, the youth who had cried while he spoke with the king. 'It was difficult. The government controlled all other methods of communication, and our messengers got sidetracked and waylaid.' He was later shot in the leg by an armed group in civilian clothes.

The crowd of students in Chitralada began streaming out through the gates and collided with spectators driven by curiosity into the streets flanking the grounds. Hours passed in increasing chaos.

'The king had given orders that Chitralada's medical clinics be opened to treat anyone injured in the crush. Mostly it was shock and hysteria,' said Vasit. 'There were more rumours of bodies in the waterways and ponds. The king had already called in frogmen and search parties and they still drew a blank. The students were jumpy, though. Since early morning, people had flocked to the scene. There were violent clashes. As many as sixty were killed around the city. A story was spread that students who went to see the king were executed. The *klongs*, the canals around the palace, were full of newcomers who either fell or jumped into the water.

'Toward dawn of Sunday the 14th, I went out bare-handed, carrying no weapon, and climbed up on top of a vehicle. The students there knew me from my writings and speeches. I told them to trust in the king and then I informed all security units that the students were going to disperse peacefully. But one group went the long way round, toward army headquarters. What happened next wasn't anybody's fault. A patrol coming down that road ran into the dispersing crowds. My psychology had been to leave the demonstrators with a clear exit. They were desperately over-tired. They ran into anti-riot squads coming the other way. This set off a chain of incidents. Unidentified groups swept around government offices, setting fire to buildings like the National Lottery Monopoly which everyone knew was a vehicle for patronage, and the tax inspection department, the purse of corrupt politicians.'

At dawn a fullscale riot along one side of Chitralada erupted. About half-a-million citizens were in city streets swept by incendiary rumours that girls had been beaten to death by anti-riot police. Traffic-police boxes were torn down, more vehicles were overturned and set ablaze to close off streets. The king suspected these were calculated provocations. More tanks and armed helicopters were thrown into the frenzy. A tank shot dead a child and student. Gunships droned low over the city and shots were fired into groups of young people. The new outbreak of shooting killed or injured unknown numbers of people. It was impossible to get accurate counts of dead and injured. Putrie, the king's personal-affairs director, bravely visited every medical post to interrogate the injured. She said, 'Trouble-makers took advantage of the confusion to make up stories. It was getting closer to civil war.'

Counter-insurgency CSOC forces reported from upcountry that communist guerrillas were launching small actions in rural areas. The king later found the reports to be invented, a last-ditch campaign against a revolution that was not against out-moded monarchy but instead sought to free a hamstrung king. Some right-wing extremists, according to Vasit, 'seemed ready to kill thousands of students if necessary'. They spread the notion that the king had talked the demonstrators into retreating, but only because he secretly supported the Three Tyrants. The Royal Household bulletin that promised a new government was kept off the air.

Lek had anticipated such betrayals and fell back on the radio station he had built for just such an emergency. He broadcast the bulletin himself. Some protesters, though, heard only the regime's propaganda that dead students had been thrown into the Chitralada waterways. Lek went back into the grounds with the Crown Prince and a group of student leaders to make another careful search. Still no bodies were found. Frogmen dived continuously in the murky waters and came up with nothing, not even the corpse of a cat. The efforts to provoke more clashes around the city were ugly. The king said later, 'There was sniper fire from city rooftops and students were killed – it seemed deliberate provocation. The burning of buildings was carried out with professional efficiency.'

The Princess Mother awoke to hear privately from a royalist, an outraged senior officer at the interior ministry that upcountry soldiers resorted to 'red oil drum massacres', clubbing to death peasants alleged to be communists, stuffing the bodies into empty oil drums and setting them ablaze to get rid of the evidence. This time she did not wait to call her son. She set out again from the Palace of Lotus Ponds, trying to think well of senior monks like Kitiwatha Bhikku who had told young soldiers – normally hesitant to take life – that killing a communist was no sin. She felt a surge of very un-Buddhist anger. This was using Buddhism to fool the credulous. The students were being broken up into small groups to isolate them and frighten them into thinking their only hope was to fight. Her car carried no identification. She said later, 'The crowds parted,' as if this had been the most normal thing in the world. Word had been sent ahead by loyal police officers that the king's mother was coming, and this had a magical effect.

She found students swarming between the gates. In so much dark confusion, they looked menacing. She left the car, to the casual eye an old woman, painfully thin and frail. But she was recognised. Word swiftly spread. The king's mother was here. A vast silence fell. She asked calmly to speak with one of the leaders. A girl, called 'the chief communist' in some later police reports, addressed her in the oldfashioned language of a commoner to royalty: 'I am dust below your feet.' The Princess Mother put her hands on the girl's boney shoulders and said softly, 'His Majesty, all of us, are worried as if we were your own mothers and fathers. You must tell your friends, please, to go home so your families are not worried for your safety.' Knowing how protesters had run into security forces, and the consequence when each side misunderstood the other's intentions, Mama knew the immediate need was to escort the students to safety. 'His Majesty has brought in private buses,' she said. 'His own guards will be on the buses. We guarantee you will be taken safely to your homes. You have our word: your concerns will be met.'

After she had finished, the 'chief communist' took up a bullhorn, repeated everything and added her own plea: 'Please show respect to the Princess Mother and go home.'

The royal family had aligned themselves with the alleged communists. Lek and his son walked through the grounds and spoke to stragglers. Ahead, unarmed but uniformed members of the Household Regiment helped those students who were weak from stress and lack of sleep to stumble into the buses. The drivers revved their engines. The 'dangerous mob' gradually melted away.

The king's mother was a friend of the Buddhist rector of Thammasat University, the epicentre of the storm, the home of moral and political sciences. He told her the trouble had been started by trouble-makers to create a crisis. The rector, Sanya Dharmasakdi, was trusted by even the most hot-headed students. The king appointed him to head a new government, stepping outside his powers, but certain he had the majority of people on his side. The threat of civil war receded.

'This is a day of great sorrow,' Lek said in a broadcast the following evening, using his own radio station because two of the Three Tyrants – Praphas and Thanom – still controlled the government news services. They were playing for time, their killer units moving into the capital. The king said he had chosen Dr Dharmasakdi to head his new government on this 'the most grievous day in the history of our Thai nation . . . I call on all to eliminate the causes of violence.'

But out of the king's presence, Prime Minister Thanom was egged on again by others who were afraid of losing the power they had always exercised even if, as cronies from the old Northern Command wartime years, they squabbled over the leadership. With Field Marshal Praphas, he ordered troops to continue street fighting around the palace, pending the imminent arrival of special Ranger detachments. The First Army, based in and around Bangkok, blocked their entry. There was a brief, tense stand-off. Army Commander Krit Sivara warned Ranger leaders that the entire country would collapse into a civil war which nobody could win. Lek's earlier 'sermon' to Krit now paid off. Krit told the Three Tyrants that all facilities were available for them to go to Don Muang airport and fly from the country. The king had again borrowed from Sun Tzu: 'The enemy should never be completely encircled. Always leave one way out, or he will fight like a cornered rat.' Praphas and Narong were flown by US transport planes to Taiwan. Thanom was flown to the United States.

Monday's headline in the *Bangkok Post* was ALL QUIET! But there had been more street fighting during Sunday night. The Yellow Tigers' Suicide Squad attacked the capital's police headquarters with Molotov cocktails and rocks, seized fire-trucks and filled the pumps with petroleum to be used as flame-throwers. Some security units continued firing, even at doctors and nurses trying to help the wounded. The fighting gradually died down.

Vasit said later, 'By Monday, Boy Scouts had taken over duties like direct-ing traffic and everything was quiet.'

The entire country accepted the king's intervention. By December 1973 he appointed a 'national convention' from which voting members would be elected to a National Assembly. He had misgivings. It might be too soon to make such an abrupt transition from a society based on ancient beliefs that encouraged people to submit to authority. Still, the civilian revolt had been against military dictatorship and the bulk of the armed forces stayed loyal to the king. Ordinary soldiers who had seen him in action were ready to follow him, provided he had the means to make his wishes known to them.

One of his channels had been Vasit, once an ordinary soldier who had started out as a poor boy in a north-eastern village where the bullying beha-viour of the local police made him vow to change things. At thirteen, he had become a secret agent against the Japanese, picked out by Force 136 to learn wireless telegraphy. He had been sent later by the king to study police work at the FBI national academy, administration at New York University, and law and political science at Harvard where Henry Kissinger had asked his views about Vietnam – 'although,' Vasit said later with a grin, 'Kissinger asked both the questions and supplied his own answers, so all I had to do was sit and listen.'

Knowing Vasit was on the scene at the critical moment had comforted the Princess Mother. She knew Vasit escaped into the mountains and med-itated alone in a cave when things got on top of him, and she read his best-selling detective novels that told the truth about drug-trafficking and other criminal activities protected by military rulers. A devout Buddhist, Vasit seemed the best proof that the king was on the right track by winning over the rank-and-file of the armed services on his way to a just society. Lek still had to watch out, for political generals demanded obedience from their own units, and might again attack him for overriding a constitutional mon-archy. Each constitution was changed to mean whatever each ruling elite wanted it to mean.

In this interval between constitutions, the king appointed a people's par-liament. It was a noble experiment which only confirmed his misgivings about introducing western-style politics too soon. There were 2,347 members with 2,347 different voices and forty-three different parties. The devout Dr Sanya Dharmasakdi of the rebellious university was unable to translate Buddhist idealism into parliamentary democracy and proved a failure as premier. He said, 'Buddha was right. The utopia of a republican democracy must wait for some change in human behaviour.' He was suc-ceeded by the two brothers descended from earlier kings, Seni and Kukrit Pramoj. Each in turn became prime minister and each turned against the other. A Thai general deplored 'the monkey-house now running the kingdom. If two brothers hate one another as these do, how can an entire country stick together without some form of higher authority to knock heads together?'

The Ninth Rama watched television scenes of the evacuation of Saigon on 30th April, 1975, with Americans kicking Asians off the last helicopters to safety. The images did a terrible disservice to the many Americans who had worked to improve the lives of Asians, but they also proved he had been right to argue that it was dangerous to depend on any single ally. He quietly approved the action of his first minister, Kukrit Pramoj, who had closed those American bases whose existence was public knowledge and asked for the closure of highly secret US intelligence-gathering installations before dashing off to see Chairman Mao in China, saying publicly that he was fearful of 900 million Chinese 'sitting on our Siamese heads'. Kukrit was portrayed in a newspaper cartoon as a virgin crying, 'Rape me!' He had played a starring role beside Marlon Brando in the movie, *The Ugly American* – as an Asian prime minister. 'I'm what Hollywood calls a type-actor,' he said. 'They only call you when they need another Oriental prime minister.' He said that the *lèse majesté* charge of disloyalty was a political tool to destroy opponents – even, the king.

He became the architect of a Thai-Chinese alliance against Vietnam. Kukrit told the Ninth Rama, 'Chairman Mao said the way to deal with Thai communists is: "First, don't issue propaganda against them, that they are bad, wrong and all that sort of thing. They won't listen to you, they are thick-skinned, those people. Second, don't kill them all, because they like being martyrs. More will come to be killed. Don't send soldiers against them because they are in the jungle and will run away until your soldiers have to leave to get back to their barracks, and then the communists will creep back into the jungle where they are at home. Finally, to defeat them, see that your people are well fed, that they have work. Then the communists cannot do anything."'

A new Thai army leadership dismissed Kukrit after 400 days of his premiership and declared him to be a fool, a jester, and anti-American. They decided that students were part of a Vietnamese plot to install a communist regime. In 1976, the new strongmen put down another 'uprising', acting this time with swift secrecy and preventing any protesters from appealing again directly to the king. Twenty years later, the education ministry still refused to sanction any references to the bloody '76 coup in history lessons. 'It was a "non-event",' *The Nation*, one of Bangkok's English-language newspapers, commented.

Three years of civilian government had given the new regime its excuse to act. By 1976, Second Daughter Sirindhorn, for so long puzzled as a child by her father's remoteness, understood why the king kept work-bases when the Three Tyrants wanted to shut them down. They were his best way of directly teaching people to think for themselves. She wished he could bridge the gap between the honest goodwill of ordinary Americans and Washington's follies. She happened to see the extraordinary final Air Commando operation when every Cambodian who had flown in secret US wars, and who could escape, was brought with his family to the 'secret' US Strategic Air Command base in Thailand, stockpiled with nuclear bombs. A tattered fleet of 175 aircraft with 1,400 refugees staggered in, with bomb arming wires trailing from ordnance stanchions after bombing the communist-occupied capital of Pnom Penh on the way. One helicopter pilot ran out of fuel above the giant B-52s on their alert pad, and came down in a controlled crash with twenty fellow Cambodians aboard. 'As usual,' Sirindhorn later reflected, 'it was ordinary people who were ready to sacrifice their own lives to help others.'

The compassion of ordinary American fighting men for allies was nullified by their government's continuing interference in Bangkok. 'US-supported right-wing groups work with police and army groups. They have immense advantages over the largely unarmed radicals they suppress by assassinations, intimidation and bomb attacks,' said a Thammasat University professor, Dr Yuangrat Wedel. Sirindhorn had a wide circle of academic acquaintances of this kind, and through them she learned the extent of the brutality which had started in 1976 and still continued. More students were running in fear to join the communists in the jungle. Her father sought them out, risking his life to offer them safe conduct home. Sometimes he let Sirindhorn come along. She found the so-called communist students were no more revolutionary than her father.

'Most young people who flee to the jungles are simply desperate,' he said. 'Many confuse the Buddhist with the Marxist dialectic but soon find that communism imposes answers. Buddha asked us to answer each question on our own.' One of the rare times when the king is seen smiling in the royal archive's photographs, he is talking with 'jungle communists', boys and girls in red scarves. 'He got along well with them,' said the princess. 'He might have done the same himself in their situation, trapped by poverty, frightened and isolated.'

She thought that for such youngsters the armed forces held out the best hope for learning the practical skills still so badly needed by a country where too many officials, from centuries of habit, wanted decisions to be made by those higher up. There was a wobbly line between the old submissiveness and outright anarchy. She talked like this to Mama who thought

Sirindhorn should be elevated to the rank of Crown Princess. She not the Crown Prince had the makings of the next monarch. But Mama said nothing of this at the time.

Her father paraphrased for Sirindhorn questions raised in the *King And I*: if allies were weak, wasn't the king better off alone? Lek was torn between idealism and the practical considerations forced upon him in a modern world. He missed being able to talk to his first daughter terribly and grew closer to Number Two Daughter Sirindhorn. He said, 'Our people have courage, not harsh – strong and gentle. Buddhists have never had a holy war.' It was the central thought to which he had to cling. Later, Sirindhorn wrote a poem for him. Like his paintings, it revealed a great deal more than spoken words could tell. She made it rhyme in both Thai and French, as if to bridge two worlds:

Through the dark jungle, very dense,
Which stretches out interminably, sombre and immense . . .
I follow without stopping the quick footstep of my Father.
Oh Father, I am dying of hunger and I am tired.
Look! The blood is running from my two wounded feet . . .
Father! Will we arrive at our destination?
– Child! . . . On the earth there exists no place
Full of pleasure or comfort for you.
Our road is not covered with pretty flowers.
Go! Always, even if it breaks your heart.
I see the thorns prick your tender skin.
Your blood: rubies on the grass, near the water.
On the green shrubbery, your tears dropped. Diamonds on emerald,
show their beauty. For all the human race does not lose its courage
In the face of pain. Be tenacious and wise,
And be happy to have an ideal so dear.
Go! If you want to walk in the Footstep of your Father.

Part Four

23

Face of Danger

'WE are in the most critical period in our history,' the king wrote on 22nd April, 1978 in a letter penned frugally on both sides of two sheets of paper to Sir William Stephenson, knighted for his World War Two work in unconventional intelligence operations. The king's English marched boldly in parallel ranks of blue ink, graceful but emphatic. He wanted 'to inspire our people, especially young officers in the armed forces . . . to combat injustice and uphold world peace by conventional and "unconventional" means . . . Even when British Security Coordination used such means, the spirit of dedication and honour is always present . . . Our country is subject to tremendous pressures from every quarter . . . although we have always been able to weather all crises using the very strong spirit of unity which emerges in difficult times. But our people are thus that when they don't see the physical danger we are facing, they tend to be lax. And the new kind of danger before us does not show its face, because it is even more than total war.'

The king felt his country was now alone in facing greater dangers than ever, and he wanted to train his young army officers to show the same spirit of self-sacrifice, and dedication to a higher cause than the political ambitions of military tyrants.

The letter was delivered by Malcolm MacDonald, an intermediary for the two men while he was British commissioner-general in South East Asia. During the war, MacDonald had represented the British Crown in Canada where Stephenson's British Security Coordination (BSC) needed diplomatic cover for a spy-training camp to which American recruits were sent during the period of US neutrality. Some of the Stephenson's highly placed secret intelligence allies later formed World Commerce Corporation, WCC. It had an office in Bermuda. There Stephenson and I lived and worked separately. Winston Churchill had described the kind of activities in which BSC engaged as having 'an element of legerdemain

... There are many kinds of manoeuvre in war ... not all take place on the battlefield.'

World Commerce was designed to help small countries like Siam resist subversion of the kind first described in Japanese insurrection manuals written by Tsuji Masanobu. *An Insurrection Manual for Undeveloped Countries* was published in Hanoi over the name of the communist Vietnamese General Vo Nguyen Giap. It was almost a carbon copy of Tsuji's textbooks. Tsuji had been reported in Hanoi by western-run agents after the American war in Vietnam. Stephenson kept extensive files on Tsuji as one of the most monstrous men of the twentieth century, and wrote of Tsuji that, 'Absolute power corrupts but absolutely secret power corrupts absolutely.'

One of Stephenson's partners in World Commerce, General William J. Donovan of OSS, had been US ambassador in Bangkok, but retired and died in 1957. Donovan, the only man in the history of the United States to win its top four medals for gallantry and public service, regarded Siam as strategically vital to Asia's defence in the cold war. This view was shared by Stephenson who admired the Ninth Rama's courage and his resolve to save his kingdom by making it self-sufficient and morally strong; but he wondered if a king who practised Buddhist forgiveness could survive in a greedy world. The king wrote that Stephenson's practical advice on how small nations could muster their moral strength to fight evil had helped his young officers to 'begin to see more clearly "the face of danger" and the means of combatting it'. Moral values, said Lek, were absolutely vital to survival.

A king's representative met me in New York and suggested I revisit Bangkok. I had read the wartime files on Tsuji. It all seemed long ago. What did tempt me was the chance to get an inside look at a royal court that appeared to belong to the Middle Ages, utterly fantastic and otherwise unknowable. I read E.W. Hutchinson's book, *Adventures in Siam in the Seventeenth Century*, re-published by the Royal Asiatic Society in London. It dealt with the fate of a Venetian, later known as 'Falcon', who had alienated Siamese noblemen who did not like any foreigner who got too close to their king. When the king fell helplessly ill, his courtiers hacked off Falcon's head. I was not in any hurry to see if things had changed.

One of the Ninth Rama's most devoted cousins had been shot and killed in 1977. She was known as the Princess of the South. For ten years, she had worked on rural development in the wildest regions of the Elephant's Trunk, that isthmus dangling down to the Malay border. Lek had assigned her Vasit Dejkunjorn, the royal bodyguard who threw away his guns at the 1973 siege of the palace. Much later, Vasit told me that, on the day she died,

(*Above*) Trekking into hill tribe villages in the Golden Triangle of northern Thailand in an attempt to get the tribes people to stop growing opium during the Vietnam War years when Communists were infiltrating from North Vietnam. (*Below*) On a firing range.

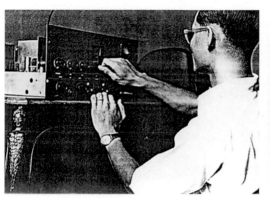 

(*Above left*) At controls of his radio station soon after he began broadcasting educational programmes from Chitralada. (*Above right*) As barefoot monk receiving alms during his retreat to be ordained, October 1956.

Hands in prayer, kneeling (in dark glasses) with other monks and facing his Teacher in the temple before his ordination in 1956.

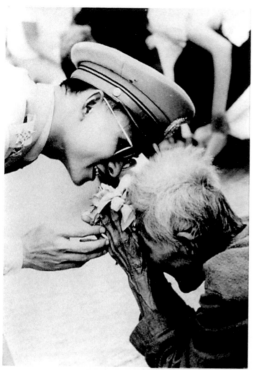

With a leper, continuing the work of his doctor-father to care and bring lepers into normal society.

(*Below*) On a night-time tour of a hydro-electric complex in the north-east.

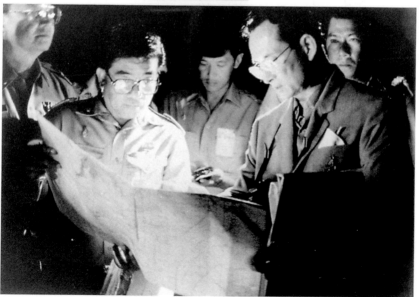

Working on one of his wooden dinghies.

At a 1960 jam session in New York. Bhumibol on the saxophone with (from left to right) Benny Goodman on clarinet; Gene Krupa on drums; Urbie Green on trombone.

Exploring the river along the Thai-Malay border.

(*Below left*) Bhumibol's painting of his wife, Queen Sirikit.
(*Below right*) An informal moment with Prince Philip, a
frequent visitor. The two had been sailing and camped on a
beach at Hua Hin, near the palace of Far From Worry.

Elephant trainers at work up in the north-east near Mama's project.

Author's daughter, Alexandra, at the palace school.

The Dance-Master fitting a mask over Alexandra's head in a blessing ceremony.

The author and
Monika, his wife, with
Than Pu-ying Putrie,
descendant of the
Fourth Rama
(of *King and I* fame)
and now secretary-
general to the Privy
Council. All dressed up
for a formal visit to the
Grand Palace.

The author with King Bhumibol.

Princess Sirindhorn.

King Bhumibol helping his mother to hospital before her last illness, with Princess Galyani, his sister, in the background.

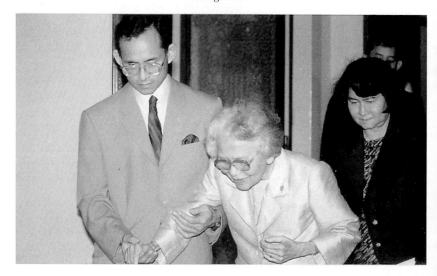

the princess was using a police helicopter to fly two monks to a remote temple. A radio message reported some police officers had been seriously injured by landmines. She dropped off Vasit to make room in case she found the injured men. On taking off, the helicopter was riddled by gunfire. It made a crash-landing at a monastery where she died from loss of blood. She was fifty-seven.

The princess was Vibhavadi Rajani who wrote popular novels under the pseudonym of 'V'. She had already raised a family, and said all she needed now was contained in her mind. She loved all forms of scholarship and wildlife. For Lek, she normally travelled through the deep jungle valleys by boat or elephant. At the time of her death, she appeared before him in his study. The apparition was as real to him as his brother's ghost. He took out a block of hand-made mulberry paper and scribbled the words 'face of danger'. And then he wrote to Stephenson about new things that worried him. Lek felt like Tom Tiddler in the old children's game of Tom Tiddler's Ground. Tom Tiddler tries to stop others from crossing into his territory while they sing about 'picking up gold and silver'. The king's enemies were both inside his territory and crossing its borders.

The monarchy was more important than ever as the means to an end. Provided it kept the people's respect, it could lead to a republic based on moral values. Lek survived because people now recognised his integrity, but they wanted him to intervene in matters they should settle among themselves and this only reinforced the old role of absolute monarchy. He decided to make Sirindhorn a Crown Princess because she had the common touch. She might be able to break the habits of subservience among so many people. In December, 1978, he provided for the possibility of female succession to the throne. Sirindhorn was seen by her pupils in the military academy to be detached from ego, from *atta*, in the Buddhist sense of being dispossessed of any attachment to power, wealth or position. Ambitious plotters, however, had put it about that the Crown Prince was not detached from *atta*: and that he said the idea of a Buddhist republic depended upon human perfectability; and people were not perfect. 'They respond to orders,' he was quoted as saying.

The king refused to hear anything bad about his son; but Lek faced the fact that he must be seen as a king who would last a long time: vigorous and in good health. 'His heart was suffering from overwork,' I was told later by the chief of Queen Sirikit's cardiology centre, Dr Suphachai Chaithirapan. 'He refused to cut back on his workload.'

Yet suppose the king died? It was not clear if the Crown Prince would succeed him. The prince had finally submitted to an arranged marriage with a twenty-year-old girl whose royal ancestry was impeccable and acceptable to Queen Sirikit. The Crown Prince was bitter after being forbidden to marry the girl he loved. Now he was surrounded by sycophants, some of whom hoped for advantages if he became king. 'Perfection was too much to ask from a boy who was Heir Apparent,' lamented an American-educated noblewoman. 'Look at these pictures of him in court dress-up! If he had to submit to old customs, then he might as well go all the way, have all the women he wanted, and behave like the earlier kings.'

One group of powerful Thai-Chinese businessmen wanted a king who protected their interests. Some had criminal connections, like Yuan of the Heaven and Earth Society. Yuan was afraid that if ever the Ninth Rama did bring about a new and just society, he and his cronies would lose their sources of wealth. Such men made mischief. They whispered to the Crown Prince that his position as Heir Apparent might not be such a sure thing with Sirindhorn in the running. 'Perhaps,' murmured Yuan, 'someone wants to kill the Crown Prince. It's an old Siamese custom.'

Yuan later denied ever saying the Crown Prince had shot a gun at his father. The denial gave birth to rumours. And rumours could not be dignified by a public refutation. The story grew with re-telling. When the accusation was said to have originated with influential Thai-Chinese, there was a danger of racial attacks on their entire community. The Chinese were successful in business and in bad times they became handy scapegoats. Eight per cent of the population was Chinese in origin but eighty per cent of the banks were Chinese-owned. Stephenson, knowing that foreigners had always used Overseas Chinese as political footballs, sent Lek a disturbing document written by Tsuji before the Japanese invasion of Siam: *How to Use the Overseas Chinese.*

Tsuji had written in 1941: 'From the time of Kublai Khan's invasion, Chinese began to emigrate in large numbers to South Asia and gradually rising from humble positions became men of wealth, and by deceiving the naturally lazy natives, increased their economic power. You must realise in advance that it will be difficult, merely by urging on them an awareness of an Asian brotherhood, to enlist their cooperation in any scheme which does not promise personal profit. Siam should be controlled [by Japan] through a king appointed by a few key men of Chinese origin.'

Refugees of Chinese origin were flooding across all the Thai borders in 1978, fleeing from brushfire wars and from the communist Vietnamese armies that swarmed across Cambodia. Eventually, more than a million refugees of all kinds had to be taken in. 'We had an obligation to do it as Buddhists,' Queen Sirikit said later. She was praised for 'exemplary leadership' by the permanent observer of the Roman Catholic Holy See to the United Nations, Archbishop Renato Martino. But Sirikit and the king knew that among this huge invasion were members of the Khmer Rouge whose genocidal leader was Pol Pot. 'We had thousands of children in the refugee camps,' Sirikit said later. 'They included ten-year-old boys who had been turned into killing machines.' Sirikit had entered camps at a border point only 180 kilometres from Bangkok. She had risked shellfire to gather lists of those executed in Pol Pot's purges. It was clear that all the leading person-alities in Cambodia had been wiped out, along with hundreds upon thou-sands of civilians. The queen was one of the first to warn of 'children's armies' which would alarm the world in the last year of the twentieth-century.

A month after the killing of the Princess of the South, the former King Savang Vatthana of Laos was arrested and taken away for 're-education' by the Vietnamese. Laos was important, not just because it once was part of Old Siam, but because US President Kennedy regarded it as the sluice-gate for communism into South East Asia. Now the Americans had aban-doned their secret armies of local Laotian hill tribes. One of the American pilots who flew covert missions in Laos, Darrel Whitcombe, later wrote: 'We just packed up and left these people. I find it hard to believe anyone in this world would trust us again.'

In February, 1979, 80,000 Chinese troops invaded North Vietnam and within a few weeks lost one-third as many men as America had lost in four-teen years of fighting the same communists. Enemies became friends, and friends became enemies. It was hard to know who to trust. The king wrote to Stephenson that the danger was 'even more than total war; it is what I would call "mental war".'

The Ninth Rama used all his experience in statecraft to place political leadership in the hands of Prem Tinsulanonda, an army commander-in-chief who recognised the king knew more about the country's problems and had more experience than any other person alive. Prem became premier in 1980, beginning eight years of fruitful cooperation with Lek; but both he and the king were challenged by coups and intrigues. One coup began at crack of dawn on 9th September, 1985 when guests in a smart Bangkok hotel found a message under their bedroom doors: 'To Our Dear Foreign Patrons – Please to be informed there is a light revolution going on this morning. Do not panic over this spontaneous demonstration. Do not fly away. We need your money. Thank you. The Revolutionary Party.' The Revolutionary Party was brought rapidly under control. There was a public trial of the rebels. It exposed nothing more than the existence of one group of powerful financial interests conspiring with another group within the same old clique of wartime pro-Japanese cronies. Lek had to patch things up and present an image of unity to get on with his private reforms.

Bangkok was the toughest nut to crack. Each time the king put forward a simple plan to end the capital's seasonal flooding, small neighbourhood groups would tell the Royal Irrigation Department that the changes should be made in someone else's backyard. Local councils were labelled 'democratic' but money dictated their decisions. Heavy rainwaters periodically reduced the capital to a jelly on which buildings tilted and sank a little further each year. The king had explored the stinking municipal drains, endless cavernous tunnels through which he trekked at night with flashlamp and map, hoping to find an alternative to displacing the streets above. 'There really is only one answer,' he said. 'You have to excuse the expression, but excrement can only be collected by flushing a toilet. A canal would do it, slicing across the top, here. But it won't get done if it's put to the vote.'

His first daughter visited him in 1981 as Mrs Peter Jensen to present him with her first daughter. She did not change her mind about court gossip and intrigue and went back to her anonymous life in California. The Crown Prince produced one daughter by his official wife, but he had four princes by a consort who had been a popular actress and singer. The court shunned her, not because she represented a return to the days of many queens and consorts, but because she was a commoner. Among those who wanted males-only on the throne, though, the pretty and graceful actress secured a place in their secret hearts.

Lek gave Crown Princess Sirindhorn duties to perform in keeping with the better traditions. She wrote more lullabies for the royal elephants and in her usual artless fashion said later, 'I researched eulogies for the sacred elephants of former reigns and cut out the usual fawning and flattering verses directed at the king and put the focus on his reform projects. There was a verse about teaching the elephant good manners, and I asked many people their opinion on this matter and one of the palace gardeners informed me that the elephant must be taught not to pull up trees and flowers.'

Sirindhorn, in line for the succession in the absence of a male heir, had become immensely popular. In 1991, she sat one day on a baked earthen road between ricefields and talked with young villagers. The sun cast ever-longer shadows until a huge harvest moon came up. The evening was interrupted by bursts of laughter. We were in a district she called the Land of the Whistling Black Snail because of a rare mollusk that whistled softly like a flute. Flying just above the tree-tops were the smallest mammals in the world, measuring twenty millimetres from nose to rump and known as kitti-bats. And there was an old abbot – 'We call him the General,' Sirindhorn told me. 'But don't tell him I said that.' The abbot was someone she recommended I visit to learn about how local conditions had deteriorated since the days when the temple was the place where every child had gone to school.

How had I arrived at this point, trusted by the king and the few closest to him? In 1990, my wife Monika had flown to Lausanne to see the king's mother who was there on a brief visit. Monika was astonished by the smallness of Mama's apartment: 'It was cramped and the furniture looked as if it had been there since the war days. I realised how totally uncorrupted she remained. She was mother of a king and nobody could possibly have begrudged her a little comfort, but she had a tiny Buddha alcove for meditation and little else. She came in, wearing pants and a nondescript blouse and gym shoes. She was pushing ninety but she seemed full of energy. She had been talking to university researchers about new agricultural technologies.'

Mama's only daughter, the king's older sister, Galyani, was there. She had divorced the army colonel and married a prince, and as Princess Galyani, she had royal status again. She was scholarly, formidably well versed in Asian affairs and skeptical of the motives of western intruders. 'She told stories of childhood,' said Monika later. 'But she said she didn't see much of her brother these days.'

After this we received a garbled message through a western embassy, telling us to go to Bangkok where someone would take us to the far south to see the king and queen. A letter had been seriously delayed and we almost failed to join what was called 'a safari,' so quaint and inappropriate a word for the king to use that it looked if he must have intended to disguise his purpose from those who might interfere. My impression in the past had been that he would have liked to show his rural reforms to Sir William Stephenson who was old and infirm, and now I was Sir William's proxy. Monika first went to see the Princess Mother in Lausanne as an author attracted to Mama's life story, irresistible to any writer. Her inclusion in this much-delayed 'safari' was meant, it appeared to us, as a kindly gesture. But neither of us after the passage of so much time knew exactly what to expect.

24

Trust

WE were taken into the region where V was killed, near the 647-kilometre-wide Thai-Malay border, and arrived at an abandoned Moslem graveyard on a 2,100-metre high mountain. Here, in a two-storeyed villa made of bamboo, was where Monika and I finished up at the end of our two days' travel.

The bamboo villa was ours for as long as we stayed in the region. It was conveniently far from Bangkok's gossip-hungry royal courtiers and almost hidden in gaudy tropical vegetation. There was a kitchen from which came sounds of soft laughter. Self-effacing attendants followed us to our rooms, carrying neatly carved exotic fruits and plates of fragrant Thai dishes. From some unseen and distant point in this jungle, the queen sent her hairdresser, supposing Monika would appreciate the attention after such a long journey. The king's private intelligence adviser took me along jungle paths around the foot of the mountain. This, he said, was Thaksin Palace. Queen Sirikit had been walking alone through the thick undergrowth here, and saw what she took to be the ghost of a dead Islamic leader smiling benevolently as if approving a plan to build a royal work-base here. It was an auspicious omen. The land was unwanted by local Moslems because of its history as a grave-yard, so nobody was upset. The base had to be called a palace for custom's sake. There were medical clinics and open-sided workrooms for craftsmen teaching their trades to young villagers. The king had designed and built a reservoir to supply the base and nearby Malay fishing villages. The moun-tain had been the home of Malayan bears with pelts of brilliant black, white-pawed gibbons, black panthers, and exotic creatures like the flying-dog. It would be a good idea to step outdoors carefully. A lady-in-waiting had been killed by a viper, and there were other deadly snakes, like banded krait, and king cobra. Workers thought they saw a tiger at night, amber-eyed, treading softly. 'Perhaps,' he said, 'they're only dreaming but they put on paper masks facing the wrong way so the tiger won't attack from behind.'

The king never gave out his agenda before time. It was his security system. Only those with a need to know saw his plans from hour to hour. We were suddenly called to dinner. Monika and I were taken off guard. We scrambled into the only clothes that seemed vaguely suitable and were led through the steamy heat to the small concrete residence at the end of a path climbing to the summit. The tropical night fell abruptly and the sky was suddenly filled with stars. 'No wonder you miss Asia,' said Monika.

There was another abrupt change. We were in an oldfashioned drawing room with Audubon-style pictures on the wall crafted from emerald beetle-wings and peacock feathers. 'It's an ancient skill,' said Queen Sirikit, showing us through. The king said he expected we must be hungry after such a long journey. I thought it best not to say I was already full of the bamboo villa's shrimp rolls. In the dining room were pictures of the children at different stages in their lives, and the atmosphere was that of a small family gathering. Queen Sirikit was fifty-eight years old by then, but she looked many years younger, sheathed in a dress of emerald green and gold made from the exquisite *mudmee* silk she had popularised. The king had on a simple blue business suit. Crown Princess Sirindhorn wore fawn-orange *mudmee* silk and had pinned back her black hair which gave her an eager, childlike quality. We sat at a Chinese-style round dining table, Monika and myself on either side of the king, with the queen and Princess Sirindhorn flanking the physician, Dr Deny, and a dear old man who had studied agriculture at Wisconsin University and who already knew Monika had graduated from there. He said disarmingly that he had flown here with a one-way ticket bought by the national electricity board, of which he was chief, because tomorrow we'd all be going to look at a big new hydro-electric project, but he wasn't sure how he was going to get back because his retirement would take effect the very next day. The king told him not to worry: he'd be a privy councillor by then. It was all quite cosy. We realised later how seldom these people could sit and chat in this relaxed way. Sirindhorn later took me aside and said, 'I've never heard my father talk about these things.'

Her father was eager to talk about anything, as if seizing a rare opportunity to exchange ideas with outsiders. I remembered what his former scriptural teacher, the Supreme Patriarch, had once told me: 'The King is a special being in our Buddhist belief, who has extraordinary power and knowledge to see you not only in this life but in previous lives. He is the Bodhisattva of Compassion whose unwavering gaze pierces you to your eternal being.'

I saw the unwavering gaze, but not a clairvoyant monk. Just a man in his sixties who seemed happy to be eighteen-year-old Little Brother Lek again, born American, full of curiosity.

This was the moment when he sid, 'I hear you call me the Revolutionary King.' He was addressing Monika who looked startled. How did he know? She had made the remark in Bangkok only the day before, talking with his principal private secretary. 'You are right!' He pressed one hand down on the table. 'When my brother died, I became my brother. I did what he wished to do.'

I asked the question Stephenson had raised so often. Could a Buddhist society survive in this modern age?

Yes, he said: what the west regarded as the 'soft' philosophy of Buddhism could resist 'hard' enemies. It was a matter of knowing when to yield, and when to pivot and use your opponent's strength against him. Good men in World War Two had defeated totalitarian enemies because they had right on their side. Churchill knew Hitler's empire was spiritually rotten, and with limited resources, he had turned Hitler's strength into Hitler's weakness. The king knew Stephenson by the wartime codename: Intrepid. It was a word he liked. It represented a continuous spirit of resistance: in wartime, resistance to external evil: and in peacetime, resistance to orthodoxy.

I said Stephenson had made enemies on his own side because he refused to play bureaucratic games. He was an amateur. General Sir Colin Gubbins, who ran Force 136 and the Siamese White Elephants, had said he looked for amateurs who must struggle for a living in peacetime: 'As a regular army officer,' Gubbins had once told me, 'I realised I didn't want military officers. They were too ready to trust each other. In real life, you can trust nobody.'

That was when the king said he trusted nobody outside that room.

The king did not trust anyone much because of the intrigues, the concealment in public of what went on in ambitious minds, the corruption of values. He recognised that most people did not think and act sensibly under certain kinds of pressure. King's Men believed in what he was trying to do; but Bangkok was probably the worst place on earth for indiscretions; sexual, verbal, conspiratorial. He had one or two thoroughly reliable supporters. He said of one: 'He's totally loyal but a little stupid and so I can't trust him to do the wisest thing in a crisis.' Of another: 'A good man, devoted, but a terrible gambler. He can lose a small fortune betting on football matches. Then, when he's short of money, he swallows a lot of valium and climbs into bed on the afternoon of a horse race or a soccer game. If he can't trust himself, how can I trust him?'

He had been struck by what Judge William Webster, the former FBI director, had said in 1987 when he appeared before Capitol Hill hearings to confirm his appointment as director of the CIA. Webster read from Stephenson's words about the need for the world to understand that during World War Two, two weapons had achieved victory. The atomic bomb was obviously dangerous. The art of covert warfare was so secret, the public was unaware of its lethal power, and it required people of integrity. 'I can't put it better,' the new CIA director had said.

Secrecy, said the king, enabled governments to put out half-truths about current history. Historians of the cold war knew little about the details because of systematic misrepresentation. His kingdom suffered from such misrepresentations. Communism had not been beaten by high-tech weaponry, but by improvisation.

Later he showed us how he was improvising to clean up a little of the damage done by the cold war. We walked through land reclaimed from salty marshland, between freshly planted rubber trees, to a jungle factory made from bamboo and palm leaves. Inside were soldiers carving wooden limbs. 'It's cheaper than importing from America,' he said drily. 'Farmers still get their legs and arms blown off by landmines, and none of the manufacturers is going to repair the damage inflicted on millions.'

Each day began early with an unheralded briefing. Vehicles appeared from nowhere and the drivers waited, engines running, until the king drove to the head of the convoy in his own roadster. Sometimes we hurtled off to an airbase and were flown to another destination. The efficiency of these operations was impressive. They were in such sharp contrast to the chaos of Bangkok traffic, we could see how tempting it must be to impose order. It was the Ninth Rama's personal influence, though, that brought it about. He was trapped. Nothing got done unless he was there to see to it. I remembered what a critic of royalty, Professor Sulak Sivaraksa, had written: 'As time passed, the king gained the upper hand. The creation became the creator.'

He flew us over the region where V was killed. By sheer force of personality, she, too, had very slowly pushed back the boundaries of docility in the face of powerful outlaws. Deforestation of mountains was causing devastating floods, and illegal logging was rampant. V had persuaded small businessmen to plant trees that would hold the watersheds, but now she was gone, the lawbreakers were back and nothing was done to stop them. The king became so engrossed in discussing a plan to build a giant dam that would hold the floodwaters, he stood map in hand as we landed. Since none of his four engineers dared tell him to sit and buckle up, he went flying down the aisle when the plane stopped. But when the doors opened, the iron mask was in place and the assembled dignitaries saw only an icon appear.

There were always monks at the site of each project, and a quiet cere-mony to bless the work, but so much of it seemed dependent upon his pres-ence as the representative of Buddha. He kept insisting that Buddhism was a philosophy; that it was folly to rely on superstition; that he respected all religious beliefs. People should not see him as a miracle-worker. What would happen when he was gone? Whenever we were in Moslem territory, local villagers appeared to accept him as their protector. But I later visited the Moslems' national leader in hospital where he had undergone a multi-bypass heart operation at the king's expense. The Sheikul Islam council was meeting around the leader's cot and nodded in unison when he told me: 'We Moslems have been here as long as the Thais. We have a right to our lands.' Bombs were blowing up trains in the Moslem provinces, but the king refused to retaliate. He had requested that no vengeance be taken when the Princess of the South was killed, but asked for an investigation into the eco-nomic causes of the rage leading to that act of terrorism.

Monika remembered a passage she had seen marked in a book in the Princess Mother's apartment. It referred to a Jewish rabbi in New York: 'He accepted that the future of his people depended upon his actions, his will-ingness to be the sacrifice.'

In New York my literary agent and lawyer, Paul Gitlin, was asked by a king's representative what should be done with royalties if the Ninth Rama pub-lished in Thai his own translation of a book I had written about Sir William Stephenson and secret-intelligence. I came back from Bangkok and said the royalties should go to the king's rural projects. Stephenson, now dead, would have liked that. There came another request for me to see the king. I flew back and this time met him at another work-base, the palace his mother had developed on the mountain-top near Chiang Mei. We talked for four hours in complete privacy about his work. I came out to find cour-tiers anxiously speculating on what was going on. I still had no clue, but the king had said he would like me to spend more time in the country to get a real sense of what he was trying to do. This was when he repeated: 'It will be dangerous for myself and for you. I still have a lot of enemies and they are stronger than I am except when the countryfolk rally to my side.'

Paul Gitlin said later, 'He wants you to write his story.' Paul was also a director and legal adviser to a big publishing house. He had calculated that the king's translation of my book would make something like a million dollars for the royal projects. This later proved close to the mark. Paul said, 'That establishes you don't owe him anything. To write an objective biography, you'll have to get inside the king's mind. That means spending a lot of time with him. Just make sure you pay your own way.' Which I did.

Monika and I moved to Thailand with our daughter Alexandra in late 1990. Authorship is a portable profession and we had other books to write. We remained in the region for several years, living mostly in Bangkok, where Alexandra entered the palace school at the age of four.

Alexandra opened the hidden world to us, because the Siamese find it difficult to talk to outsiders about it, but feel no embarrassment with a child. She would walk with her teachers among the Chitralada trees and hear about the spirits that dwelt in every growing thing and how these kindly spirits were enshrined in small wooden houses garlanded with flowers. One day we found her sitting alone in the lotus position, palms together. 'I'm waiting to go *up*,' she said.

One of her classmates was Vajravira, a son of the Crown Prince. His mother was the actress-consort, Yuvadhida. Everyone called him the Little Prince. He would arrive each day in a chauffeur-driven limousine bristling with military radio antennae. There was an accident in the schoolyard that involved the Little Prince and a girl who was left crying and bleeding while the staff rushed to comfort the boy. It was not his fault that all the attention was concentrated upon him; he was royal even in this new palace without official concubines. He had put his arm around Alexandra on the day she cried because her closest friend was going away, and after that he would help her with her books and console her when things went wrong. Even at this early stage, we glimpsed a reason why Princess Ubol, Lotus Blossom, ran off to America. The Little Prince was being slowly smothered by the habits of centuries. He began to fade from sight behind bodyguards escorting him to and from school. He was like a small ghost in the classroom, the only place where he could be his own mischievous and yet also kindly self.

Alexandra's sources were not confined to that exotic setting. We lived by Siam Square where she spent most of her time outside school chattering with people who brushed the leaves from the pathways and ran their tiny foodstalls. One of them made flower arrangements for nearby hotels and made me think of Mama's mother long ago, painstakingly stitching together huge garlands of gorgeous petals for the palace. The flower-lady was married to a detective who told us that he sometimes saw and heard ghosts from the days of Dowager Queen Sawang when he made the night rounds of the Palace of Lotus Ponds. It stood on the other side of a waterway on which floated enormous lily-pads, big enough for white egrets to use them like emerald-green aircraft carriers. Here also was the temple containing the ashes of the king's father.

The temple was being renovated by Police-General Vasit whose honesty had made him politically unpopular. The king had placed him there, as he placed others who might be in danger into sanctuaries as long as they were 'Out of Sanction'. The phrase caused Vasit some wry amusement. In his time as a secret agent in Laos he had been 'Out of Sanction', meaning he could expect no US government help if he got into trouble. Vasit's job at the temple satisfied his natural inclination for Buddhist duties. And across the street was police headquarters. Sometimes I would glimpse his monk-like figure slipping on foot through the dense traffic to where we first met in his police-general's office. He continued to speak quietly to young police officers about the need to stay away from every form of bribery and corruption.

One day he told me, 'Too much time is taken up with police escorts for every politician and bureaucrat going from one cocktail party to another. Ordinary people are not getting the protection they need.' For being so outspoken, he had been punished. The king had saved him with a task that met Vasit's spiritual needs.

But who or what would save the king from the consequences of his own frankness? His mother avoided malicious misquotation by working as far from palace in-fighting as she could get, in the furthermost tip of northern Thailand, on the highest mountain ridge. The tides of court intrigue were sweeping away the Little Prince and she saw little of the Crown Princes's family. She dispossessed herself of everything not essential to her creation of another Chitralada-style Inner Kingdom.

Alexandra mastered the palace language employed to address the highest-ranking royalty. One day, at the Princess Mother's northern base, Alexandra spoke in the language appropriate for someone entitled to a many-layered purple umbrella. 'We are away from all that,' said Mama, laughing. She was wearing her usual jogging pants, blouse and gym shoes, and was at work on tissue-culture on a wooden deck overlooking the territory of a local brigand known as the Highwayman.

25

Mama and the Highwayman

Mᴀᴍᴀ was as far from the cramped little Lausanne apartment as she was from the shop-house where she was born, but she was back among the poor and the disadvantaged. The Highwayman whose fiefdom she bordered was a vigorous brigand who looked ageless astride his caparisoned mule at the head of 15,000 well-armed soldiers. Whenever she approached his armed camp, and crossed into Burma over the little bridge at Mae Sai, his people fell to their knees to honour her.

Around her mountain-top home were straw-thatched bamboo houses and cheap foodstalls where the cuisine was infinitely varied, thanks to the new crops she introduced and the old ways of preparing food with *nam plaa* sauce made from rotten fish which the true northerner could not live without. There were landscaped gardens with hardy flowers and plants she had transferred from her Swiss mountain haunts, and other botanical splendours. At first sight, they seemed incongruous in valleys of savage beauty. These gardens, though, were not purely ornamental. Village girls had been taught to grow long-stemmed flowers, and how to package them to be flown to hotels in the cities of Asia riding the crest of an economic boom nobody had ever thought possible. The money that came flowing back competed with the body-brokers. The sale of little girls to brothels seemed at an end.

Mama, paddling her own boat once more, was just as self-effacing as when she was the little orphan girl near the start of the century, although she was revered in her Inner Kingdom of Doi Tung. It covered 300 square miles of highlands wedged into the Golden Triangle between Burma and Laos, rich in forest colours and streaked by the bright plumage of exotic birds. When Lek came to the throne, there were still rhinoceros and mouse-deer, sun bears and the huge 900-kilogram gaur, hoopoes and hornbills and antelope. Mama's projects included a small sanctuary to preserve the specimens that escaped extinction. Eighty per cent of the forests had been destroyed by illegal loggers, by slash-and-burn nomad farmers, and by the Highwayman. Mama approached him in Buddhist fashion. It was a test of wills.

The Highwayman accumulated enormous wealth by taxing every drug smuggler who passed through his domain. He operated like the warlords that once split up China. He was called General Khun Sa in a ten-count indictment against him announced in Brooklyn, New York, by the US Attorney-General, Richard Thornburgh, who did not regard him as a roguish tax collector, but as the mastermind behind a business grossing US$200 million a year. He was said to break opium production records yearly, and to account for seventy per cent of the world's heroin, pure enough to snort or smoke. He had once controlled villages nestling in the high valleys around Doi Tung, Mountain of Flags.

Doi Tung was where Mama began to push out the Highwayman's lackeys when she was in her eighties. Her home looked like a Swiss chalet, except that the architecture was that of the old Lanna kingdom, probably the original home of the Thais, encompassing that part of Old Siam once accessible only by elephant or by rafts moving slowly upstream through narrow gorges. This part of Old Siam stretched from the Shan plateau of Upper Burma into the Chinese province of Yunnan, and across the great Mekong river fed by the snows of Tibet. Here, Tsuji of Japan had cut his wartime deals with Chinese gangsters and the young Siamese officers of Northern Command who, from Phao onward, took turns governing Bangkok by coup for the next four decades.

Mama relied on a man she called her Chief Gardener, Pi-Chai. He walked barefoot and dressed in the grey tunic and pants of a labourer when he was with the villagers but in Bangkok he had to wear a business suit and was better known as Prince Disnadda Diskul. His father had been a friend of Dr Mahidol and knew Mama when she was a girl freshly arrived in Boston, Mass. Pi-Chai had gone to Sutton Valance prep-school in England, competed at White City as a champion sprinter, and was placed among the world's top marksmen at Bisley. He went on to business-school in the United States. Like so many bright young Thais, he did all this on King's Scholarships that austerely covered only school and board. Money was so short that he took no vacations home for years on end. 'Then, just before returning for good,' he said, 'I wrote my Dad two letters in blue and red ink. The red said what I did *not* want to do – work for the palace or government. In blue ink I wrote that I was now part of the modern world. Dad met me in Hong Kong to talk about what the present king was trying to do. Dad died, and the king asked me to replace Dad at Chitralada. A lot of courtiers said I was too young. Also I kept beating the king at badminton.

I'd have him on his back and sweating. The court might disapprove but the king was glad to have someone who wasn't afraid to thrash him. He asked me to talk to his mother and, within seven days, she suggested I work for her. And that was twenty-three years ago.'

Pi-Chai was fifty, stocky, muscular from tramping over the mountains, and low-key in an English schoolboy kind of way. We drove his Land Rover through the villages once controlled by the Highwayman. 'I carried a gun under the driving seat for months after I first came here,' he said. 'I kept the gun hidden. I didn't want to scare the locals. Their only real cash-crop was the opium and they made little out of that, just pennies. The profits went to buyers, the price doubling at each stage – US$5,750 per kilo in Chiang Mei, and so on until it reached US$150,000 wholesale in America. The biggest demand was for Uoglobe No.4 heroin, with a logo of two lions resting their forepaws on a globe.'

The Highwayman spent a good proportion of his drug money on an army and arms. He had boys as young as twelve who practised with wooden rifles, and veterans of Nationalist Chinese campaigns against communist insurgents. The Nationalists had lived off the opium trade and he showed me a white house that looked as if it belonged in a Chicago suburb: it was owned by a Chinese dragon-lady who ran mule-trains smuggling opium out of General Khun Sa's territory.

The Highwayman liked talking to Mama who was open-minded about his claim to be fighting for the independence long ago promised to the Shan people. Police-General Vasit, tending the temple containing Papa's ashes, regarded the man as purely evil, and that any claim that he would give up the opium business in exchange for help in establishing his Shan State was a sham.

The Shan people were tough and the British had steered clear of them after annexing north Burma in 1880. During World War Two, the British had promised the Shan independence from central government for fighting the Japanese. When the British ended colonial rule in Burma in 1948, they forgot the Shan whose leaders felt they had been tricked. By 1960 they were in rebellion and had to live on 'jungle food' like *chakachan* grasshoppers smeared in honey – unless they made money from the opium which the British had once collected.

Mama believed the conflict could be resolved if people applied simple Buddhist logic. She recalled historical hypocrisies: nobody was without guilt. In the 1850s, the head of one of the largest opium smuggling companies was US President Franklin Delano Roosevelt's grandfather, Warren Delano II, competing with the British East India Company in the illegal sale of opium to China. Later came the Chinese *chiu chao* whose underground operations originated as a conspiracy to defeat Mongolian conquerors. As failed rebels, they survived through crime and drifted into the most lucrative business: opium.

'Khun Sa's battlefield is down there,' said Pi-Chai, looking out from the Princess Mother's home toward the bald hills that began where the frontier wriggled along the high ridge. 'I'll cream him yet.' But the words were cheerfully spoken, as if the Highwayman was just another personage to be beaten at badminton. Before Mama's residence was built here, Pi-Chai had lived 'in a kind of tree-house', preparing the way for the Princess Mother, talking with villagers by day, promising them the king's full protection. The Ninth Rama had trekked through the area by mule, and although he thought it physically dangerous for his mother, he knew better than to try and stop her. General Khun Sa was Falstaffian, a noisy braggard in some ways, and yet he put up portraits of Lek and Queen Sirikit in the open-sided, thatch-roofed wooden pavilions he built in the Shan State. His real problem was that, although he was a warlord, his resources were controlled by the Chinese *chiu chao* gangs in Thailand.

'They do his banking in Thailand,' said Pi-Chai. 'All his logistical support, his arms and ammunition, everything is here. Every other route, through Burma or China, is blocked. For a time, his bankers tried to stop what I was doing. We had some shoot-outs. The Princess Mother came and talked to the hill tribes. She had their support. She had no illusions. She found just how many young girls were being sold into prostitution, and how ignorance, desperation and poverty made such evil things possible.'

She started a Buddhist rehabilitation centre for local opium addicts. She appointed a Black Panther of the Border Police Guards, now a monk. He was slender and sinewy as jungle vine. He wasted few words. A majority of the addicts were cured, he said, 'through harsh but compassionate religious discipline' that began before dawn and ended late at night. Back-sliders were given two more chances. 'After that, "incurables" get just enough opium to ease their pain'.

Mama had up-to-the minute statistics to tell her when young girls quietly disappeared from the villages: she knew how parents were only too ready to believe the body-brokers who bought girls, the younger the better, promising they would work as waitresses in city restaurants. Mama knew how girls were sent overseas: in places like Tokyo, they became prisoners, never able to pay back the cost of their airfares which had been advanced by the brokers at iniquitous rates of interest. The business was in small boys as well as girls, and it was hugely profitable. Like the opium trade, it could easily afford big bribes to keep officialdom quiet. Mama kept records on each hill tribe and village. Local people had identity cards; but Pi-Chai said, 'We don't want a police state and we explain these i.d. cards are for the people's own protection.' His way of undercutting the body-brokers was to make it possible for villagers to earn a decent wage all year round.

The booming Asian economies created markets for new crops. Mama still clung to the belief, though, that rice was key to the kingdom's prosperity: the Thai word for exports still translates as rice-out. A new high-yield variety had changed the structure of the rice plant, producing shorter tougher stems. The increased use of nitrogen resulted in bigger seeds, or panicles, with a genetic resistance to fifteen of the traditional pests. Mama had reservations about the forecasts that there would be 4.3 billion rice eaters in another thirty years in the region, requiring an increase in production of 10 million tonnes a year every year from now on. Too much depended on the wild-eyed optimism of bankers who thought Asia was going to overshadow the west in terms of wealth. She would rather concentrate on developing inner resources, making the kingdom self-sufficient, so that when foreign markets dried up, her villages would be reaping the benefits of their own produce. Modern industrial development was eating up the ricelands. Mama found a super-rice, directly seeded to avoid the laborious transplanting of seedlings. There was a certain mystique to rice, she said. The Emperor of Japan was God of the Ripened Rice Plant. Lord Vishnu created rice. Indra taught mankind to raise it. Rice was a state of mind, not just a food.

'The Princess Mother made these valleys so relatively prosperous that Khun Sa can see what we're achieving. If he's honest about wanting a way to get out of the illegal drug business, we've shown him how,' said Pi-Chai. The Highwayman's Nationalist Chinese soldiers had been useful in the cold war, though, and all they knew or cared about was the growing of opium. The use of other mercenaries in the nearby Laotian highlands had been financed by drugs.

US Army Major Wade Sheridan Lnenicka, at twenty-one, had been asked to join a covert operation. 'I was told if I was captured, the US government would disavow me,' he said. 'I declined the offer of a monthly salary paid in thousands of US dollars, cash, tax free. Drugs were far more dangerous to Americans than any military threat, so we became the cause of our own defeat.' He put this into a Pentagon paper seen by the Ninth Rama whose chief of narcotics-control told me, 'I'm tired of telling each new American drug tsar that Americans have to reduce their own market and its huge profits. We cannot cover every inch of our borders. There's such enormous money at stake. In the years of American Prohibition, law-enforcement was impossible for the same reason. In those days the Americans had only themselves to blame and that is still so.' As he talked,

I could see an endless vista of narrow mule trails for one-time use by smugglers. The dusty trails passed below Mama's house which was almost invisible from below the ridgeline. The smuggling routes were switched constantly, and they looked like holes in a sieve. No army in the world could plug those holes.

Mama put no barriers between herself and the villagers. She dressed in working clothes, just as they did. She mobilised villagers who built roads with the same speed as those at the Palace of Phu Ping, and with the same sense, or so it seemed to me, of helping themselves by serving the Princess Mother. Pi-Chai twisted the arms of business executives to get them to invest, but they had difficulty grasping the way Buddhism was being put to work by a woman who conjured up volunteers. If they could not assess labour costs, western-trained accountants said they could not fathom the cost of anything else. International corporations wound up making donations to improve their business chances in Bangkok. The cold war had justified foreign aid because the region lay north of the Khao Khor mountain range, which was a natural barrier to the southern plain. When there was a visible danger that frightened the west, aid was forthcoming. It dried up when the danger was gone. To create more reliable longterm help, the Princess Mother visualised road and rail lines passing through warlord territory to south west China where a sublime climate made it possible to harvest three crops of rice a year. She ignored political frontiers, as did the local people, and thought in terms of a region that would share in mutual prosperity. The US Drug Enforcement Agency had the Highwayman's fields bombed from inside Burma. The west had fixed ways of doing things that clashed with her baffling Buddhist bolshevism.

She knew the Asian bubble would burst. The threat of largescale physical violence had receded, but she said passive violence was growing in the form of exploitation and greed. This would cause a crisis, and the first to suffer would be the people in these remote valleys. She dealt with this at the Midnight Museum.

It stood on the outskirts of the nearby town of Chiang Rai. When I first landed there, it boasted one small airstrip. Anyone looking for it had to rely on a small wooden post in a side lane that said TO THE AIRPORT. Then it became the hub of international tourist traffic, and a distressing percentage of this was sex-tourism. Foreign newspapers blatantly advertised the cheapness and availability of 'young virgins', boys or girls. An exquisite little monastery bordering the old airstrip was suddenly surrounded by hardtop runways. 'Massive machines and cement mixers violate the soil,' wrote a Bangkok columnist who signed himself Somsak J. 'Someone maliciously opened up the holds of a few hundred Japanese superfreighters and let out all the Toyotas, Isuzus, Mitsubishis, Nissans and pulled the bolts on motorbikes called Kawasaki, Suzuki and Yamaha so that we have now no less than 253 internally combusting and noxious exhaust-spewing cylinders per square block. In the Terribly New Testament in today's religion of the Supreme Worship of Financial Gain No Matter What Impact It Has Upon Thy Neighbour, the Word is – "What wealthy scoundrels lust for, let not the masses put asunder."'

Mama challenged the despoilation of Chiang Rai and the Ninth Rama said to me, 'I don't know what I shall do when she dies. In her sixties, we said she should slow down. We said it again in her seventies. And now she is in her nineties, and still she has these five-year plans. But after she goes, I shall be the old one.'

The Midnight Museum was unplanned. It now rescued the past for the tribes of the Wa, Ahka, Lahu and of Laos. It was a school, a temple, an experiment in humanity and in architecture. It was built by another former Black Panther, a border guard named Nakorn Pongnoi who had been sent to Stanford University in California on a King's Scholarship. Nakorn sat monk-like and barefoot on a wooden bench in fifty acres of recovered swampland. Behind him rose a multi-tiered wooden temple, so strange that it was easy to miss a lifesize sculpture of the Princess Mother with one hand outstretched, sitting on a grassy mound outside. Others had wanted to raise the statue on a platform, but she insisted it blend into where she was happiest, in the wilderness, with children who boarded at the Midnight Museum. They were brought in from outlying villages to learn the ancient Lanna crafts. She covered all the costs; but as in everything she had ever done since she was a young widow, she made her children earn their keep. They had to follow the regular government curriculum as well as carve and paint and design; and then they had to help with the chores.

The temple was called the Midnight Museum because inside were thousands of candles, as if here it was always night. It balanced on massive legs of teakwood, brought in from the smashed temples of Laos and polished with age. Inside were scores of wooden carvings covered in the same dark patina. On a night of the full moon, a few narrow beams of natural light descended from an open-sided tower some 100-metres above. The tower sat on tiers of pavilion-like structures, each larger than the one above, surrounding a narrow three-storey wooden enclosure whose bars encircled a 300-year-old statue with the large and distinctive ears characteristic of the Buddha images in the old Kingdom of Lanna. The building was uncannily silent. It was built from hundreds of individual pieces of wood. 'We scoured the countryside,' said Nakorn. 'We dragged back timber from ancient buildings destroyed by bombing or falling down from neglect.' His Buddha was cast from gold and brass in accordance with the 108 auspicious signs of a true Buddha. Its long ears signified royalty. The original Lanna Buddha was said to have manifested himself as King of Kings to a proud but foolish king of the south who refused to heed Buddhist teachings until an explosion of flame gave forth this Buddha robed as the transcendental monarch. I was reminded of the Buddha in the temple where the ashes of the king's father were kept, and the note that it was 'made by a highly cultivated ancient Laotian tribe'.

This Buddha came from a temple in Laos where a 300-year-old abbot was said to still sit upright and uncorrupted, his spirit having silently crept out of his body, nobody was sure when. It was an odd story, made odder because it was investigated by a Soviet Red Army medical team in Laos. Together with Igor Lisevitch, a Soviet orientalist, they reported the abbot's body was perfectly preserved, even to bones and internal organs. I had found the report in a Moscow publication. There were photographs of a mummified monk sitting upright in the lotus position; and X-rays that showed a normal skeleton. The Russians wrote that the abbot had meditated without food or water until his followers could find no sign of breath, whereupon they sealed his body against termites. The Russians said they were satisfied the abbot had indeed lived three centuries ago. They offered no explanation, but their scientific tests had been part of Soviet research into paranormal events, conducted on behalf of the KGB. How this would serve a secret service, it was hard to imagine. I told Nakorn the story and he said, 'You'd be surprised how many western intelligence agencies have looked into such things.'

One day I found the Princess Mother sitting at her work table on the balcony overlooking the Highwayman's fiefdom. She was cloning King Mongkut's favourite breadfruit tree in the Grand Palace. The technology seemed as miraculous as the 300-year-old abbot. She knew about him: the temple was founded 650 years ago and still displayed a stone toilet seat and clay sewage pipes from 'the oldest sewage system known to us'. There was a bronze cannon made in the 1400s that was built for use on the backs of war-elephants. It had been lying in the unsorted debris of the Forest-of-Teak Monastery over there, in the direction of the Blind Bonze of Luang Prabang in Laos. The Blind Bonze was consulted by western intelligence agents in the 1960s when they wanted to know what he predicted to credulous communist leaders. Then the western spies could anticipate future communist moves.

'Credulous communists?'

'O yes,' said Mama, 'in Laos, they were simple farmers.'

The Revolutionary Party of Laos had only professed communism to keep their Soviet Russian, Chinese and Vietnamese visitors happy. A Russian transport plane had made a forced landing here, and she had arranged for the crew to be provided with food and lodgings until the aircraft could be repaired and go back to wherever it came from.

She took a group of cells from a piece of plant, immersing it in a chemical solution that stimulated the cells to reproduce into something resembling the protocorm of a seed to grow into a plantlet. This is tissue-culture's version of a seedling, and she wanted hundreds of such seedlings to replace watershed forests destroyed by nomadic farming. In villages below, there were small sheds employing young girls trained in the delicate art of cloning. A Japanese electronics and bearings manufacturer, Minebea, had invested in the work and now claimed that the Thai tissue-culture industry was the biggest in the world. The Swiss company, Nestlé, searched the world for a coffee plant that would grow well at Doi Tung. 'It was a kind of corporate intelligence operation,' said Pi-Chai. The Princess Mother chuckled quietly.

A fog drifted along the tops of the mountains: smoke from thousands of fires set by cultivators burning off the vegetation to prepare new ground for opium poppies. It came winding down from the lower slopes of Tibet and Nepal, and the phantom scarves crept eastward through Laos as if an aeroplane trailed an incredibly long advertising banner for the narcotics trade.

'The king banned the sale and consumption of opium,' said Pi-Chai. 'But of course he couldn't pass any laws. He could only hope people would listen, and meanwhile he offered ways to kick the habit of earning a living from the poppies.' He showed me small allotments of opium poppies grown for the incurable addicts. The poppies had no petals after a recent harvest; there were bare pods instead, like large dark nuts, scored by the tappers who collected the raw gum of opium, saplike, which quickly oxidised to the deep brown familiar to opium-smokers.

Pi-Chai's programmes depended so heavily on the Princess Mother's extraordinary charisma that I felt a chill of apprehension as he rolled out his charts with such enthusiasm. He had shown farmers how to grow and profit from oranges, lemons, limes, red kidney and pinto beans. 'But developing substitute crops and then marketing them takes time. I've searched for a mix of quick-return and longterm crops. And now we pay the people here a salary, lend money without interest, and give them a stake in the land. To foil speculators, the land can't be re-sold except by common consent after a certain period. When I see an unexplained peak in a village's income, I take a closer look. It usually comes from the sale of children of

Chinese origin as Taiwanese sing-song girls. They command a much higher price in the brothels of Bangkok.'

The king's mother could not legislate virtue. She said any improvement in human behaviour had to come from within. So long as the enormous markets existed for the buying and selling of children, of human slaves, of illegal drugs, precious stones and timber, wealthy lawbreakers could always corrupt the lawmakers. Mama worked within a small community, but even here it took time to prove that it was worthwhile to follow Buddhist rules.

Lek now issued warnings without regard for what politicians might say about his interference. He feared that progress being made in voluntary reforms would be undone if the country became infected by more greed in a blind race to industrialise. 'The Poor Man's Way' would provide markets for all these new crops within the kingdom. Food exports earned foreign currency, but Thailand must keep its head in the wave of excitement about becoming an Asian Tiger. If it relied on outside investment, and financial institutions collapsed, how would these new farmers repay the loans; who would buy all these oranges and lemons? The country had to enrich itself from within, not by selling itself to foreign speculators.

But in Bangkok, few who were busy making serious money listened.

Mama's world was self-contained. She did her best to change the habits of the several thousand people who were now living amicably together, despite big differences in tribal origins. Other than her stacks of detective novels, her only indulgence was the old two-seat helicopter tethered by her home. I like to think it was one of the two machines Lek wanted to borrow from President Johnson. She used it to nip around her projects, and on days like this one, fly along the margin of that sinister scarf of smoke in search of clues to its distant source.

The old helicopter came out of the Border Patrol Police leftovers from the cold war. Its pilot never discussed his past. It was Pi-Chai who told me, 'He rescued eight badly wounded soldiers trapped on a ridge after being ambushed by insurgents. The damage to all our aircraft in that skirmish was extensive but this helicopter was still operable, although damaged by small-arms fire. He had to dump enough fuel to make each flight until he brought down all eight men. If he'd miscalculated by a decimal point, they'd have all been killed.'

When Mama wanted to cross into Burma, she went in a little Swiss electric go-cart. There was an American magazine in her quarters, with an account of a bold reporter's dangerous journey into the Highwayman's Shan State by mule train through narrow mountain trails. This was how the warlord liked to be seen in the west; mysterious, unreachable except with his consent. The bold reporter failed to mention two hardtop roads built by the Thais straight into the Highwayman's Tiger Camp.

From time to time, Crown Princess Sirindhorn drove there. She saw the fantastic possibilities for expanding this northern Inner Kingdom peacefully in the old way when national boundaries were meaningless. She said the soft resolve of Buddhist non-violence would outlast the harshness of our times and quoted an exasperated Catholic priest. He had written, back in 1670, that the 'confidence of Buddhist priests is the principal cause of their refusal to accept Christianity'. Now, after 400 years of foreign evangelism, only half-a-million professed to be Christians out of some 65 million Thais. Yet some of the most prestigious schools were Christian: the Catholic Assumption College in Bangkok took up one side of a city block. 'The Siamese had confidence in their own beliefs,' said Princess Sirindhorn. She recalled a Bishop Bigandet of Rome who, 200 years before, wrote that in Buddhist monks 'strength and energy maintain a vitality throughout convulsions of all descriptions. It is impossible to account for such a phenomenon, deeply rooted in the very soul of the people.'

These deep-rooted beliefs came up in startling ways. One day, Pi-Chai's mother died in her eighties. 'She donated her remaining years to the Princess Mother so that she will have that much longer to live,' said the former Bisley sharpshooter who had once refused to work for the palace because he wanted to make money the modern way.

But Mama's era was coming to an end. Her death was approaching. And with it, the chaos feared by her son, the Ninth Rama.

26

Coups and Intrigues

THERE was a bent and grey-haired old woman who always knew when a military coup was brewing because she carried in her head the secret of making an almost indestructible paper to be found nowhere else in the world. Each time there was a coup, a proper constitution had to be inscribed upon this special paper, even by the most arrogant of army strongmen. Lek, as a king whose mother was born in the back alleys of the city, knew each community whose name indicated its dominant and traditional skill. Fireworks, for instance, were still made in the district known as Ban Dol Mao which meant the place of fireworks. Ban Kradaat was where the craftsmen lived who made this unique paper whose full name was *kradaat khoi*. The Ninth Rama could tell when trouble was brewing because he had an advantage over most generals ambitious for political power: he knew where *khoi* was made, and who made it, and when.

All the *khoi* makers had died out except old Mrs Bang-orn, but her neighbourhood kept its name. In the winter of 1991–2, she got out her wooden hammer and board and set about the secret procedure known only to herself. She looked for aspen bushes of a species not found outside the kingdom. She needed branches, not too old and not too young, growing near ricefields. Nobody else had the secret of just when the branches were right; and how to blacken them with ashes from the burned trunks of banana trees. When all this was done, the *khoi* had to be dyed gold. *Khoi* was highly resistant to insects and other tropical enemies of paper. It did not turn yellow nor crumble. It lined *khon* dance masks to soak up sweat. *Khoi* had the strength to hold the mask's shape.

Alexandra studied Thai classical dance and when she was blessed by the Dance Master, the gravity of the moment was reflected in the faces of palace dancers who had grown old and were able once again to feel the spiritual buoyancy of the ritual when the Dance Master blessed the mask on our daughter's head. Monika reached out to the mask and stopped in mid-air as if it gave out a tremendous heat. A director of the king's personal affairs cried out in alarm, '*Don't!*' If an onlooker touched the mask at this perilous moment, demons would glue it to the dancer's head and a special priest would have to be called in to loosen it with complicated rituals.

Khoi was used for centuries to make temple books, folded horizontally. When opened, each volume became a continuous piece of paper dangling downward. These imperishable temple books were vanishing rapidly as Japanese 'tourists' roamed the countryside buying them cheap from remote temples, knowing their value as the only records of early Siamese history. A precious and ancient copy of the sacred Tripitaka scriptures of Buddhism, inscribed on *khoi* long ago, had been presented to the Ninth Rama by the President of China. Royal orders were issued on *khoi* paper recycled from old archival documents. But for a new constitution only fresh *khoi* would do.

Mrs Bang-orn made it from scratch. She had done this so frequently that she knew what was coming when the order reached her for a continuous twelve meters of *khoi* which would fold into sixty pages, the proper length of a constitution. And so the king was forewarned.

It was three hours after midnight on 29th April, 1992 that the Ninth Rama was playing the saxophone at a private Chitralada dinner. The queen danced with General Suchinda Krapayoon. Later, Suchinda went to talk to the Crown Prince who sat at his own table. 'It's strange the Crown Prince is here,' said one of the king's close aides. 'He doesn't usually come to these things. And look at the men at his table. They're all crooks.' Then Suchinda left the room without bothering to bow to the monarch who sat with his jacket slung over the back of his chair, as usual. He had put an old cartoon from *MAD* magazine on a rostrum: in the centre of the cartoon was the single word, THINK!

Just below the surface of such evenings, there were invisible cross-currents, and some were benevolent. Tonight was special: this was the fortieth wedding anniversary of the king and queen. My dinner partner was an expert on 'elephant language'. I had asked Crown Princess Sirindhorn for more information about Auspiciously Significant Elephants. She had drawn the points that identify a White Elephant, and also the way work-elephants are made to obey the mahout by the clever application of a goad to specific areas of the animal's body. There were also instructions on how an enemy war-elephant can be brought down by pricking it between certain toes or joints. My partner described 'the only village in the world where the people knew how to talk to elephants'. The inhabitants passed their secret by word of mouth down through the generations. They would talk to me if the king wished it. He had marked the secret location of the village on a map.

The other undercurrent this night was unease. Courtiers wore tight smiles. Few danced. The old prince who first investigated the King's Death Case tried to inject some jollity by dancing with the queen. He said that in the early years of the reign, 'There were wonderful parties – everyone so happy!'

Suchinda re-entered the room. The political wind was changing. As Suchinda made his rounds, people bowed.

The Ninth Rama was curiously detached. All he could do was wait for the general to make his move. 'At such times,' he said later, 'I prepare for whatever is coming. I store away advance information. And then I wait . . . Buddhism is very complex. It has many grades. The highest level is to attain absolute purity in yourself. You may call that selfish – a selfish motive. And that is true – it is selfish, purely selfish, but to attain this purity you must do everything that is not selfish. That will seem a paradox to you. One has to discard everything that one thinks is one's own. In Buddhism, one doesn't want to be on top because there's no bottom and no top. And there is no sin. There is only an original purity which has been spoilt or covered by what we call sin. You may believe in the doctrine of original sin, but in Buddhism, there is original purity.' And so he made no judgements, and tried not to think ill of those who might be plotting against him.

The end of the intermission was signalled at the piano by Manrat, who had started playing jazz with Elder Brother Nan and Little Brother Lek back in 1946. The king swung into one of his own favourite compositions. It was 'Blue Night', and I had only just learned that this and another five he had written for Mike Todd's *Peepshow* had generated royalties that he turned over to his reform projects. The balladeer king was immersed in his music again. There was nothing else he could do until the Armed Forces Supreme Commander showed his hand.

Suchinda's men seized the government broadcasting services next day. Soldiers replaced traffic policemen and soon the Bangkok traffic was flowing so evenly that in Siam Square, stall-holders and shoppers told each other what a good thing it was to have the army take charge.

Then Suchinda broke his own promise to hold free elections, and he made himself prime minister. The appearance of fax-machines, though, had brought a new freedom of expression. It was hard to use the old device of invoking the *lèse majesté* charge of disloyalty against anonymous authors of faxes flying around the country and contradicting government propaganda. The law could not be invoked as it had been in the past to prevent the king himself from 'bringing the monarchy into disrepute'. It was an absurd abuse of Article 112 of the penal code which stated: 'Whoever defames, insults or threatens the King, Queen, the Heir Apparent or the Regent shall be punished with imprisonment.' If Lek said anything that a dictatorial regime decided was a criticism of the Crown Prince and his supporters, the king himself could be charged under the law of *lèse majesté*; but this was increasingly unlikely. In this new crisis, he stayed in his study, reading a sampling of the wildly flying faxes. They attacked Suchinda and the Crown Prince and supported the king. Then counterattacking faxes smeared Suchinda's opponents, but still left the king unscathed. He bided his time. If he moved ahead of public opinion, he might be piously accused of imperilling the sacred institution of the monarchy by exceeding its authority.

Riots erupted. The young and growing middle class in Bangkok was angry. Many called for a counter-coup by General Chamlong Srimuang, an ascetic former governor of the capital who led a well-publicised austere way of life. Chamlong was a skinny figure with close-cropped hair and a grin that split his narrow face in two. He had come across Alexandra once when we were walking in one of the king's big new public parks, and hoisted her onto his shoulder while he talked to us about the impact of foreign investment. He said Japanese golf-clubs destroyed the fertile plains because the Japanese found it cheaper to play golf here, whatever the cost of hotels and the five-hour flight from Tokyo. Each day, six new Japanese factories were opened and 400 new cars appeared on the roads of Bangkok.

He wanted to free Thailand from all foreign influence. From personal experience, he condemned foreign powers who treated the kingdom as a pawn. In the 1960s he had been hired by US Special Forces. In Laos, where the American government denied any military involvement, Chamlong had defended Site 85, the highly secret US installation that was used to direct high-flying US bombers onto targets around Hanoi. Chamlong had seen 'primitive' Vietnamese scale the mountain on its supposedly impregnable side and take Site 85's American specialists by surprise, killing or capturing them. He had learned, he said, a lot of lessons from this; not least, that arrogance of power leads to disaster. He was regarded with suspicion, though, by people who doubted the sincerity of his claims to have rejected the pleasures of the flesh. They saw him as power-hungry. And he had made powerful enemies in the US defense department by speaking about the use of nerve-gas in Laos. A growing volume of the 'freedom faxes' denigrated him with stories of his double-life and sly pretensions of being a true Buddhist.

However, by the third week of May Chamlong was at the head of a citizen uprising against General Suchinda's heavily armed troops. Chamlong vowed to go without food until Suchinda backed off, and he began a hunger strike. The world watched TV pictures of bloody fights between soldiers and students. Hundreds were said to have died and the wounded ran into thousands. All-night curfews were imposed so that the dead could be removed in army trucks with their tarpaulins down, unseen by the public. My wife was lecturing in Dallas, Texas, and TV-news coverage there gave an impression that civil war had broken out. She flew back, and after midnight on 20th May had to get a special police escort to our home, passing the long lines of shrouded trucks. 'They were filled with bodies,' she said. 'Nobody will ever know where they've been dumped.'

From abroad came a stream of urgent messages for the king. A former Danish ambassador who had been a good friend wrote that the Ninth Rama's inaction was a disgrace. King Baudouin wondered if Lek was cut off. Crown Princess Sirindhorn was in Brussels and got through by phone to say that the world's impression was that a bloodbath was in progress. The Crown Prince disowned Suchinda who had gone too far.

Still the king waited. If his timing was wrong, he would cease to exist. 'I must be seen to be impartial by the poor who don't have power,' he said. 'This ensures stability, because those without power know that if they destroy someone who is impartial, they destroy themselves.'

He would not disturb Mama who had broken her hip at Doi Tung, and was in hospital, isolated from the disturbances. It was ironic. The rest of the world knew what was going on. International television news now reached into even the most oppressed communities; but Mama did not have television in her sick-room. The equipment in Lek's study could intercept all radio communications and monitor domestic and international TV channels. His King's Men reported to him on his personal radio net, or they came by foot. When he was sure the people wanted him to act, he sent for the warring generals. They came.

Shortly after midnight, King Bhumibol appeared on live television. He sat in a business suit in the Chitralada room where we had often met. A local TV channel's cameras were feeding pictures to all the networks. The world saw General Suchinda and General Chamlong approach him on their hands and knees.

The king spoke in the manner of a monk but the broadcast of his words was unusually and strangely muffled. His own audio-tapes also recorded what he said: 'It may come as a surprise why I asked you to come to meet in this manner. Everyone knows the situation is very complicated. It can lead our nation to ruin. There may be many other performers and actors involved. You two have been invited because from the very beginning you were confronting each other. If this were to continue, it would lead only to the destruction of Thailand. What is the point of feeling proud to be the winner on top of piles of debris that once constituted the country we have spent so long building up?'

The two generals sank back on their heels and responded in soft tones. Both agreed that a civilian government should take over. They backed out on hands and knees again. Cameras showed the king with iron mask in place. The hour-long scene was Shakespearean theatre, transmitted live by satellite. For the first time in history, the world saw an unarmed king in the very act of subduing men who had the physical power to destroy him.

KING OF THAILAND ORDERS END TO VIOLENT UNREST headlined the *Financial Times* of London next day. The *Washington Post* editorialised: 'Who will soon forget the remarkable picture of the military ruler and the opposition leader together on their knees before the King on an otherwise powerless throne?' *Time* and *Newsweek* magazines put the king on their covers.

But once he was back among his fellow conspirators, Suchinda denied he had surrendered. He had backing from financial institutions. Some Thai-Chinese businessmen were now among the world's leading hundred billionaires, and they wanted a king to be the opium of the masses. Instead, Lek's publicly expressed views in recent months had challenged the power of some of the wealthiest families in Bangkok. He was concerned that Thais provided some of the world's cheapest labour and that factory-owners kept wages low to bring in more foreign investors. A million young Thais had been sold abroad, for construction projects or for the households of oil sheikhs. Would-be organisers of trade unions in Bangkok disappeared. There was a miasma of fear among workers who dared not ask for better salaries and conditions. The king was active on their behalf. In his Buddhist fashion, his parables had become more blunt. He opposed the sale of agricultural land to foreign companies. Japan wanted to buy a vast region where it could park unwanted old people at little cost. The king's land reform projects seemed even less like the harmless fancy of an under-employed monarch. There was a lot of money to be lost if the king was allowed to keep the reputation of a living Buddha.

A totally false impression of what had transpired between the king and the generals was broadcast over the army's radio stations. They relayed a tape of the royal audience all next day. General Suchinda's voice overrode that of the king. Lek could hardly be heard. It sounded as if the general was telling the king what to do. Listening to the broadcasts in Bangkok markets, I thought nothing so dramatically illustrated the monkey-tricks played on the king over the years.

He showed me how the distortion had been accomplished technically. He sat again in the same ordinary chair below which the generals had crouched. He had positioned his own microphone close to his elbow to pick up all that everyone said. However, the local television crew that arrived at Chitralada had been tipped off in advance. 'The army used the mike brought in by the television crew. It was over there, too far to pick up my voice clearly,' he said ruefully. 'It wasn't difficult to tamper with a tape that muffled my voice. Of course my own tape was available to the media.'

In the past, when attacked abroad, army strongmen had been bellicose about 'defending military honour'. Now, it was impossible to prevent western opinion from sweeping through the kingdom. The students I met in Siam Square were well informed, and together with a growing middle class, they exercised a populist democracy. They were disenchanted with the well-publicised austerity of General Chamlong who had ended his hunger-strike almost before it began. Young Thais wanted a civilian cabinet and a civilian prime minister, free from corruption. And it was no longer easy to condemn these students as 'communists'. They knew who they wanted for a civilian prime minister, a man driven into exile as a communist by coup-makers in the 1970s. Khun Anand Panyarachun was a diplomat and a scholar. He had been charged with subversion and jailed, with nothing but rumour and gossip for evidence. After months of investigation that produced nothing untoward, he had escaped to West Germany where, in his outrage and disgust, he declared, 'I am no longer a Thai!' Now he returned and agreed to serve for a year as premier. At his formal royal audience, the Ninth Rama said, 'Ah – Zorro rides again!'

Khun Anand gave up the premiership after a year, as he had promised, despite appeals for him to continue. He refused to play politics. He told me, 'I can't do this to my family.' His wife had been almost destroyed by the cowardly accusations that he was a communist, and he knew that still lurking in the background were military cliques and their corrupt backers who made parliamentary democracy impossible. The Ninth Rama had wanted him to stay in the post. 'Only when I became prime minister,' said Khun Anand, 'did I feel for the first time that I knew my king.' He saw my surprise and added, 'The king must trust you.'

As an outsider, it was always hard for me to appreciate how remote Lek must appear to even the most highly placed Thais. Khun Anand was free from humbug, he had made a new life for himself as a highly successful businessman in an open society, and he had come back to a world of invisible barriers erected by others around the king. He had come to see that a good king was still the only safe leader for a country bound by tradition. When he gave up the premiership, jealous courtiers again kept him outside their circle. Khun Anand should have been able to sit down with Lek as a close and trusted friend. Drawn within the orbit of the throne, he had arrived with only the haziest notion of what the Ninth Rama was really all about. Just when his obvious integrity had prompted the king to confide in him, political realities made Khun Anand withdraw.

Another man whose profession brought him into daily contact with Lek asked me: 'Do you understand him?' I had imagined that I did; but caution tied my tongue: I was infected by the atmosphere of intrigue, the fear of saying too much about a god whose magical aura was guarded by others. In the countryside, ordinary people were at ease with him; but their contacts were fleeting and they withdrew in reverential silence, and were soon swallowed up by swarms of minor officials anxious to keep the magic touch of a king to themselves.

In the end, Khun Anand understood his king too well, and the ways in which the Ninth Rama's rivals tried to monopolise the magic. Army commanders staged a spectacular event in the natural theatre of the ruins of the old capital at Ayudhya. The climax showed the king as a legendary Great Being walking over the backs of the people. Queen Sirikit innocently sent a letter of congratulation to the military organisers, taking the performance to be a tribute to their god-king. But Lek was quietly furious. He was not a god-of-gods. He had gone through what he called 'my twilight zone'. Before this, he had many times considered giving up.

27

Perseverance

MAMA returned to Doi Tung. For a woman of her age, a broken hip could be fatal. Yet she seemed sprightly. 'If ever there was an example of the power of mind over matter,' said Pi-Chai proudly 'she's it.' Her resolve was hardened by what she learned belatedly about the latest attempt to curb the king.

Lek climbed into the mountains east of her Inner Kingdom. He found a spiritual tranquillity in the rarefied atmosphere of temples carved hundreds of years ago in rock, two or three miles above the hot plains. There were abbots who gave sermons and abbots who reported on local conditions, and other abbots who collected news from distant places. 'The hill tribes have friends, they have relatives, all over the routes from Tibet through Yunnan and down to here,' said Lek. 'They have communications, very good communications. Apart from what you can seen in the mountains, there is something you cannot see. It is the spirit of these people.'

A few, swathed in embroidered head-dresses, were trickling one day along the mountain trails of Laos. We watched them in the early morning light, like tiny beads of coloured water dripping into the valleys and vanishing into thick grey mist. By noon, we heard their cheerful shouts, and more of them coalesced on a distant ridge. They moved at a steady pace but seemed days away. By dusk the stream had become a river to the foot of the mountain where the king was going to spend the night consulting the Abbot of the Gung Saen Stone Bell. It was eerie. By the time stars pricked the sky, countryfolk had silently washed up the hundreds of polished stone steps to the Temple of the Stone Bell. There was no visible explanation for this rising flood of deathly quiet humanity. Lek had not signalled his intentions before arriving.

'This is a different world where you accept what seems strange,' he said. 'The hill tribes come and go and they spread information. They are better and swifter than the radio services of Bangkok.'

He was still careful to avoid suggesting that some supernatural force was at work. He remarked, though, that the disastrous defeat inflicted not far from here on the French in May 1954 at Dien Bien Phu had etched into western minds a fixed way of looking at these things. Quite a different picture occupied the minds of the local people, which was why his mother's work spread so freely across borders. Even while an undeclared war was fought against communists in Laos by the Americans, his King's Men had been buying electricity from the Laotians. The majority of Laotians had no interest in communism, and paying them a fair price for surplus electricity was both compassionate and pragmatic. Thailand's expanding national grid needed the power.

He recalled the sad conclusion of a former supreme commander of his armed forces, General Saiyud Kerdphol: 'He was dependable and I sent him abroad to attend conferences on Laos. He told me when he came back, "Small countries about which such conferences are called seem to suffer as the result of international help. In spite of all the talk, the foremost concern is the interest of the great powers."'

Here, near Laos, was no sense of frontiers drawn by the great powers. People moved freely along ancient Himalayan trails. Five hundred thousand years ago, people lived here by hunting. They left the evidence in pebble tools that were only now being dug up. Their cave paintings were only lately known to outsiders.

The tranquil abbot meditated high above what had long ago been Chiang Saen City State. He occupied a temple that was bare except for the stone bell said to be a thousand years old. He repeated a story from Buddhist scriptures that might well have been preached by the Buddha's disciples travelling through these parts. The parable stuck in the king's mind. He wrote a book based on the parable and commissioned artists and designers to illustrate it with scenes similar to ancient temple wall paintings. He called it *Perseverance*.

The book was basically his own improvisation in English. He had told me that his knowledge of written Thai during the early years of his reign was nonexistent and he had to pretend to read his speeches when in fact he had memorised key words. Now, at Chitralada's yearly celebration of his birthday in December, he spoke conversationally in the style of a monk and the crowds who came to listen said he had undergone a mysterious transformation.

'I may sound Marxist,' he said. 'But the Marxist dialectic has only a superficial likeness to a classical style of thesis opposed to antithesis, leading to synthesis. Sun Tzu follows that formula, so does the Master of Tao and Confucius. Logical questions lead to logical answers whereas

Marxist-Leninism dictates the final answer . . . I oppose an opinion with a question that throws it back to the other person who must seek the answer honestly, in that individual's own heart.'

This was the method of the Buddha. At Chitralada, notables sat in the reception hall. The outer gates were open to everyone. Folk drifted among hot-food stalls under rainbow-striped umbrellas. Incongruously, closed-circuit TV sets perched among the trees and the crowds fell into a respectful silence while the king posed his questions. In the winter of 1992, under a crisp blue sky, the Ninth Rama debated the industrial expansion that drew water away from the ricefields, and asked: 'What is more important – to make things for export to compete with the same things made by other Asian Tigers or to preserve the natural resources that made Siam self-sufficient and prosperous?' He told folktales and said, 'A country losing touch with its legends is like an old man losing his glasses, a distressing sight, at once vulnerable, unsure and easily disoriented.'

Beyond his gates, the roads were choked with Suzuki Spacecabs, Mazda Galaxies, Toyota Dynamic Diesel Jets. Vehicles bearing more prestigious names were permanently parked outside shops to advertise the owners' wealth: Jaguars and Mercedes and a Rolls-Royce or two.

The time was approaching when the owners of those status trophies would not be able to sell them at fire-sale prices.

Lek's book, *Perseverance*, anticipated the crisis. He wrote of a king who had seen two mango trees, one bearing fruit and the other barren: 'When the king returned, the mango tree full of tasty fruits had been vandalised and felled, whereas the barren tree still stood. Thus we see that good things of good quality will be the target of greed and will stand in danger.'

Most striking about Lek's book was the account of how a palace courtier had lied to this mystical king, saying his Little Brother had plotted to kill him. 'Little Brother said, "Elder Brother, chain me up and if I am innocent of High Treason, the chains will fall away."' The chains had fallen away. Elder Brother was killed nonetheless. His queen escaped and gave birth in another land to a prince who later sailed across oceans to recover his kingdom. His ship sank. The prince, alone, swam and swam, having no idea where land might be. An angel asked, 'What mighty use do you see in swimming in the midst of a great ocean?' The boy replied, 'We have reflected on worldly behaviour and the merits of perseverance.' And angels lifted him up and he became the Great Being.

Lek had earlier told me that he felt like the legendary prince who just kept swimming. For his book, he drew navigational charts after the style of the old sea-kings with divine angels hovering above. *Perseverance* was an allegory to defy those who tried to hurt him with the old allegation that he killed Elder Brother Nan. Lek was no longer hamstrung by *lèse majesté*. He defined the law's origins in a note: 'It is French from the Latin *laesa majestas*, injured or violated majesty, a legal phrase denoting High Treason.' There was no treason in a king pursuing the vision of a Buddhist republic. He made this plain in his book: 'The King would have achieved supreme tranquillity more readily if he had completely fulfilled his worldly duties first.'

This alarmed those who still hoped to confine the monarchy. His book contained diagrams of the two mythical mango trees. The fruitful mango tree was shown as containing the goodness of Thai beliefs in the form of angels, and ancient scientific knowledge was symbolised by clockwork gears. Then this good tree was shown being destroyed by greed, with familiar scenes of modern dissolution: depraved men haunting brothels and the live-sex shows of Bangkok's most notorious red-light district, Patpong. Under another illustration was the caption: 'Methods of restoring the mango tree', with scientific agriculture on one side, and modern education on the other.

'We are the richest country in the world for folktales,' he said. 'People gathered at night to recall the past. The stories were used to teach. They became especially important after a large part of our written history was destroyed. That's why we collect our history from folktales . . . They should guide us now in practical matters.'

Overwork was blamed by his chief of cardiology after the king passed out while taking his twice-daily jog. Nobody talked about it publicly. 'I went through the twilight zone,' the king said. 'I came out wiser and with better perspectives.'

Those around him tried to persuade him to go abroad for a rest. He needed a quiet retreat in the west, absolutely isolated from the daily worry of a kingdom under tension. Queen Sirikit herself needed such breaks. She had tried unsuccessfully to take Lek with her to see *The King and I* on Broadway and had gone backstage to assure Yul Brynner that royalty was not offended. Lek had seen the movie version and thought it portrayed 'the spirit' of their great-grandfather, even if it was mostly wrong on facts. He liked the idea of 'a strong and agile king, always ready to learn'. But he refused to reverse his decision never to leave the country again.

The twilight zone had been a warning of impending trouble, though. 'When I recovered,' he finally disclosed, 'I felt I had been in the twilight between what we think of as being real, and what is real but appears to be mythical.'

'He knows the kingdom better than anyone,' said Major-General Anu Sumitra who had resolutely remained a colonel in the first years of our friendship, preferring the real jungle to the jungle of politics at higher levels, until Lek made him an intelligence chief. Anu had served in Malaysia with British Special Forces and he was exceptionally tough in the physical demands he made upon himself and others. So it meant something when he said things like, 'HM punishes himself with duty. He's covered every inch of this country. What he doesn't know about the people isn't worth knowing. And because they are so different in different parts of the country, he has to talk almost with each one . . . You've seen HM sitting for hours on end, personally handing a degree to each graduating student.'

I dreaded these ordeals, sitting in a pool of perspiration while the Ninth Rama received each graduate; but he had said, 'You wanted to know exactly what it's like to be a king, so come.' And so I did. The numbers of graduating students was growing to a point where it seemed physically impossible to see each one. His argument was: 'It takes a few seconds of my time to give out a degree, but for the student it is a lifetime memory.' So he sat bolt upright in steaming heat while long lines of mortar-boards and gowns moved slowly forward, each graduate performing the same skilful act of opening the palms outward in a gesture of trust, and then receiving from the stern figure a beribboned scroll, while the rest of us strained to keep awake. Nobody could have guessed the stress he was under, planting his feet hard into the floor to relieve the agonising pain of the spinal injuries he had suffered in the 1949 car crash, and which were never publicised.

Crown Princess Sirindhorn was the only person who could persuade him that this particular duty ought to be shared. She tended her own development projects, but took on some graduation ceremonies. Between furious bouts of activity, she had the good sense to fit in adventures abroad: journeys of discovery along the Old Silk Road which had once linked Persia overland to Siam by way of Mongolia; explorations to find the lost written history of the Mongols; a search of the South Pole regions for evidence of a prehistoric civilisation buried under ice; visits to experts abroad after she found that certain dinosaurs, recently unearthed, were unique to Siam. She had become a workaholic and slept hardly at all.

I walked one day behind Lek along a narrow trail. We were among north-eastern farmers, tortured by months of drought. A wind rustled through the trees and brought with it the unmistakable tang of soil suddenly refreshed by a distant rainfall: the bitter-sweet, unmistakable breath of an approaching deluge. He stopped and said, 'It rains. How come?'

There was a burst of relieved laughter. Later I asked, 'Why is it that people think your presence brings rain? You reject divinity.' He gave a fleeting smile. 'If you try to do good, the Almighty sometimes gives a hand.' He had long ago formed a squadron of aircraft for experiments in seeding clouds to induce rain. He had become an odd combination of magician and technocrat. He used the things in which the people truly believed while in his study he had computer systems that linked him to new technologies abroad.

He was studying satellite weather-maps when a tropical storm came churning up the Gulf of Siam. I happened to be in the headquarters of the Border Patrol Police. The telephone rang. The general answered questions from the person at the other end, and listened, and quickly turned to his wall charts. Later he explained: 'HM said, "The storm is going to develop into a typhoon." I said, "With all due respect, Your Majesty, the forecasters say it will head directly north and blow itself out in China."

'He said, "No. Here are the coordinates and the time when the storm will turn through ninety degrees and become a typhoon that will strike at a certain time at a certain point on the coastal highway at Chum Phon. I am faxing you the details. I want you to get emergency crews out immediately ... Yes, I know we have at least five neighbouring governments whose forecasters all say the same thing, that it's a storm and so on. You must act now because this is going to do tremendous damage."'

The general told me, 'There's only one highway south from Bangkok to serve this huge region where HM said the typhoon would make landfall. I had to move the crews before the highway was cut.' What was uncanny, confessed the general, was that the tropical storm became a typhoon exactly where and when the king said it would. The only help available to the people in the typhoon's path were the Border Patrol crews who had raced down the highway with aid and heavy equipment before it became impassable.

I now got another glimpse of the political quicksands in which the king habitually trod. The BPP general was telephoned by an angry minister of the interior. The minister demanded: 'Who told you to move those crews down there?'

'His Majesty,' said the general.

'You take orders from me! You do not take orders from the king!'

Lek's intervention was never made public. This had always been the case when he acted fast.

I asked the BPP general how he explained the king's prescience.

'He had an inherent sense of how air and water interact.'

'But this was like extrasensory perception.'

The general looked at me for a long time, perhaps measuring the degree of my skepticism. Finally he fingered a small gold Buddha hanging from a chain around his neck and smiled: 'You said it, not me.' The general had worked with the king to make the BPP's paramilitary forces serve the people in remote areas. The Buddha lockets were presented quietly by Lek to those who helped him: good men in the armed forces who were ready to risk punishment for showing him loyalty. The BPP general was still in political trouble because a new prime minister was in even bigger trouble. The public blamed him for having underestimated the damage done by the typhoon.

Crown Princess Sirindhorn flew into the devastated region to survey the appalling damage and report back to the king. His prediction had been only too accurate, and the only action he could take through the BPP was not enough to save hundreds of thousands of people from being uprooted by the storm. The figures on dead and wounded were played down by the government. Livelihoods were wiped out. Some 850 fishing vessels were taken by surprise at their open anchorages or while at sea. Sirindhorn stayed to help rescue workers, without publicity.

Her aide was a disarmingly frank young man I knew as Ting who was eventually overwhelmed by court intrigues. He had once told me, 'I'm descended from six queens but I'm not supposed to boast about it.' He described how Sirindhorn carried small children to safety from islands of mud. Ting had been richly educated in the west but he still followed the old Siamese beliefs. He explained: 'My family doesn't approve of my brother because he works in Hollywood and wins awards in the United States as a writer of science-fiction.' The brother's distinction, however, the king admired. It was Princess Sirindhorn who did not like to hear of talented Thais who stayed overseas when they were needed at home. She could not be told, for instance, that Ting planned to educate his son in western schools.

I asked Ting why she had not taken the press with her to examine the devastated region. 'She works behind the scenes,' he said. 'She has to be careful not to arouse the jealousy of the Crown Prince. She's already the people's choice as the next monarch.'

Her private report to the king so enraged him that he called in the current premier, Chatichai Choonhaven, one of several hundred army generals whose ridiculously high numbers were the tip of an iceberg of self-promotion. His inner circle of cronies promoted each other and quarrelled among themselves, but they had held together as the dynasty founded when the Northern Command worked with the Japanese. This inner circle still believed that the king was easily hood-winked and, despite all his knowledge, simple-minded. Lek asked Chatichai what would have happened if the Border Patrol Police had not acted ahead of the emergency? Chatichai resigned. The Ninth Rama had taken the measure of these secretive cliques and their days were numbered so long as they intrigued against the monarchy and so long as he stayed alive.

'I cannot afford to die,' he joked. All he had worked toward would be in jeopardy the very moment it might seem that his life was running out. The Crown Prince would never allow Crown Princess Sirindhorn to inherit the throne. She had upset her mother long ago when she decided she would never marry. The question of how much longer the king had to live was endlessly debated. Those who planned to monopolise political power could not afford to ignore the future of the Crown Princess. Even if she remained a virgin and even if there was no chance of her bearing an heir to the throne, provision had been made by the king for her to succeed him. And a majority of the people were so devoted to her that they would readily welcome her as the next monarch, however startling an innovation this might be. She was seen as a young version of Mama. Both women commanded an oldfashioned reverence that increased against all the calculations of men who fancied they would keep an exclusive grip on affairs in the years to come.

The future already cast a shadow in ways unforeseen. Ordinary people could no longer be deceived by censurious bullies. News and opinion from around the world poured freely through cyberspace. Ironically, the arrival of the global village reinforced the structure of kingship. At least so long as Lek was there, the peculiarities of Siamese monarchy seemed more democratic and a lot less violent than the foreign alternatives whose failings were laid bare for all to see on their desktop and living-room screens. The king knew by now his people's deeply conservative ways. He had once told US congressmen, agonising over the likely collapse of Siam under communist pressure, 'You Americans have more communism in your own backyard.' Now he felt the west and the remnants of communist dictatorships had new post-cold war problems that could devastate Siam. What he had called, twenty years ago, 'the most critical period in our history' was coming to a climax, unforeseen by his enemies.

28

Mama's Death

THE king's mother, they said, weighed no more in 1995 than she did as a child. Her Chinese father grew up in an age of imperial rule sanctioned by a Mantle of Heaven which could be withdrawn by the people if they lost confidence in the ruler. Now the people had elected someone whose leadership seemed godly, too. It was ironic. Both Mama and Lek were deeply opposed to the old notions of divinity. Yet her final public act was seen as that of a divine being who saved the life of the Ninth Rama.

She had been brought back for more treatment at Siriraj Hospital and the king became a patient there soon after to face heart surgery. Siriraj was full of memories. This was where Old Gran had unwittingly paid for Mama's training as a nurse. The Grand Palace was just upriver. The hospital was hot and noisy and crowded and confusing, a collection of dozens of small villages with all the odours of rural life mixed in with the smells of disinfectant. This community life humanised Siriraj. Fewer patients died from hospital infection than in the west. The inmates were in good spirits. Our daughter, Alexandra, went often to see nurses she had befriended and she grew up feeling this was just another, very normal, part of life. These impromptu villages grew organically around the high concrete medical wings and spread into streets banned to general traffic. There were Thai food canteens where we could sit and talk with doctors over delicately textured meals costing a few cents. Because Mahidol's nursing college was at the core of the hospital there were always young trainees helping out with the chores. Mama refused to be cut off from them as they flowed along the corridors. They adored her because she had been one of themselves. When her strength allowed, she insisted on being wheeled out to talk with them.

She was not expecting to have the king as a fellow patient.

'It began while I was fast-walking for exercise,' Lek said later.

'I was feeling gradually more uncomfortable. My strength was failing.

My blood pressure was very high and it would not come down.' It was Monday, 6th March, 1995. Four days later, he was admitted to Siriraj. 'I wanted to see Mama but I was knocked out. The doctors brought me a piece of paper. I could hardly grasp it. I was supposed to sign it before the surgeons could operate. I could not. Mama signed it for me. Only then could the doctors go ahead.'

Nothing would have happened without her firm signature, as mother, as widow of the doctor and one-time Heir Apparent who was the patron of this massive hospital. All the physicians called the king 'Big Doc'. But they were not prepared to go ahead without the sanction of the ninety-five-year-old Princess Mother. She knew the risks and was prepared to take the blame if the heart surgery went wrong. Big Doc rejected the rest of the family's preparations to fly him out to a big western medical centre where he was promised priority treatment from the most prestigious specialists. He wanted to demonstrate faith in Thai doctors.

The first surgery was successful. 'When I woke up from the anaesthesia, what a relief!' said the king. 'I could breathe, everything was bright. At that moment, Mama came to see me in her wheelchair. She said, "Eh! I am glad, so glad that you are strong now."' She continued to hover over him, like any worried mother. Finally, the doctors said the king could go home.

He said, 'So I asked Mama when she would be allowed to go home, too. She said, "The doctors already told me I could go home any time – I just waited so that we could go out together." Then she added, "Eh, that's good! Mother and son leaving together!" So I accompanied her to the Palace of Lotus Ponds.'

Mama, though, had not much longer to live.

Lek recalled, 'Ten years earlier, she said to me, "This mother of yours is quite old." At that time, very old meant more than eighty years old. I told her, "To be old is good; the longer you live, the better it is for us because our parents' longevity encourages us." At that time, she ate very little. She got thinner and thinner and weaker and weaker. She said, "What is the good of going on living? When I go to the dams, or to other projects, it is a burden to others who have to come and look after me." I guaranteed to her that officials and villagers were happy and willing, they called her Grandmother, her example encouraged them to keep on trying. She listened and began to eat and got stronger. While she was at Doi Tung, I would fly to see her. She still acted with Buddhist logic, breaking down problems to their smallest parts, and then asking, "Now, what are the consequences if – ?" Once, the queen and I stayed until it was late and Mama wanted us to fly back to Bangkok in the helicopter because I had duties there. Still we lingered until she said, "Eh! It gets dark. In these parts, what does darkness bring? Danger. So go, before the danger descends with the night."'

She had not been in good health when I had been to Doi Tung with Monika and Alexandra to see her before she was forced to leave forever. And yet there was a radiance about her, a quickness of wit. She discoursed on the love that gave birth to all religions, and how ancient languages like Greek, Persian and Sanskrit carried ideas between east and west.

Mama's search for enlightenment ended almost three hours before midnight on Tuesday, 18th July, 1995. The entire country was plunged in grief by her death. The economic crisis that followed was so profound that people in every station of life had a superstitious sense of cause and effect. Many blamed it on their failure to listen to what she had been trying to tell them for such a long time: that they could rely on nobody but themselves.

'The love and respect of the people throughout the land was so evident,' the king said. 'I was touched and glad. They all considered her to be their Grandmother. It was unique. It means those who call her "Grandmother" are my nephews and nieces. We are therefore all relatives and we all feel bereaved. Even after death, she continues to contribute, and will for a long time to the country's welfare through her foundation. It is a unique contribution. People from all lands, speaking all tongues, even those who dislike Thailand, see this unique situation and this deep respect. They say, "Thailand is a strange country", and indeed it is, because we have a different spirit, a different view of how to deal with things while we are alive.'

Lek and his sister Galyani had been with her when she died. 'And Crown Princess Sirindhorn, her favourite grandchild whom she had reared and who took care of her,' said the king. 'The three of us held her hand until she passed away peacefully. And we did as she had asked. "Don't cry," she said. "I forbid it!"'

Her death came when the king felt liberated from the old restrictions. He followed the same rituals that his mother observed for his brother, and her body was folded into the Great Golden One. But for reasons that were different to those that delayed Nan's cremation, the cremation of the Princess Mother was put off while the whole nation went into a year of mourning.

29

Queen Sirikit's Court

'Why wasn't the queen at the death-bed?' asked a lady-in-waiting nicknamed Barra by a King's Man who dismissed the women around the queen as 'barracuda ladies' after a strange accident killed Sirikit's closest and oldest friends. Sirikit had gone with Lek many times to look after the Princess Mother in the final weeks but the queen was a victim of rumours leaked from the royal court. 'And where were the Crown Prince and Princess Chulabhorn?' asked a self-styled critic of royalty who then hastily begged not to be quoted.

Early in the Princess Mother's last illness, I had been sitting alone with the king when he said disarmingly, 'You must excuse me, it's time I fed my mother. She won't eat if I'm not there.' He drove himself to the hospital and slipped inside through an obscure entrance. Other royals could not do this, although his sister had an arrangement with his Number Two Daughter, Sirindhorn, for skirting protocol.

Queen Sirikit had no such option and tried to cut down on journeys inside Bangkok because of the horrendous traffic jams caused by her motorcades. The routine chaos of the capital's traffic was so bad that it almost put a stop to normal social life: people would do anything to avoid an evening engagement. It was bad for the royal image to cause even more tie-ups, and Sirikit passed more and more time at country palaces like Phu Ping above Chiang Mei or wherever she could cast off formality within her own group. Lurid stories about her private life had gathered strength since those told to US intelligence by her friend, Clare Booth Luce, a member of the US President's Foreign Intelligence Advisory Board. The queen retreated into an informal court of her own. She was lonely and vulnerable.

Two of her children were drifting away from her. There was a period in the early 1990s when Sirikit would appear with the Crown Prince to join in the ballroom dancing at Bangkok hotels but she could not recapture the

239

feeling of freedom she had known in Europe: here, the floor would clear suddenly at her entrance, and armed security guards would rob the occasion of any spontaneity. The Crown Prince became more preoccupied with his own affairs. He had been to see Mama at Doi Tung before she got sick, to talk about his actress-consort. Why, he had asked, should the palace object because his actress came from humble origins? It ought not to prevent her from having royal status so that their sons might be in line for the throne. After all, the Princess Mother's origins were even more humble. Mama replied tartly that she did not understand what he was talking about. Sovereigns no longer had the latitude given to previous kings of Siam, and an Heir Apparent must earn the respect of the people. The Crown Prince had never been to see her again.

The youngest princess, Chulabhorn, kept away from her mother's changing court. The daughter feared she was dying from the kidney disease that 'runs in the family'. She had acquired a formidable list of foreign degrees in chemistry and physics and confided that she hoped to win a Nobel Peace Prize. She had taken me to see the work she was doing among victims of a typhoon. Under a huge purple umbrella, she rode in an infantry-carrier at the head of a column of armoured vehicles to where she had modelled new villages on Israeli cooperatives. 'I've been getting threats against my life,' she said. 'The threats come in faxes from people who resent that I use the army to construct new homes instead of giving the work to local businessmen. My aunt [the Princess of The South] was shot down here. I loved her very much. It's a very dangerous area. Every household has a gun.'

The king voiced concern that her Chulabhorn Research Foundation was open to criticism from the government for misusing funds. He was baffled and hurt when she wrote him impersonal letters addressed to 'Your Majesty' and signed 'Professor Doctor Air Marshal Princess Chulabhorn'. He never saw her to talk with any more, and yet, while cooking a Japanese meal in the way she had learned in Tokyo during one of her periods of study abroad, she told me how closely she tried to follow her father's example. Something was clearly wrong. Our visit to the flood-stricken regions came after a glitzy party in Bangkok to help finance Chulabhorn's campaign against AIDS. 'My father asked me to take over the AIDS programme because he would never live long enough to see the problem solved,' she said. She asked Elizabeth Taylor to preside at the party in an expensive hotel, and invited New York's most prestigious jeweller to exhibit a collection that required special Thai forces to guard it, so that the corridors were filled with armed troops. The history of Old Siam was re-enacted in the ballroom, with some of the most beautiful women in Thai society scantily but elegantly clothed. Muscular semi-naked young men performed mock duels and Liz Taylor, stunned by the spectacle, told her companion, Norma Heyman, the producer of the movie *Dangerous Liaisons*, 'We must make a movie based on Siamese history – it's so spectacular.' All of us then flew south in a King's Flight jet, pausing at the exclusive resort of Phuket only to deposit Taylor and her companions. A large delegation waited on the tarmac to greet the princess before we took off again to the flooded region. Taylor assumed the reception was for her. As she progressed regally along the lines of uniformed bureaucrats, dressed in an ankle-length *muu-muu*, she waved one languid hand in the manner of Queen Elizabeth. Princess Chulabhorn suddenly stopped at the top of the aircraft steps, seeing it would be embarrassing if she stole the limelight, and got her husband, a wing commander, to radio the local dignitaries from the cockpit. By the time the actress rode into town, a large banner had been hastily strung across the main street with the words: WELCOME QUEEN ELIZABETH TAYLOR.

The princess and her husband admitted they were tired of being constantly under the public eye. 'I have to fly a helicopter to some remote spot where we can be alone,' he said. Later, he was assigned to a diplomatic post in Washington where Chulabhorn dressed up as Air Marshal and insisted she must have a bigger house than the military attaché. She disturbed society dames in the American capital by making her servants come to her on hands and knees at dinner parties. A Thai ambassador's wife said to me later, 'It is impossible to tell her this leaves the worst possible impression on foreigners. My friends beg me to tell her, but how can I risk my husband's career – ?'

The youngest princess had always felt under-valued. In our conversations, she spoke of her father with awed respect. She desperately wanted to please him. Yet, like her brother, she was losing favour. Like her brother, she eventually divorced.

The Ninth Rama was now by far the world's longest reigning monarch, but he had to undergo two major heart operations. After making a swift recovery, he appeared on television and armed with charts and a pointer, described the surgical procedure in detail, and then sounded a warning note. He fully expected, he said, to live for a long time yet.

The warning was meant for those who were already clustering around the likely Tenth Rama, the Crown Prince. Lek, like any father, was reluctant to believe the stories he heard. The hesitation to publish anything less than reverential was destroyed by computer networks that proliferated in a country where young geniuses made unauthorised copies of anything from designer clothes to the most intricate electronic circuitry. It was impossible to trace the authors of reports that alleged the Crown Prince took elaborate precautions before sleeping with any woman who caught his fancy because of the rapid spread of AIDS. The users of fax machines and modems claimed his selected companion had to go into quarantine long enough for doctors to be sure she was free from infection. He was now forty-four and lived in his own heavily guarded palace in Bangkok. Queen Sirikit proposed that he should use his military skills in Laos. As part of the Golden Triangle, its conditions were similar to those at Doi Tung. There, a return of banditry since the Princess Mother's last illness threatened to destroy all her work. Laos, went the argument, had always been part of Old Siam. The Crown Prince would impose order in place of what his new allies regarded as Mama's wishy-washy idealism.

The king preferred his mother's ways and invited to Bangkok the Laotian leader Kaysone Phomvihane, the first general-secretary of the original Communist Lao People's Party. 'Kaysone is a man who fought fifty years in the jungle,' Lek said privately. 'He should be honoured.' Kaysone looked very frail when he arrived. He was seventy-six and the Ninth Rama met him at the military aviation complex at Bangkok airport and did something nobody remembered seeing the king do for any visitor before. He took the old enemy by his arm and helped him climb the steps to a reviewing stand for a march-past of Royal Thai troops.

Lek said Laotians had tried to shake off western colonialists and innocently fell victim to communist propaganda. Laos was still suffering the after-effects of covert warfare. The British-based Mines Advisory Group, MAG, backed by Diana, Princess of Wales, had officially confirmed reports, denied during the 'secret war' between 1964 and 1973, that one payload of US bombs had been dropped on Laos every eight minutes day and night to a total of more than 2 million tons, 'making Laos the most heavily bombed country in the history of warfare'. Even now, 200 Laotians were estimated to be killed each year by leftover bombs and mines. Eight million live bomblets and mines were said by MAG to still lie in wait for victims. The Ninth Rama had built on the Laos border the kind of thatch-roofed factories for artificial limbs that he had shown me in the south. Laos was a victim of operations launched from his kingdom and he wanted to make amends.

He had Laos in mind, and other racial groups whose different ways made them fair game in the Cold War, when he published a biography of Tito, and wrote that the Yugoslav leader had held together a republic made up of many different clans who, after Tito's death, resumed age-old feuds. He warned that religious and racial intolerance could break out again when peace and order depended so heavily upon one man. 'You will see how people are fighting each other in that country today,' Lek told a Chitralada audience. 'If we are prudent, we will not be like them . . . The bottom line is, when it comes to preserving our own ways, we all must help each other.' He included the old jungle fighter from Laos. 'Each of us, according to his conscience,' he said, 'has been on a road to revolution.'

Within his own royal court, though, he had to deal with divisions. He did not want to be a Tito whose calming influence evaporated after his death. Silence about majesty had been cracked by modern technology. Whispers in the darkness of cinemas were now shouted over the Internet which carried stories that Queen Sirikit, fighting age, had fallen under the influence of 'a female Rasputin' who prescribed medications that were hallucinatory in large doses. Sirikit had been for so long an astonishingly svelte and lovely woman and courtiers either flattered her to get her help and favours, or told mischievous tales. Lek's work left her on her own more often now. Her companions' motives were mixed. One of the good ones was a ballerina from Europe who privately helped Sirikit with daily physical exercise. The queen invited her to move permanently to Bangkok when her husband died after a cruelly long illness that left the ballerina penniless. The court's innate suspicion of foreign intruders eventually showed itself when the ballerina was named in the yearly honours lists: she was never informed until it was almost too late for her to appear at the awards ceremony. Her absence would have been a fatal breach of etiquette. At the very last moment, Queen Sirikit learned that others had tried to sidetrack her European friend. It sounded like an echo of the unexplained delays in conveying to Monika and myself the original requests to see the king.

The story of the 'female Rasputin' was more sinister. Queen Sirikit had difficulty coping with the rumours, the intrigues, the court chatter which cut her off from normal intercourse. 'She feels she missed out on chances to educate herself,' her principal private secretary, Than Phu Ying Suprapada Kasemsant, had once told me. 'She has more common sense in her little finger than anyone around here, but she suffers from this feeling of inadequacy.'

We were at dinner on the site of a large Japanese project, a combination of power dams, reservoirs and irrigation channels initiated by the king. It had been a long and exhausting day, walking great distances, sitting through ceremonies, studying charts, talking to individual villagers and local officials. Repetition made such activities tiresome. Only the king had the detailed knowledge to plug stoically on, absorbed in the technical information and buoyed by his passion for maps and those things which can be pinned down solidly, not like the abstractions of ritual. Sirikit remained queenly and gracious. I wondered if the lively young seventeen-year-old of yesterday might have changed her mind if she had known what fate had in store: days like this one, always smiling, always ready to respond to a kneeling villager by kneeling in return, finding the right things to say in a carefully modulated whisper. Now she sat beside her wordless king. He looked drained. His body had that stony stillness that said his mind had gone off somewhere. The queen had to carry the social load: her smile always special, her soft words and her attentive look designed to make each Japanese company executive feel special, her radiance encouraging timid murmurs from local officials.

Than Phu Ying Suprapada was a rare friend to the queen: worldly, always up-to-date on events in distant capitals, utterly loyal. That night she let her hair down, out of compassion for the queen, feeling I would understand and sympathise. Later she was killed with two of Sirikit's ladies-in-waiting and ten others of her staff when a Super Puma transport helicopter crashed on its way to one of the queen's projects near the palace in the south where we had first met. Queen Sirikit had lost the few courtiers she could trust. And, of course, the rumours flew over the wires that the helicopter had been sabotaged.

The queen withdrew more frequently to Phu Ping. She felt secure there, away from the tension and gossip. Whenever she left Chitralada with her rapidly shrinking court, she always said, 'Please take good care of His Majesty' to the man Alexandra had come to call Uncle Woodie, the one man who now sat through the long nights talking with the king alone. Woodie was a compact, muscular man who so hated the rigmarole of military pretension that he wore his own funny combination of old army jackets and jungle gear as an act of defiance that the king could not make, although he approved. Woodie had quick brown eyes and an infectious laugh. He had once gone with me to see a movie about American Secret Service agents who risked death for the President: 'I would die for HM,' he said later. He told me anything I wanted to know about Thailand, warts and all, and his devotion to the Ninth Rama did not stop him from pointing out the king's failings and failures because what he told me was what the king discreetly wished me to know. 'HM is betrayed by greedy men who take advantage of the fact that a king can't be everywhere at once,' he said. Royal projects are often ripped off by these opportunists, and ordinary people, the victims, are afraid to tell him. Land on which the poor are settled is quietly purchased by speculators, in spite of rules against re-sale. HM knows what's going on. He says these crooks will hurt themselves – but they might drag down the country at the same time.'

'Can't he do something – ?'

'If he does, he goes against what he believes. People have to learn for themselves. He gets very angry but he tries not to show it. Sometimes he tells me, "Get rid of that woman," when the queen wants to interrupt him at work in his study. He loves her but the queen is surrounded by "barracuda-ladies". They fill her head with disturbing notions. She's exploited by these barra-ladies and the husbands who stay behind the scenes.'

Barra, one of these barracuda ladies, proposed that she and I should have an affair and explained how easily these things were managed. Her sinuous conversations in private made me suspect she hoped to provoke me into comments she could report to the queen as representing some secret hostility to royalty. It was difficult to avoid being cornered by her at palace functions. She provided an insight into the little treacheries of the royal court with her widespread stories: that hypochondria caused the queen to withdraw into a coterie of bad advisers; that opportunists curtailed her good works; that Sirikit was now the king's wife in name only. Barra claimed to have love letters from the Crown Prince and said she was now 'very close' to the king.

The tragedy was that Barra had been a brilliant graduate from western universities and her former fellow-students all agreed she had been a stunningly beautiful girl. She was now, she admitted, 'bored to death here. There's nothing to stimulate the mind, no good western theatres and cultural activities, nothing else to do but stir things up or have affairs.' She had been to bed with many important men, she said; and when I failed to join their ranks, she put it that her purpose was 'to find out things, like a spy. I talk to chauffeurs and other common people and wheedle out of them their real thoughts about the king so that I can report them.' She suffered from spy-fever and talked endlessly about those Thais who were, in her words, 'always trying to find out what's going on inside the queen's court now that she's no longer really living with the king.'

Her frustrations translated into her remarkable performances whenever she appeared with the queen on ceremonial occasions. Then Barra swept haughtily through the ranks of other courtiers and prominent personages. 'I imagine I'm back to being the great warrior queen I was in a previous life,' she confided one day. 'Enormously rich, free to do anything I please.' At the next ceremony, she looked straight through me as if we had never met. This disconcerting technique, however, was used by all the royal courtiers on public occasions, leaving me to wonder how Queen Sirikit could ever hope to discover what betrayals were concealed behind their masks.

The queen said to me one day, 'Thank you for helping my husband.' Members of the royal court were keeping their distance, forming a wide circle around her like benign captors who were also held captive by what she might do for them. Her words were softly spoken. Her eyes were moist and almost pleading. In her early sixties, she kept the style and grace of someone who had made it her life's work to do what seemed right. Her hand trembled in mine. She wanted someone from the outside world to reinforce her husband. She was now marooned on another planet. She could watch distant events through images beamed through space from distant places on earth. Without interaction, these marvels only contributed to her sense of isolation. It was increasingly difficult for her to see things for herself. When she had escaped to visit New York or Paris, her companions went off on shopping sprees and loaded down their aircraft with booty that was not taxed by Thai customs. Or so foreign newspapers reported. The offending reports were scissored out of incoming newspapers by Thai police; but then these well-intentioned protective censors were forced to explain their actions to hostile politicians. When senior police officers quoted from the censored stories to explain their actions, they were charged with *lèse majesté* for airing them! 'It is safer to say and do nothing,' said one. 'The politicians are clever at making us scapegoats if we try to serve the queen's best interests.'

Sirikit had thanked me for helping the king by taking an interest in his projects. The only other way I could help was in the matter of his brother's death and Lek did not want to go over that again. I believed Tsuji, Japan's God of Evil (or God of Strategy, depending on who you believe) had been in the vicinity of the Grand Palace that fatal morning but that he had come in the guise of a monk. To say this was deeply offensive to many Buddhists. Only the Ninth Rama could discuss it. For others, it was dangerous to overstep so many invisible boundaries. The instinct that made courtiers snap, 'Let the story die with you!' was still deeply entrenched. Tsuji, though dead, might still win. He had planned to divide the kingdom by destroying kingship, and one thing Barra had taught me was that unresolved mysteries were greedily seized upon by the idle and the mischievous within the queen's court for conversion into dangerous gossip.

30

Economic Collapse

Mama had taught her children to be self-reliant. Her younger son preached the same kind of self-reliance on a national scale. Competing businessmen with influence among politicians dismissed his warnings of an approaching economic collapse that would be catastrophic. So he delayed Mama's cremation until the storm broke. Then it would speak to people in the language of imagery they understood. He had said Thais united when they saw 'the face of danger behind the mask' but were otherwise lax. By 1996, the country's financial institutions were on a binge that would end in disaster.

Support for his views came from an unexpected quarter. 'The Pope like the King could not always speak out. The global crisis gave the Pope his opportunity,' the Catholic Archbishop of Bangkok, Cardinal Michai Kitbunchu, told me. 'The Pope's words gave the King support.'

Pope John Paul II said publicly, 'Asia has spiritual wisdoms for the rest of the world.' Like the king, he warned that every society must nourish the best aspirations of its people. Unbridled capitalism could not produce a civilisation worthy of man. Global capitalism was 'the idolatry of the market.' It reduced human beings to mere bundles of appetites, shorn of dignity. These were revolutionary views, coming from the Vatican, and a monarch who voiced them in his own way.

'The king has *to be seen* as detached from politics,' said Cardinal Michai. He had a broad Chinese face and benevolent eyes magnified by cheap spectacles. His polished pate grew wings of tufted black hair. His simple white cassock with cardinal's red buttons were as impressive as Lek's ceremonial robes. He said 'The King always responds at once to my requests for help in social projects.' The cardinal's projects were in the unspeakable slums of a capital where wealth rode roughshod over the humble. 'Where the King's mother was born might have seemed a slum,' said Archbishop Michai. 'Compared with today, it was a decent little shop-house in a community of the decent poor. I deal daily with decent, poor people struggling to keep their dignity to stop from slipping into despair. They are victims of the greed against which the King acts in the only way he can.' Lek always had to keep in mind the past: the Venetian '*Falcon*' had lost his head when courtiers thought he tried to convert King Narai to Catholicism in the 1680s; and Lek's great-grandfather King Mongkut was circumspect in his friendship with a Jesuit bishop. But the present archbishop was a valuable source of information and a channel to the Vatican and the moral support the Pope could provide.

His Eminence had been hatted in 1981 as one of the Vatican's youngest cardinals. He had given hope to millions of Catholics in East Asia struggling to survive against communism, especially in Vietnam. The cardinal met clerics like the Bishop of Ho Chi Minh City. He opened pathways into forbidden zones. He saw the Ninth Rama as a lonely man who could not look to saints or a single religious institution to tell him what to do during fifty years of constant crisis. Now came the worst. Crony banks and businesses built on corruption and special favours had ruined the country. Some generals whose cronyism dated back to collaboration with Tsuji's wartime opium-rich northern states were dead or in exile, but their relations and dependents still shuffled the key cards among themselves.

'Drug dealers in a Thai Cabinet? There's nothing new about that,' a veteran American correspondent, Stanley Karnow, wrote for *Time* in an essay headlined 'Holier-Than-Thai'. 'We didn't mind when the generals ran the opium shipments because they were lovely anti-communists.' His comments followed the US State Department's warning in July 1995 that relations would be 'complicated' if the Bangkok government gave high office to politicians denied visas to the US because of drug dealings. Drug traffickers made pious protests against US interference. It was hard to measure now, but their power could still remove the king.

He delayed the cremation of the Princess Mother until 1996, the year in which he had hoped she would share the Golden Jubilee of his reign. He did not want himself to be celebrated, but the cremation would be an assertion of all the things she stood for. There was to be no unveiling of monuments to himself. Money was still squandered on massive multi-storeyed Japanese-funded supermarkets. They were solid concrete and steel mausoleums, not like the false-front Japanese supermarkets made of straw for wartime propaganda; but they too were about to collapse as suddenly as the economy. The new ones were still besieged, even with the storm clouds gathering, by elegantly dressed housewives whose chauffeur-driven limousines crammed the underground car parks. Mama's home at The Palace of Lotus Ponds faded behind a multi-storeyed car park. Siam Square was overshadowed by costly condominiums.

Lek asked the tourist board not to turn the Golden Jubilee Year into a bumper commercial for kingship. He did not want it to become another opportúnity for the rich to cluster around the throne to show off their supposed influence. Now it was the turn of the humble: they had trusted Mama's distillation of their most cherished beliefs. Mama would want him to draw upon this spiritual power.

The cremation provided Lek with a platform that foreign eyes missed. Nothing like it had been staged in living memory. Those ceremonies for King Ananda that Mama could not bear to attend were now re-enacted on a grander scale. The little orphan girl once rejected as an intruder in royal circles now ascended to the gods in a spiritual coronation. When the BBC televised a documentary with the funeral as a centre-piece in the late summer of 1998, one London reviewer commented on 'the medieval extravagance . . . Her urn was dragged through the streets in a monstrous golden chariot, eleven metres high and weighing forty tons.' Outsiders were unaware that this extravaganza was a substitute for the Ninth Rama's golden jubilee.

Lek warned that problems would pile up if the kingdom continued to forget that the foundation of its independence was its agriculture. 'Eight million in this country of 65 million earn less than the equivalent of one hundred American dollars a year,' he said. 'Yet twelve of the world's hundred richest billionaires are listed as Thai citizens. We have the third highest sales of Mercedes Benz cars in the world, but in our countryside, royal foundations are lending money to people for whom the most important thing is to own just one pig.' He began saying such things with greater candour. The very rich came to his annual birthday sermons for reasons of social status, and thought the boom would go on. US DOLLAR IS GOING BROKE was a gleeful cover story in *Asia Magazine*, circulating throughout the region.

'Expect another 400 million Asians to move to megametros in the next ten years,' forecast a report on the king's desk from the International Rice Research Institute. 'Mega-cities will each contain 25 million inhabitants.' Bangkok was moving so fast in that direction that nobody was sure how many people lived there. Citibank distributed a confident forecast that 'by the year 2000, the Asian market will be more economically powerful than the European Common Market.'

One ominous indication of impending trouble was deeply personal. Lek went to look at the restoration of the shop-house where Mama was born. It was in the slums, but beside it had been ricefields, and these same ricefields were still taken as the Asia model in the late 1940s by American anthropologists. Now, huge discount superstores, real estate developments and factories covered this place where Mama had once paddled her vegetable boat. Lek saw that these buildings would soon be derelict, and that the vanished ricefields would never be restored. The soil was poisoned, and a slum would grow out of broken concrete and rusting girders such as no slum-dweller in Mama's infancy could have imagined.

All through his reign, careful management had kept the *baht's* value steady. He knew this could not continue but his warnings fell on deaf ears in the capital. Nobody knew the exact population of Bangkok because of the hundreds of thousands of countryfolk who came to work on construction sites. A major crisis might bring people to their senses. Businessmen wondered why, in the midst of a commercial boom, the king talked of 'cooperative groupings' in which farmers could help one another, pool resources, and meet the kingdom's essential needs without spending foreign currency.

He no longer played the simpleton, no stutter, no pretension, before thousands of well-wishers on his birthday at Chitralada in December, 1996. 'You are composed of many different people: police, civil servants, Village Scouts, students, business people, members of the armed forces.' He discussed the globalisation of information technology and said, 'I have to use the word "globalisation" or you'll say I'm not with it . . . In fact, I don't know what the word exactly means . . . systematic mass killings in other parts of the globe? That implies, if we are "globalised", we go in for killing, too. But the Thai terminology gives another meaning – "*to live better than*". And this is what we must continue to do. We know better than to kill one another.' And he told the tale of quarrelsome families in the Valley of the Shadow of Death. Only this was not an old Siamese folktale. It came from John Bunyan's *Pilgrim's Progress* and told of the good man Christian who, overcome by the sense of his own sin and the death that soon awaits him, makes a journey to find enlightenment. It was couched in plain man's language. Any unlettered person could follow how Christian fell into all kinds of error from which he had to be rescued constantly. And so spoke the king, like Christian. 'When one has to endure hardships, one's patience is often put to the test. You're at your wit's end. For all of us, it is the same: a day, two days go by. You have to take a firm grip on yourself, remove the confusion in your mind, think carefully.'

But he also spoke of *devas*, the gods and angels whose advice was worth heeding. He had to, because so many of his listeners still lived in that invisible universe governed by divinities and demons, even though he emphasised modern education. College enrolment rates were high, and all children of primary age had schools to go to, although many were made to work by their impoverished parents. Family-planning had been introduced thirty years ago: the Thai population was better stabilised than anywhere, even China where family growth was limited by law.

He calculated that each man, woman and child in the kingdom owed more money each year to powerful foreign-dominated institutions than each Thai could earn in several years. 'Accountants run everything,' he warned. 'The poor countries owe more than a hundred billion American dollars to foreigners because foreign financial institutions say we cannot develop if we don't borrow.' He was speaking months before such things were said by stock-market analysts in the west when they finally panicked over a global recession caused by Third World debt. 'Meanwhile,' he continued, 'our own agricultural land is disappearing to a point where we may not be able to grow enough food for ourselves.'

On this last birthday before the crash, those growing wealthy on real-estate development still lavished expensive gifts on him in the hope of winning preferment. But the most devoted of his woman aides, Putrie Viravaidya, the descendant of King Mongkut, habitually gave him a dozen sharpened pencils. 'That's all he really needs,' she said. 'Maps and pencils for his surveys.'

Then Putrie became secretary-general of the Privy Council, made up of a dozen distinguished Thais who debated with the king on actions he could take. A woman had taken a seat at the council table. She spoke with Mongkut's voice. Lek was empowered to use his sermons to deal with the economic catastrophe ahead. Putrie saw to it that a document was drawn up to untie his tongue. 'For the first time in Siamese history,' he said, 'a new constitution is being drafted that will transform the nation into an open, democratic society where transparency will be the norm, not the exception.'

He spent most nights in his study working on what he thought of as a 'New Theory'. He believed there had been nothing innovative in politico-economic thinking since World War Two. Mao's Chinese revolution had only underlined the failure of Soviet concepts. The king had good connections with scientists in Kunming, the capital of China's south west province of Yunnan. He had known since the late 1950s that engineers there, working with American factory equipment provided during the war against Japan, had been bitterly critical of the Soviet Union's advisers. 'The American machinery was old but it was still better than what the Russians forced upon us, along with politically educating our craftsmen when they ought to have been working,' a Chinese plant manager had once told me. Lek had no illusions about China's disastrous submission to Soviet tutelage. Mama had envisioned Yunnan as part of a region where artificial borders did not count.

Lek relied on the ability of villagers to endure and adapt. The vitality of small shops and stall-keepers kept at bay the waxen-faced misery of neighbouring countries trying to climb out of the depths of Soviet-inspired doctrinal development schemes. If things worked out in his kingdom, others could join in.

He played on folk memory. In 1996, there had been a sudden transition from near-drought to heavy rains during Songkran, a water festival in mid-April that marks the traditional New Year and approximates to Easter. This was a time to visit the temples, 'make merit', and sprinkle water over passers-by. 'Water is the river of life,' he told another gathering at Chitralada. 'Many people grumbled there was no rain this Songkran so I contacted the gods to send junior *devas* to join our water-festival celebrations. So the celestials joined in, on a grand scale, to the point where the people said, "Enough!" I consulted the Chief *Deva* of Mount Meru who told me the celestials were not heavy-handed, it was just that my artificial rain-makers had also participated. I spoke to my officials and I found that overall, the abundance of rain had been more beneficial to the greater number of people. This response was a kind of referendum in which you ask a large number of people their opinion. And in this case, most said it had been better to have too much rain, and so those who suffered accepted this vote . . . I have started out speaking of rain and now I end up speaking about voicing one's opinion in a democratic way, so that the minority accept the opinion of the majority!'

It was the nearest he had yet come to lecturing on his own version of political science. Elder Brother had envisaged a Buddhist democracy, but Lek translated Buddha's thoughts on this: democracy was possible when people reached the level of compassion needed to work together; and this required knowledge of physical causes of trouble. 'Every year during August-September, a monsoon trough appears in the upper north. The temperature rises from hot to extremely hot because of low pressure areas that induce the high temperatures. However, in this month there is also a high pressure area in China that moves down to cover the upper north of Thailand causing rain, thunderstorms and hail which lower the temperature . . . When high pressure areas twice move from China and blanket Thailand, two airstreams intermittently converge . . . In Bangkok on this Songkran, the highest level of rainwater was measured at 134.2 millimetres.' These were facts. It was no good relying on the intervention of the gods. How, he asked, could people fail to agree on the concrete steps that should have been taken long ago to reduce the huge impact of floods in Bangkok? He had outlined ways to save the excessive rainwater for use in droughts. The models had always been there at Chitralada, for people to copy: from small concrete water-traps to weirs, ditches, and 'wet forests' that would also act as firebreaks.

Despite all the talk about Asian Tigers and economic miracles, farmers and their families were at the mercy of the elements and the land developers. By democratic processes of their own devising, they could change this, he said later to the inhabitants of a valley who had voted against an irrigation system. He brought them to the adjoining valley where local villagers had voted in favour of the king helping them to build such a system. He knelt to release fish fingerlings into the new reservoir: 'A few fish,' he said. 'But one day they will feed thousands.' The other villagers had been afraid to vote in favour of the king's project. It went against the wishes of local politicians anxious to keep on the right side of local businessmen. These resented royal competition, and their money ensured the re-election of obedient politicians. The trouble was that old habits were stronger than new concepts of parliamentary democracy and the king therefore appealed to true Buddhists. He published small books Mama had written on Buddhism. People had only to work together, respecting each others' differences, to make their lives better, she wrote. Buddha was not a mystic. His awakening was not a shattering insight into some transcendental truth about the universe. 'He taught simple rules that might save humankind by bringing it into tune with the countryside,' Mama had written.

The king was not always helped by some of his own family's failings. Mama's cremation diverted attention from London newspaper reports that the Crown Prince had posted a proclamation stripping his new wife, the actress re-named Princess Sujarinee, and her alleged lover, sixty-year-old Air Chief Marshal Anand Rotsamkhan, of all privileges. Sujarinee was living in London and was said to have called the police when her daughter, Princess Busnamphej, failed to return home from a private school. Scotland Yard reported that her father had recently arrived in England and that he had taken the child. 'The princess was distraught but for reasons best known to her,' said a Scotland Yard spokesman, 'she did not officially allege abduction.'

When it seemed the scandal would die down, the Crown Prince plastered the capital's walls with photographs of his actress-wife and the air marshal together: 'These two people have been declared persona non grata and expelled from the palace. If anyone sees them, they must be shunned . . . Anand Rotsamkhan has been expelled from his position. If he does anything else, he will be given serious punishment . . . The Thai Government does not want him to return to Thailand. Rest in Peace in Foreign Lands.'

Those backing the Crown Prince as the future king withdrew into a discreet silence. He had no authority to speak for the government but already he sounded like an absolute monarch.

The financial collapse of July 1997 marked the beginning of the dramatic failure of all Asian economies. The hard decision was taken to devalue the *baht*, and it fell to half the value it had maintained with such sturdiness throughout the Ninth Reign. The king's usual critics were subdued by the dramatic spectacle of Bangkok's population of migrant workers draining away. The capital's residents were thought to have dwindled to 5 million from the previous, unofficial estimate of 10 million. Many farm workers now no longer had land to go back to: it had been sold to developers.

Lek had approved devaluation, whereas other Asian countries had tried to prop up their currencies until forced to suffer much sharper declines. More people looked to him for leadership. Foreign newspapers commented on the Crown Prince's unpopularity. 'Many would like to see the crown pass to his sister, Princess Sirindhorn,' reported the international edition of the London *Daily Express*. Sirindhorn did not want a conflict with her brother, but continued her father's work, knowing he must stay alive to save what had been accomplished. He was still secretly opposed by a few powerful figures. Some were called in the Bangkok press 'formerly rich', a coded reference to the likelihood that they had squirrelled away their money abroad. A grand chamberlain spoke of transferring Princess Sirindhorn's assets into a foreign bank account, which was untrue. There was talk of a plot to discredit Sirindhorn and boost the Crown Prince by those who had money enough overseas to finance another junta. The old lies about Lek as killer of Elder Brother Nan were whispered again.

By November 1997 a squabbling and discredited parliament produced its fifth prime minister in as many years while luxury limousines and private aircraft were sold in Bangkok's flea markets. The world's fastest growing economy was becoming Asia's biggest economic embarrassment. 'The turmoil is a far cry from the brash confidence of what was Asia's slickest Tiger economy,' editorialised the London *Sunday Telegraph*. An annual growth of eight per cent had been taken for granted. A new Mercedes showroom had opened every other week. Skyscrapers had risen like souffles out of the polluted logjam. The outgoing premier, Chavalit Yongchaiyudh, another member of the generals' club, had been so sure of Japanese money pouring into new golf clubs that he had boasted only a year before, 'Where else can you play golf with a girl to hold an umbrella against the sun, another girl to carry your clubs and a girl to give you a sexual massage?' Now he was alleged to have spent more than US$100 million to get himself

elected by buying votes, drawing some of the money from Japanese partners before the currency crisis clipped the tiger's claws.

Just before his resignation, Chavalit begged his former military cronies
to stage a coup. They refused. They backed Lek's appeal to save Thailand's
fragile democracy rather than recycle the old system of rule by military
dictate. They were influenced by a dramatic statement from Siriraj
Hospital where the king was again a patient, his heart giving new problems.
His physician called publicly for an end to the political bickering that
threatened to tear the nation apart. 'It is making His Majesty seriously ill,'
he said, which was as close as he dared go to saying the king was near death.

But Lek recovered from more operations, saying 'The best medicine was
public support and the loyalty of a new generation of military officers.'

What the 'formerly rich' were forced to sell at the flea markets was as
astonishing as the things they had been prepared to buy: gem-studded cat
collars; a mini-hovercraft for the backyard swimming pool; a four-seater
aircraft offered as a bonus to anyone willing to buy two Mercedes for
US$100,000; a wine-cellar with bottles of the century's best vintage,
Chateau Lafite 1981, going for forty dollars each. The dwindling number
of luxury cars had raised the average speed of Bangkok traffic. 'Traffic that
once moved at two miles per hour now moves at two-and-half,' observed
the *Bangkok Post*.

Lek acted as many ordinary people clearly wished, as an outspoken king
from the age of absolute monarchy. It was ironic. His Buddhist republic was
always just out of reach. People looked to him for answers, even when he
repeatedly said they must find their own. He gave me a typical example: 'A
committee asked my help in cleaning up the river. I told them to work out
their own solution. Nothing would get better until people learned to do
things for themselves.'

He quoted Simon Linguet before the French Revolution. The words
sounded like Bangkok before the crash: 'Industrial capitalism promised
heaven and delivered hell . . . It created a new god, the entrepreneur, and
made subhuman troglodytes of urban people living in regular
burrows . . . dark holes where herds of laborious animals hide out, breathing only a foetid air, poisoning one another with the contaminations
unavoidable in that crowd, inhaling at every moment the seeds of death,
while toiling without respite to earn enough to protract their wretched
lives.'

Before the crash, as property markets boomed, ragged families from the
north had been herded like cattle to construction sites. One scene stuck in
my memory: a mother with a child strapped to her back, tied by a rope to
her husband and four walking infants, all grimy and apparently half-

starved, jerked along by a broker in tinted sunglasses. Little townships had grown on the building sites where children fended for themselves while the parents laboured up and down bamboo ladders with heavily loaded baskets. Fatal accidents were so commonplace, they were seldom investigated.

The king cancelled the Capitalist Cronies List: a nickname given the annual announcement of titles that he normally signed on the recommendation of government. It had become a sharing out of privileges to the wealthy instead of an acknowledgment of selfless service to the nation. He announced a new foundation: in English it meant 'Our Loss Is Our Gain'. He had previously asked for two more major dams to be built for his Jubilee Year. There had been opposition from politicians still riding the gravy-train. Now the times were on his side. He spoke to ordinary people who happened to be in the Grand Palace when he had to join his privy council. 'These meetings with casual passers-by became my coffeehouse assembly,' he said later. 'More and more people came with ideas. We worked "Our Loss Is Our Gain" into the new theory. What seemed an overall loss in money raised for new reforms would become "our net gain" as a nation . . . the Poor Man's Way.'

Local communities would make use of local materials and donate labour. Lek published a formula called '30-30-30-10' for dividing up plots of land to be given to the landless: thirty per cent for fruit and wood-fuel trees; thirty per cent for a ricefield; thirty per cent for a house, vegetable gardens and livestock; and ten per cent for a pond to hold water collected in the rainy season. The details were carefully worked out to suit different conditions. It would be a partnership between the people and local businesses willing to assign funds to the projects. It was not something likely to attract hard-nosed foreign investment bankers or international monetary fund bosses.

The king called the first stage the Monkey-Cheek Project and said: 'As a boy, I thought monkeys were very wise to store food in their cheeks for a time when essentials would be in short supply. Each community is to be assisted to build local reservoirs and storage centres so that water can be conserved in times of flood and certain foodstuffs kept against times of famine.' It would draw upon the emotional force of Asian nationalism. 'What brought about the crash in Asian economies,' he said, 'was not communism but unbridled capitalism.'

In villages where Mama had slashed opium production by eighty-five per cent in ten years, each household in her valleys had seen income rise eightfold to the equivalent of US$2,000 a year because markets had been opened up for new crops in the cities. Now, though, some villagers were heavily in debt. Cool-weather vegetables had sold briskly in steamier parts of the country but city-dwellers could no longer afford such luxuries. The village of Nonghoi, population 710, had been one of dozens of tribal settlements relying on opium as their only cash crop. With Mama's assistance, Nonghoi had been shown how to produce lettuce, carrots, leeks, beets and Chinese cabbage. With income rising, farmers had been tempted by city brokers to purchase tractors, refrigerators, television sets and Toyota pickup trucks on private loans which now had to be paid back with interest. A farmer who prospered from growing strawberries had never found it difficult to borrow from a Bangkok food broker – until the demand for strawberries fell to zero and no money was available to buy next season's fertilisers.

'Yet this loss can be turned to our gain,' insisted Lek. 'The migration back to the farms from the cities will put agriculture back on its feet.' The need was to recover arable land and this was opposed by the moneylenders. Buyers of property during the boom spoke of him as a neo-Marxist.

He was growing tired. He could no longer sit for hours, back straight, legs firmly planted in the ground, never once crossing or stretching them for hours on end. He would have liked to shift some of the burden onto the Crown Prince whose misbehaviour, he felt, resulted from frustration. In middle age, it was difficult for any son to remain under his father's shadow. In Laos, they were saying that the king's son could carve himself a niche. Its people were forming a new Lao People's Liberation Front with a return to monarchy as its aim. It was widely reported that a Thai-American mining consortium would back the Crown Prince as ruler of Laos. This had not been in the Ninth Rama's mind when he received the old Laotian communist jungle fighter, Kaysone Phomvihane, in Bangkok. Kaysone was typical of Asian nationalists whose rebellion against imperialism had been twisted into submission to big-power communism. The good work Lek had done in befriending Kaysone was imperilled if Laotians feared another wave of colonial exploitation.

Peter Jensen, the husband of Lek's first daughter, Princess Ubol, was reportedly a member of the consortium entering Laos. On recent visits to Bangkok with Ubol, he had been described as 'the royal consort'; and the couple's three children included one son, Bhumi, short for Bhumibol. Gossip-mongers said Bhumi Jensen, although a fourteen-year-old schoolboy in California, could find himself in line of succession.

The Ninth Rama could not let speculation distract him. Great-grandfather, the Fourth Rama, at the age of twelve had commanded armies in Old Siam's outlying regions; but he had then made his own journey toward enlightenment. When his own time came to die, Lek hoped he would leave like his ancestor, not as in *The King and I*, but in the manner recorded by palace scribes. He would hear a report on the nation's affairs, ask forgiveness for the mistakes he had made, and finally turn onto his side and murmur: 'This is the proper way to die.'

Physically exhausted, he sent Princess Sirindhorn to a rice-planting ceremony at the military academy in January 1998. The army chief-of-staff, General Charn Boonprasert, said, 'My officers are carrying hoes instead of guns. Every military camp now sets aside land for integrated farming.' Sirindhorn, wearing the plaited straw broad-brimmed conical hat of a peasant, waded through a demonstration plot, scattering rice seeds. A French expert from the Loire Water Basin, Jacques Talec, lectured on the management of water resources through 'a nature-oriented strategy, according to geographic basins, not administrative boundaries'. Talec asked if the king felt angry that his own plea for such a strategy had been sabotaged. Lek shrugged: 'Read *The Ten Duties of Kingship*. The Seventh is *akkodha*, bear no grudges.'

He wrote a how-to book on the way to escape dependency on other countries. It was distributed free. 'Social capital' would be based on small cooperatives and elected local committees. Workers who were pouring back to the land could volunteer to join pilot projects on New Theory farming. They would get grants to buy seeds and animals for the first year and a large plot. More technical help would be available from officials trained at Chitralada. At last there seemed a chance to expand Chitralada's ideas without running into the obstacles put up by governments run by greedy generals with big business partners.

Dr Mahidol's work among lepers had resulted in boarding-schools for the children of lepers and Lek looked for ways to employ millions in enlarging schools for handicapped children and other make-work projects. He called for volunteers to dig fish-ponds and stock them with 'King's Fish', the *pla nil* that his how-to book recalled 'has been easily raised anywhere including brackish water, growing to marketable size within six months . . . In the shallow ricefield water in the rainy season, the fish feed on insect larvae and weeds, and by the time the rice is harvested, they are big enough to eat.' When asked where the the money would come from, he pointed to the millions eager to work and the abundance of raw materials that made it possible to stop thinking in western terms of financial accountancy.

In May came the Royal Ploughing Ceremony. Lek had dreaded this in 1946 when he waited to fly back to Europe as a simple engineering student. Now he presided. The countryside crept back into a city sobering up. The giant Chivas Regal billboards were in tatters at the far end of the Grand Palace field where five white-clad Brahmin astrologers led two sacred white bulls, Rung and Roj, pulling a plough. Four silk-clad maidens followed the furrows, scattering rice seeds blessed by priests. The bulls came up to the king and were offered seven different foods in banana-leaf bowls and chose only to eat rice and drink grain alcohol. This signified an abundant harvest. A royal official made a blind choice from three proffered belts. The one he selected was in length five *keub*, an ancient measurement of distance from the tip of the tongue to the end of the index finger. This promised above-average rainfall wherever drought was the farmer's enemy. The minister of agriculture, in tall wizard's hat and toga, walked ahead of the prettiest young women from the palace, barefoot and loose-robed, to signal to the huge crowd of ragged farmers that they could now collect the scattered seeds made sacred by a ceremony dating back to when land was first culti-vated. 'Rice-goes-out' had made Siam the world's biggest exporter of rice. But now the ricefields had mostly vanished under factories and golf-courses.

These magical rites had been so scorned at the peak of the rush to indus-trialise, the premier known as 'the flavour of the week', Chuan Leekpai, had said ideally only five per cent of Thais should be farmers. Now, four years later, Chuan was long gone and sixty per cent of the population was back to farming nonexisting land. The last time I had attended the cere-mony, the king had the feeling that the thick clouds of gas fumes rising from traffic inching along the borders of the great field would choke the very life out of the country. The Lord of Life River lay under a thick scum of indus-trial waste. The scene had inspired one of the paintings in his book, *Perseverance*. Greedy opportunists were shown using imported machinery to bend back and strip the fruitful mango tree, while others fell in drunken stupors, and skulls of dead cattle littered the landscape.

Lek had talked of his Ten Duties. It cannot have been easy to live by them, I realised when a button-eyed Bangkok socialite asked me to an inti-mate dinner. Halfway through, she dumped a leather bag between us and scattered heavy gold coins across the table. 'I had them minted in Switzerland at the very best place,' she said. Each coin bore the profile of King Bhumibol. Altogether she had spent US$950,000 on this special and limited edition, using money stashed away during the fat years. She pro-posed to sell each coin for about US$500, and donate an estimated million-dollar profit to the king's charities. She pushed a handful of the coins to my side of the table, and put the rest back in the bag. I looked down at the coins, and she looked at me. 'Take them,' her tiny brown eyes said. I gently swept them back to her side. 'You know the king,' she ploughed on. 'Show him these. Ask his permission for me to go ahead.' She slid six of them at me. 'Three thousand dollars,' I thought, and shoved them hurriedly into her lap. What preferment did she hope to get from this remarkable enterprise? Fame? A title? Financial gain draped in good deeds? I glimpsed the world of hidden traps Lek had been treading through all these long years.

He was seventy-one. He kept a sort of innocence, despite having had to learn about human nature during fifty-three years as an unwilling migrant from the west. It was an innocence found among ordinary Thais that may not have protected them physically from the evil that crowded around them, but yet gave them inner strength. A woman cleaner in Siam Square thanked the king for advising her not to sell her land. She had been tempted to dispose of a coconut plantation when speculators were scooping everything up at phenomenal prices. Now she was glad she could still do what many workers in Bangkok did: escape by bus once a week to her patch of soil where she did not depend on foreign bankers, to where her small salary went a long way. These patches of soil would add up, said Lek, and contribute to the land he needed for his new plan. But those who owned such properties were not always excited by such a vision.

He relied on the support of the poor. 'Have you forgotten to speak Thai?' the workers in Siam Square would tease Alexandra when we came back from a lengthy break. And it seemed she had, until Sunday morning when she returned to the little Thai classical-dance school run by sisters whose ancestors had been dancers at the Grand Palace. They worked for love of their art more than for money. Their teaching method was to stand behind each pupil, and by physical touch prepare each girl to complete the intricate movements of a new dance. They transmitted a kindness to which Alexandra responded. Soon she chattered fluently in the language she thought she had forgotten.

Such people remained untouched by fat years or lean. Noi, the seamstress, had to take care of a sick grandmother in a distant village. Her neighbours, without even thinking twice about it, kept her business running until she returned. Big Tek had tried to break out of his fifteen-hour day running a food-stall by borrowing money to develop some land: it was confiscated by the banks; but his family had kept some other land where he now cultivated trees and shrubs whose leaves and bark were used in traditional medicines.

So much had been destroyed of old Bangkok by wild speculators. The second-hand bookshop near the Erewan Shrine had been erased overnight to make room for a ghastly neo-Nazi hotel and its dozen expensive restaurants, now mostly empty. The shopkeeper was the historian and descendant of ancient kings, Manich Jumsai. He would bargain me *down* about the price of a book: 'It is not worth so much – give me half.' Whenever he located an obscure book, he would phone: 'Meet me in my office.' The office now was a corner table at a McDonald's, opposite a big sign in English: 'Accidental Police Hospital'. On the other corner was a shrine so sacred, it had always drawn visitors from all over Asia. They donated a few coins to the girls who danced at the shrine under the blazing sun rather than sit in aquarium-like showcases with numbered placards around their necks in nearby massage parlours. One day a mammoth new hotel had jammed up against one side of the shrine and a Japanese department store had leaned against the other, obliterating the shrine. The elephants from the shrine had lumbered into Siam Square, looking forlorn. Now the superstore had no customers. The mammoth hotel was derelict. The elephants' eyes shone again as young women ran under their bellies for luck. The shrine reassembled itself beside old women who released doves for a handful of coins. Each dove flew up, circled, and always returned to its cage. 'Life is like that, a cycle of good and evil,' said the king wearily. 'People taste freedom but want the certainty of the cage.'

One of his King's Men who had been an agent with Force 136 met me in the Throne Hall one daybreak when the king knelt to fill the bowls of monks. The ex-agent wrote in the neat hand of a one-time wireless operator a list of White Elephant codenames. It was difficult to get an account of his own role. Absence of ego had been bred into him. This had caused a British army instructor to misjudge him and call him 'Ping, the bloody pampered prince'. Ping knocked him out. 'I had to do it,' he said apologetically, 'to prove "bloody princes" were as good as those Siamese agents who were in revolt against "blue-bloods". Now the whole country sees the face of danger and it feels like one big family again.'

A bent little old man sat with me at a cremation ceremony; a typically cheerful affair; an occasion for old friends and relatives to exchange news and speak well of the dead. The ceremony went on for days and nights in a royal temple, and soft-footed mourners brought trays of sugared tamarind seeds, crisped shrimps and sweetmeats. The old man was alone. I asked about the rest of his family. 'I have none,' he replied cheerfully. 'I began to serve the Princess Mother as a doctor some thirty years ago. I never had time to marry and raise children.' His name was Dr Montien Bunnag and he helped run Mama's Flying Doctor Service. 'More than 3,000 doctors, 300 dentists, 10,000 nurses,' he said. 'Volunteers, part-time, unpaid. In one year, we treated a million cases. It was our version of

China's "barefoot-doctors" and helped us build chains of local clinics.' Then commercially-run hospitals offered higher salaries to government doctors; some ran businesses on the side; fewer were willing to move to rural areas. With the national crisis, said the little doctor, the numbers of volunteers had risen again.

Deng, the daughter of a village headman, was in charge of the intensive-care unit of a big army hospital built around one of the old palaces. She was an army lieutenant and won a scholarship for post-graduate studies in England. I asked why she didn't become a doctor. 'Doctors form a hierarchical system,' she said. 'A woman doctor wouldn't have a chance. I can do more good as a nurse and I want to work in the countryside 'like the king's father. He collected old medical prescriptions on *khoi* paper, rolled up in cylinders and kept in our temples. We'll value the old medicines again, now we're all poor.'

Crown Princess Sirindhorn had given Alexandra the tape of a sad little song about a mistreated elephant, lost in the polluted streets of Bangkok where once there had been ricefields. Now, with so many motorists forced to sell their cars, elephants reclaimed the capital's streets. The spectacle was strangely moving. People still remembered how every country household once kept working elephants, whereas the tractors that replaced them had been reclaimed by the money-lenders.

It was tempting to believe the romantic vision of a Buddhist republic would work. Or was it too much like Tolstoy's infatuation with Buddhism and a kind of socialist paradise that the great Russian novelist created on his lands and in his imagination?

In this respect Lek was trying to use that hidden world to rally his country. His critics did not think his idealism would solve the strange new problems of today. Some still had a lot at stake. They did not want to lose it by letting the king push through his Poor Man's Way. Was it practical at the end of the twentieth century? I was in no position to judge. I never felt worshipful of him but I did judge him as heroic at a time when we in the west didn't recognise heroes that come in such strange garb. It was everywhere fashionable to ridicule qualities like his. A new middle class, a fresh generation of Thais, did not always want to listen to sermons.

By 1999, there were divisions within this new generation looking to America and Europe for guidance. 'The noble truths of Buddhism are being ignored – the importance of suffering, humility, absence of greed,' said the critic of royalty, Sulak Sivaraksa. 'Monks handled social responsibilities a hundred years ago. Now some monks smoke and take drugs and call it medicine, and would open bank accounts if they still could.' He reached his audience through the media which gave no voice to the silent masses of ordinary people who still insisted on waiting for answers from the man who had no wish to be an omniscient god-of-gods.

One night the Ninth Rama climbed a thousand rocky steps to another cave temple. On every step sat small families in eerie silence. There had been no warning of his arrival, and there was no explanation for the way they rose up out of a vast and poorly populated countryside. They waited patiently for dawn to touch the tops of the nearby mountains of Laos. The king knelt in the presence of an old abbot who sat placidly in a mound of saffron robes. They talked softly until daylight filtered into the cave and lit up one stone wall and its only decoration, a skeleton. The skeleton had an amused tranquillity, as if declining to affirm anything except that we are born, live, die and for unknown reasons, stay silent.

When Lek could see the crease in the palm of his hand, he pressed his palms together, bowed his head to the abbot, withdrew, and began a slow descent. It was easy in that icy dawn and at such a godly altitude to imagine Elder Brother following too. People silently held out bunches of carrots, wildflowers, woven baskets containing berries, whatever seemed fitting for this isolated figure whose presence blessed them with an opportunity to give. Lek knelt before the infirm, the old and the sick. For a moment in the half-light and a cold drizzle of rain, he might have been any forest monk with only his umbrella, robe, toothbrush and pencils.

He kept under his robe a piece of paper, tattered and torn now from his travels, in which his mother had written lines from Dean Jonathan Swift's *Gulliver's Travels*, where the King of Brobdingnag 'gave it as his opinion, that whoever could make two ears of corn, or two blades of grass, to grow upon a spot of ground where only one grew before, would deserve better of mankind, and do more essential service to his country, than the whole race of politicians put together.'

31

Journey's End

Our ways part. Lek continues a journey whose end he cannot see.

I look again at the symbols that abbreviate stormy passages along his path. Each is like a Chinese ideogram. A few bold strokes compress whole lifetimes.

Lek's early ideograms cover years when I was writing immensely wordy reports that no longer seem to matter:

Here! See this painfully long account of what happened when I opened a Cairo door and found Johannes von Lehrs under an Arabic name broadcasting his same Hitlerian venom against Jews long after he was allowed to escape justice. Who cares now?

Here, I chronicle the movements of a KGB boss, out of place in his broad-brimmed trilby hat and wide-bottomed trousers among the Afghans. I write down the evidence of Russian intentions. Has it made any difference?

Here is Nehru recounting how the Dalai Lama has left Tibet, and telling me tiredly, 'Of course the Chinese say he is running away.' In America later there was much Hollywood-style huffing and puffing about saving Tibet. But it remains under Chinese control.

Here a Russian takes me up a Kazhak mountain to study the site of China's atomic-bomb tests. China's nuclear arsenal continues to expand.

I raced cocksure through a black-and-white world of absolutes while Lek was drawn, unwittingly at first, onto a path confronting him with questions to which he could find answers only within himself.

Lek's calendar is so marked by brevity that it can be rolled into a scroll and hidden in the tiniest of worm-proof temple cylinders.

Here, he has drawn a symbol summing up a schoolboy year in World War Two when my father is airlifted out of France after helping prepare anti-Nazi resistance groups and my mother is teaching secret agents. Lek is learning from his dead father through his mother to let the wicked punish themselves. I cannot reconcile the two extremes, but neither could Lek in those days.

Another squiggled symbol shows where he began moving from western certainties into his separate Siamese world: he gives Elder Brother Nan the cremation that socks you in the eye. At such an age, I was on a rusty Liverpool tugboat with Bill Kempe and Nigel Fisher and other hard-faced naval fighter pilots watching an improvised wreath sink in the dark waters where Len Hardy's body might have fallen after his aircraft blew up next to mine at 30,000 feet.

Here, a symbol covers Lek's mastery of modern warfare while he is also studying Sun Tzu's *Art of War* and the use of spies and booby traps. I am sketching Soviet missile launch-pads in the Crimea when he reaches out to moderates in China. He anticipates an abrupt reversal of American policy that will leave his kingdom suddenly abandoned when I am in Beijing demanding the return of Squadron Leader Andrew Mackenzie, shot down over Manchuria and said by hard-nosed Red Army generals to be dead, although we all know he is not.

Lek confided to me his encounter with his brother-king's ghost after waiting until he was sure I would understand. Our separate worlds touched because I was no longer embarrassed to talk about the night 'Spud' Murphy appeared at the end of my bunk at the moment he was killed night-flying.

But then I remember the ghost in *Hamlet* that will never rest until murder is avenged and I think about Tsuji who set out to kill Elder Brother Nan. I have assembled all the facts. Lek reduces them to a five-stroke ideogram signifying nothing but pity.

He has doubts. I have plenty more. We agree that terrible things move through the stillness of the deep after I tell him about the first search for the *Titanic*, when I dived to check underwater cameras and later re-played videotapes in the US research-vessel *Fey*, and watched in astonishment the image of a great white shark moving slowly beneath my dangling legs. Lek asks me what I would have done if I had seen the shark at the time, swimming through shafts of sunlight? I have to reply that my frightened threshing would have drawn the monster to me.

Terrible things. He saw them but taught himself to be still until the moment came to move. He still searches for a middle way between self-defence and compassion. I ask him if his father's compassion, fired up by World War One, might in the 1920s have robbed the great dictators of the grievances on which their evil empires fed. Or would Nazism have grown anyway, so that my kindly parents, and millions more, had to use violence to destroy it?

There is no answer to these questions except what we may find within ourselves, replies the king. Life should be a hymn to the imagination; the pure imagination of a child. If that is poisoned, everything else is meaningless.

His story demands a happy ending. It isn't over yet. By the ethics of the world to which I return, Tsuji should never have been allowed to escape. 'One of the worst men on the planet,' concluded British hunters of war criminals. An expert on Tsuji, Ian Ward, says: 'The man and his grotesque machinations have been allowed to warp and mangle history.'

Just before Elder Brother's murder, and again and again afterwards, Tsuji faked his own death. The Japanese government officially declared him dead on 7th July, 1968. His body, though, is not under the gravestone erected by the Self Defence Alliance at a temple in Japan. The Japanese Foreign Office continues to get reports of Tsuji in China and in the Soviet Union after his absolutely final and never-to-be-repeated official death.

But what if Tsuji had been captured in 1945? Perhaps Elder Brother would not have been killed. Little Brother Lek might never have become the Ninth Rama.

Acknowledgements

Among the personalities who deserve prominence in any history of the twentieth century, one man is little known outside his country. I felt compelled to tell his story, not because he was a king, but because of his uniqueness. He had been captured as a western-educated youth by a people who needed him in a part of Asia that the world thought it knew from cold war rhetoric. Through him, I learned that nothing is what it seems. Thailand is still called Siam in royal language, and I had to search into its beliefs and its long unwritten history to discover why it remains as mysterious and misunderstood as it always has been. Some of the background draws on my own experience and acquaintances like Malcolm MacDonald who brought about the secret and extraordinary meeting in a Singapore rest-room with a communist Chinese leader at a time when 'Red' China threatened to invade the king's domains (described in Chapter 15). Such large events, undisclosed at the time, endangered the Ninth Rama's reign but his focus was on bringing about an internal and singular revolution. To tell this story, I needed the help of hundreds of Thais. These talked to me freely in formal interviews. Many more hundreds made my family and myself feel, as they would say, 'born in the wrong place', because we were foreigners who settled into their unique ways. For the best part of ten years, they took us into their lives. Most were poor by western standards but we envied their richness of spirit.

The frank answers to all questions left me with thousands of pages of interviews and research. Carol O'Brien, editorial director of Constable, first suggested this book and brilliantly organized and edited it. Without her, I should have been lost. Of the many in Thailand who contributed to the story, some prefer anonymity. Of the others, I list here only a few, more or less in the order we met. Obviously nothing would have been possible without the goodwill of King Bhumibol and Queen Sirikit. Crown Princess Sirindhorn was an amusing companion with a formidable knowledge.

Princess Chulabhorn confided the difficulties of doing good works while living 'in a goldfish bowl'.

Privy Councillor Thawisan Ladawan was Principal Private Secretary to the King when my daughter Alexandra was enrolled in the palace school. The Grand Chamberlain in charge of the Crown Property Bureau, Dr Chirayu Isarangkun Na Ayuthaya, was an urbane go-between. 'Hom', Dr Chittrapat Krairiksh, tolerated with good humour many years of my questions. Chantanee Thanarak, chief of royal protocol, became our 'Auntie Chan', and travelled thousands of miles with us, tireless, patient, and always with jokes that needed no translation.

'Wud' was a walking encyclopaedia: as a boy, he got to know every corner of the kingdom and then studied in the west before becoming expert in all forms of warfare. He would disappear into distant jungles and return with strange tales to tell the king. 'Wud' became one of our dearest friends, a physically tough intellectual with few illusions. His cousin, Major-General Anu Sumitra, I first knew when he was a colonel resisting promotion to a desk: he had fought with British special forces and in the end his first-hand knowledge of jungle warfare and other skills put him in charge of military intelligence where, despite his general's rank, he still contrived to vanish into his beloved jungles.

My understanding of the past was enriched by a descendant of the Fourth Rama, fictionalised in *The King And I*, Putrie Viravaidya, and by her father, His Serene Highness M.C. Chidchanok, a graduate of Sandhurst Royal Military College. Her husband, Mechai, was extraordinary in his knowledge of village life and his work among the poor and unprotected: his father was the palace doctor who took into the Grand Palace the mother of the Ninth Rama when she was an orphan from the slums.

Of singular help was Suprapada Kasemsant, Principal Private Secretary to the Queen, killed with 13 others of Queen Sirikit's entourage on 19th September, 1997 when their helicopter crashed during a survey of a project run by the royal SUPPORT foundation for saving ancient Siamese crafts. Dr Ladawan Souvannakitti rescued me from death and incidentally taught me the essence of Buddhism as well as the way to escape Bangkok traffic jams through a network of alleyways. Her father, Mongkol Navikapol, was equally practical in proposing ways to incorporate modern science within a Buddhist society. My life was saved again on another occasion by Dr Suphachai Chaithiraphan of Siriraj Hospital who had once worked at a veterans' hospital in Brooklyn, New York. He called the king 'Big Doc' and in 1986 helped him recover from his first heart attack by gently insisting that the monarch continue jogging a great many miles each day.

'Piya' Piyathida Sucharitaves must be among the world's best story-tellers. Her puns both in Thai and English pop out like bullets and her remarkable life is punctuated with funny anecdotes; and yet there were times – in Vietnam for instance – when she behaved with incredible coolness. She had been a TV star and I asked her why she stopped. 'I shot my husband.' How did that end her career? 'He owned the TV station.' It was all an accident but Piya had to find another husband. He is 'Nick', a man of immense integrity. Piya now works for another most helpful source, Pi-Chai, Mom Rajawongse Disnadda Diskul, secretary-general of the Mae Fah Luang Foundation established by the king's mother.

My understanding of Buddhist social reform derives from Buddhadasa (Servant to the Lord Buddha) Bhikkhu, formerly a merchant's son who, at fifteen, had to take responsibility for his siblings when the parents died, and later became a 'forest monk'. During much of the Ninth Rama's reign, he had a quiet influence and revived the philosophy of Buddhist 'socialism'.

Among others to whom I am so deeply indebted are some who helped the king's 'revolution': Police-General Vasit Dejkunjorn; Supphaluck Srisamoot of the Grand Palace staff; Khwankeo Vajarodaya of Dusit Palace and the Association Des Anciens Eleves/Lausanne; Sanh Hongladarom of the Office of the Narcotics Control Board; the staff of the Chai Phattana Foundation; Peter Studd, former Lord Mayor of London; George Abonyi of the National Economic and Social Development Board; Rosarin Smitabhindu of Royal Chitralada Projects; former US Marine pilot Roy Heinecke, his wife Connie, and their son William Heinecke, Chairman of the Minor Group; Suthat Pleumpanya of the Royal Projects for Northern Agricultural Development; Pratuang Hemathat, Director of Household Affairs, Chitralada Palace; Prince Bhisadej Rajani who served as a 'White Elephant' agent with British Special Operations Executive in World War Two; General Saiyud Kerdphol; Ting Tirawat Sycharilakul of Personal Affairs Division of Princess Sirindhorn; Dr Sumedh Tantivejakvl; General 'Pete' Pichitr; Police-General Phairoyana Phusayanawin; Temsiri Punyasingh of the National Identity Board who collected some 3,200 folk tales 'constituting our oral history'; Kanitha Vichienchuen; Privy Councillor Kamthon Sindhvananda who went 'from muscle power to nuclear power' when the king appointed him to bring electricity to all parts of country; Miss Pompimon Jai-ngam, secretary to the President of Siam Cement; Chumpol NaLamlieng, who frequently interrupted a busy life to help my family wrestle with housekeeping in Bangkok and to steer me through the complexities of a hidden universe.

And I am indebted most of all to 'Mama'. She died while I was still writing a story that is also about her, the slum child who single-handedly raised two infant sons who became kings of Siam.

William Stevenson
Bangkok 1999

Simplified Genealogy of the Thai Royal Family

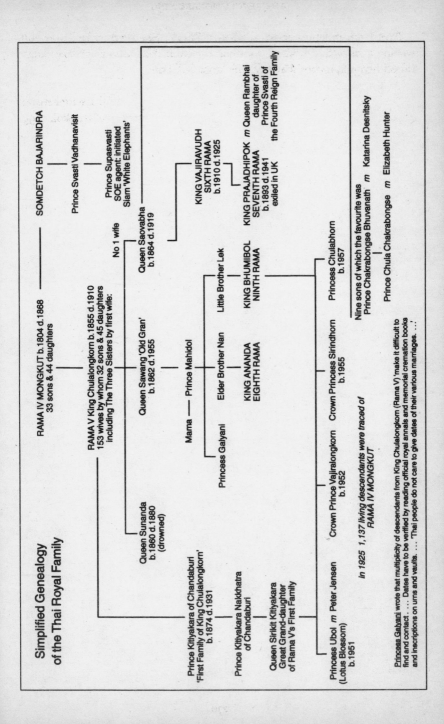

SOMDETCH BAJARINDRA

Prince Svasti Vadhanavisit

Prince Supasvasti SOE agent: initiated Siam 'White Elephants'

RAMA IV MONGKUT b.1804 d.1868 33 sons & 44 daughters

No 1 wife

Queen Saovabha b.1864 d.1919

KING VAJIRAVUDH SIXTH RAMA b.1910 d.1925

KING PRAJADHIPOK SEVENTH RAMA b.1893 d.1941 exiled in UK   *m* Queen Rambhai daughter of Prince Svasti of the Fourth Reign Family

RAMA V King Chulalongkorn b.1855 d.1910 153 wives by whom 32 sons & 45 daughters including The Three Sisters by first wife:

Queen Sawang 'Old Gran' b.1862 d.1955

Queen Sunanda b.1860 d.1880 (drowned)

Mama — Prince Mahidol

Princess Galyani

Elder Brother Nan

KING ANANDA EIGHTH RAMA

Little Brother Lek

KING BHUMIBOL NINTH RAMA

Princess Chulabhorn b.1957

Crown Prince Vajiralongkorn b.1952

Crown Princess Sirindhorn b.1955

Prince Kitiyakara of Chandaburi 'First Family of King Chulalongkorn' b.1874 d.1931

Prince Kitiyakara Nakkhatra of Chandaburi

Queen Sirikit Kitiyakara Great Grand-daughter of Rama V's First Family

Princess Ubol *m* Peter Jensen (Lotus Blossom) b.1951

Nine sons of which the favourite was Prince Chakrabongse Bhuvanath   *m*   Katarina Desnitsky

Prince Chula Chakrabongse   *m*   Elizabeth Hunter

In 1925 1,137 living descendants were traced of RAMA IV MONGKUT

Princess Galyani wrote that multiplicity of descendants from King Chulalongkorn (Rama V) 'make it difficult to find and contact . . . . Dates have to be verified by reading official royal annals and memorial cremation books and inscriptions on urns and vaults. . . . 'Thai people do not care to give dates of their various marriages. . . .'

Index

Adam, William 80
Adventures in Siam in the Seventeenth Century (Hutchinson) 196
Alexandra, Princess 146–7
Anand Rotsamkhan, Air Chief Marshall 253
Ananda, King (the Eighth Rama) 2, 3, 5, 6; childhood 18, 21, 24–5, 38–9; love of jazz 5, 25, 55, 64–5; invited to be Eighth Rama 3, 24; his response 26–8; uncrowned king 29–30; visits Bangkok 32–7; 44–5; returns to Bangkok 45–9; first threats to life 36, 50, 51–3, 55, 56; his murder 3, 57–9; funeral rites 61, 62–3, 65; inquiry into death 61, 62, 63, 69, 72–3, 137; cremation 86–8; his spirit 2, 65–6; *see also* King's Death Case
Anand Panyarachun 226–7
Angleton, James Jesus 156–7
Anna and the King of Siam (Landon) 4, 72, 103–4
Anu Sumitra, Major-General 232
Armstrong, Louis 83
Asia Magazine 249
Ayudhya 11, 129, 130, 227

Bangkok 11, 12–13, 34, 112–13, 132, 200, 220, 252; Back Palace 12,

13–14, 22, 36, 37, 149; Boromphiman Mansion 13, 34, 36, 47, 55; Chapel Royal 36, 91, 134, 152; Chulalongkorn University 169; Grand Palace 11, 12, 13, 17, 21, 34, 54–5, 105, 134, 172; Palace of the Lotus Ponds 17, 19, 21, 34, 69, 73, 87, 93, 131–2, 207, 248; Siriraj Hospital 12, 15, 19, 236, 255; Wat Bovoranives 123
Bangkok Post 155, 187, 255
Baudouin, King 96, 108, 115, 144, 224
Bedell Smith, General Walter 117, 120
Beech, Keyes 46
Bennett, General Gordon 149
Bhanabhandu Yugal, Prince 59, 61, 111, 169
Bhumibol, King (the Ninth Rama) birth and childhood 19, 21, 24–5, 27–8, 30, 39; love of jazz 4–5, 25, 55, 56, 64–5, 77–8, 79, 83, 94, 147, 170, 221–2; visits Bangkok 32–7; return to Bangkok 45–7, 54, 55–6; murder of brother 57–9; acclaimed Ninth Rama 60–1; launches inquiry into regicide 61, 62, 63, 69, 72–3; alleged

Vajiralongkorn, Crown Prince (*cont.*)
182, 186, 191, 197–8, 200; and
Suchinda coup 221–3, 234–5,
239, 240, 253–4, 257
Vajiravudh, King (the Sixth Rama)
15–16, 18–19, 23
Vajravira 207
Vasit Dejkunjorn, Police-General
147, 178, 181–2, 188, 196–7,
207–8, 211
Vejjavivisth, Major Nitya 58, 83
Vibhavadi Rajani (Princess of the
South) 196–7, 199, 202, 205,
206, 240
Victoria, Queen 31, 47, 125, 126–7
Vietnam 82, 158, 198, 199; War 116,
160, 164, 166, 178, 189, 190,
229
Vo Nguyen Giap, General 196

Wales, Quaritch 152
Warner, Jack L. 155
Washington Post 177, 225
Watson, Arthur K. 153–4
Waugh, Alec 19

Webster, Judge William 204–5
Whitcombe, Darrel 199
White Elephants, the 42, 43, 53, 204,
261
Wild, Colonel Cyril 70–1
Willoughby, Major-General Charles
70
Wilson, President Woodrow 16, 100
Woodner, Beverly 97
World Commerce Corporation
(WCC) 4, 162, 195–6
World War One 15
World War Two 22, 36, 39, 40–4, 82,
205, 211

Xaveria, Sister 21

Yamamoto, Kumaichi 70
Yuan 198
Yuangrat Wedel, Dr 190
Yuvadhida 207

Zimmerman, Gereon 169–70, 172
Zhou Enlai, Premier 121–2, 158, 159,
160

Other titles available from Robinson Publishing

Belly Dancing   Rosina Fawzia Al-Rawi   £7.99 [ ]
A revelatory story of the origins and the life force of Arab dancing.

Attila, King of the Huns   Patrick Howarth   £7.99 [ ]
The true story of the warlord who was called 'the Scourge of God', which draws
on the wealth of evidence from modern archaeological finds, as well as Hungar-
ian sources not previously known in the West.

Cardinal Richelieu   Anthony Levi   £7.99 [ ]
The much-acclaimed biography of the man who created a unified France now
available in paperback.

Pilgrim Princess   Maria Fairweather   £7.99 [ ]
The extraordinary story of Princess Zinaida Volkonsky, a member of one of
Russia's oldest families, who later took a vow of poverty and dedicated the last
decade of her life to helping the poor.

Robinson books are available from all good bookshops or direct from the publisher.
Just tick the titles you want and fill in the form below.

TBS Direct
Colchester Road, Frating Green, Colchester, Essex CO7 7DW
Tel: +44 (0) 1206 255777
Fax: +44 (0) 1206 255914
Email: sales@tbs-ltd.co.uk

UK/BFPO customers please allow £1.00 for p&p for the first book, plus 50p
for the second, plus 30p for each additional book up to a maximum charge of
£3.00.
Overseas customers (inc. Ireland), please allow £2.00 for the first book, plus
£1.00 for the second, plus 50p for each additional book.

Please send me the titles ticked above.

NAME (Block letters) . . . .

ADDRESS . . . .

. . . .

POSTCODE . . . .

I enclose a cheque/PO (payable to TBS Direct) for . . . .

I wish to pay by Switch/Credit card

Number . . . .

Card Expiry Date . . . .

Switch Issue Number . . . .